Education and Society in Plurilingual Contexts

Participants from the Vrije Universiteit Brussel who took part in the international conference *Plurilingual Hubs in the New Millennium* are all members of The Centre for the Interdisciplinary Study of Brussels. Their participation was partially financed by the Fund for Scientific Research, Flanders, which is part of the framework of a major Scientific Research Network Grant for a project on 'Research into Brussels and other multilingual (capital) cities'. The project team includes members from Switzerland and Canada as well as Belgium.

Education and Society in Plurilingual Contexts

Edited by

Daniel W. C. So and Gary M. Jones

VUB BRUSSELS
UNIVERSITY PRESS

VUB BRUSSELS UNIVERSITY PRESS
Waversesteenweg 1077, 1160 Brussels – Belgium
Fax: +32 2 629 26 94
Web Site: http://www.vubpress.org
E-mail: vubpress@vub.ac.be

ISBN 90-5487-322-1   NUR 610
D / 2002 / 1885 / 08

Distribution Agent for orders <u>outside</u> Europe
Academic & Professional Book Centre
Unit C, 5/F., Casey Aberdeen Centre, 20 Wong Chuk Hang Road,
Hong Kong
Web Site: http://www.apbookshop.com
E-mail: apbook@netvigator.com

Cover: Cliff Fan
Artwork & Layout: Salie Fung, Patrick Tse, Ida Ip, Rebecca Lam, Winnie Chan
Printed in Hong Kong by Kin Kwok Printing Press Limited

Contents

Preface

Daniel W.C. So and Gary M. Jones

The Contributors

References

Index

Acknowledgements

Preface

Two themes thread through the 15 papers in this volume. Towards the end of his seminal *Bilingualism: Basic Principles,* Baetens Beardsmore enters a plea that individual bilingualism should be considered normal rather than exceptional (1986: 120). Twenty years later his plea has been taken as a matter of course by the authors in this volume: that societal bilingualism is a common phenomenon worldwide and that knowing or trying to know more than one language is a normal condition in human society, past and present. The other thread is the recognition that an understanding of the phenomena of individual and societal bilingualism has to take into account the socio-cultural contexts in which the phenomena are found.

These two threads are most evident in Lüdi's paper which sets the scene for the rest of the papers in this volume, first by showing how unilingualism can be understood as an exception and a handicap, then by showing why it is in the interest of all concerned to incorporate bilingual norms in language-policy making, and finally, with examples from the schools of Switzerland, by suggesting how such norms could work.

The next nine papers of the volume address the issue of achieving individual bilingualism through schooling. They cover experiences in eight countries – Belgium (mainly Brussels), Brunei, Canada (particularly Quebec), China (including Hong Kong), England, Germany, Italy, and Singapore. The programmes examined range from those designed for minority students with disadvantaged backgrounds, to those for students in the mainstream, as well as to those that cater to students from relatively privileged backgrounds, such as pupils in the European School system. While the reasons for incorporating the development of individual bilingualism as one of the major aims of education vary from country to country and from programme to programme, indications provided by these papers make it quite evident that it is a very common aspiration among people and governments worldwide. As predicted by Genesee, it is quite probable that individual bilingualism is going to be an important agenda in education of most, if not all, countries of the world in the New Millennium. The benefits that come with the success of this agenda, such as mother tongue maintenance and/or facilitation of intercultural communication, may be obvious, but the costs and the technology involved in implementing this agenda are not yet clearly understood. Also the costs may differ according to context, as shown in the papers of Gao, Jones, So and Tsou.

In recent years the application of the methodology of Content and Language Integrated Learning in schools and programmes that have individual bilingualism development as a primary goal has produced many encouraging results, as reported in the papers of Genesee, Coyle, Wolff, Gajo & Serra, and Housen. The principal feature of the methodology is the use of an additional language, which is normally the students' less familiar language, for the teaching and learning of subjects other than the language itself. From these papers it is obvious that the methodology holds a lot of promise that might develop individual bilingualism among a large percentage of the school population, rather than for a small elite, as is the normal situation today. Accordingly, these papers should be of particular interest to readers interested in the technology of additive bilingualism through schooling.

The papers of Teng, Jernudd, Saxena & Sercombe, Janssens and Witte are in various ways all about societal bilingualism, particularly languages-in-contact. The primary focus of these papers is on the importance of the sociolinguistic context in the study of linguistic developments and/or attitudes derived from these situations. Teng's analysis of the syntactic characteristics of Taiwanese Mandarin speech demonstrates the complexity of contact-induced linguistic features of a rapidly evolving language variety in a truly plurilinguistic community. Such a community defies simplistic classification and needs new taxonomies in language-contact studies that take into account more fully the dynamics of cross-linguistic interactions.

According to Jernudd, hubs like Hong Kong, Brunei and Brussels are 'a crucible of languages from which new linguistic species and language attitudes are fostered.' His paper discusses the impact of these contact-induced sociolinguistic changes on people and communication in hubs like Hong Kong. It appeals to sociolinguists concerned to re-think what they teach about 'the linguistically complex, plurilingual and intra-linguistically differentiated, environments of the hubs', and concludes by asking for more effort in developing textbooks and pedagogy that will open windows for students to better understand such sociolinguistic dynamics, particularly with reference to their own language experiences.

Saxena & Sercombe focus on contact-induced changes in language attitudes and language choices among the young people of Brunei, another hub that is undergoing rapid sociolinguistic change. The findings of their study should be of interest to students of social studies who have examined the reproduction theory of Pierre Bourdieu and Jean-Claude Passeron.

The papers of Janssens and Witte are about the complexities involved in studying contact-induced language attitudes and sociolinguistic changes in a hub like Brussels. Janssens' paper discusses the inadequacy of existing theoretical resources *vis-á-vis* the study of hub bilingualism, particularly by way of sociolinguistic survey and, based on his ample field experiences, shows the reader how such inadequacies may be overcome. Whereas Witte's paper traces the sociolinguistic developments in Brussels with special reference to the vagaries of the French-speaking and Dutch-speaking communities from a historical perspective and in the course of doing so shows the reader why Brussels is such a fascinating topic for historico-sociolinguistic study. Witte also gives the reader, based on her own first-hand experience, the background to the genesis of the *Centrum voor de Interdisciplinaire Studie van de Brusselse Taaltoestanden* (Centre for Interdisciplinary Study of the Brussels Language Situation) in 1978. Since its founding, the Centre has played a significant role in fermenting multi-disciplinary studies on societal bilingualism in Brussels and in other hubs of the world, of which the present volume is a good example.

The Contributors

Georges Lüdi was born 1943 in Baden (Switzerland). He is married, has four children and has lived in Basel since 1982. He studied Philology and Linguistics at the Universities of Zürich, Madrid and Montpellier, gaining a doctorate from Zurich in 1971. He then studied French and Spanish Linguistics at Zürich, receiving his Habilitation in 1976. He first taught in Zürich and Berne before becoming a Full professor for General Linguistics at the University of Neuchâtel 1979-1982. Since 1982 he has been Full professor for French Linguistics and Director of the Institute of Romance Philology at the University of Basel. He was Dean of the Faculty of Arts (Philosophisch-Historische Fakultät) of the University of Basel 1994-1995 and has been President of the Planning Committee of Basel University since 1996. In addition, he was President of a group of experts that were mandated to propose a whole language policy for Switzerland (1997/98). He has been Counsellor of the Council of Europe for language policy since 1997; Member of the Executive Board of the International Association for Applied Linguistics since 1996 and has been nominated *Chevalier de l'Ordre du Mérite* (France). Professor Lüdi's main research interests include: Second language acquisition, contact linguistics (bilingualism, diglossia, code- switching), language policy, and semantics.

Fred Genesee is Professor in the Psychology Department at McGill University, Montreal, Canada. He has conducted extensive research on second language education, including foreign language immersion programmes for majority language students and bilingual education for minority language students. This research has systematically examined the long term effectiveness of immersion and bilingual education and individual student and programme variables linked to programme success. His current research interests are on children who acquire two languages simultaneously during the pre-school years. This research focuses on the phonological, syntactic, and communicative development of bilingual children with typical and impaired patterns of acquisition.

Do Coyle is Director of Learning and Teaching, and Vice-dean in the School of Education, University of Nottingham, England. Her postgraduate studies were in applied linguistics and modern language teaching methodologies. The first sixteen years of her career were spent in the field, teaching modern languages in secondary schools, before transferring to teacher education in 1990. Since then, she has been instrumental in setting up innovative teacher education programmes – notably the joint European initial teacher education diploma (Austrian, French and British) and the only UK bilingual initial teacher education programme to train subject teachers to work through the medium of a foreign language. She participates in a variety of European Lingua Teacher Education projects and has coordinated two major studies in reflective practice and bilingual education. In 1997, she was awarded the honour of *Chevalier dans l'Ordre des Palmes Académiques* for services to French Teacher Education. Her current research supervision focuses on sociocultural and linguistic processing in FL classrooms, developing learner autonomy, second language acquisition, teacher education theory and practice and bilingual education. She is now involved in developing two major European projects for bilingual education, regularly publishes and researches in the area of CLIL (Content and Language Integrated Learning), and is active in several national and international bilingual networks. Her most recent work is in the application of new technologies to bilingual learning and teaching. Her innovative *Teaching Observatory* linking remote classrooms with the university for pre-, in-service and research purposes is receiving international acclaim.

Dieter Wolff was born in Germany in 1939 and completed his postgraduate studies at the University of Saarbrücken in 1969. Since then he has taught at the Universities of Berlin, Essen and Düsseldorf. Since 1989 he has been Full Professor (Chair) at the University of Wuppertal (Applied Psycholinguistics) where he has also held the posts of Dean of the Faculty of Philology and Pro-Vice Chancellor. From 1987-1998 he was co-editor *of Die Neueren Sprachen.* He is currently co-editor of *Neusprachliche Mitteilungen aus Wissenschaft und Praxis* and is a board member of both 'CALL' and 'Applied Linguistics'. He is also currently Vice President of AILA, advises local and regional governments on Content and Language Integrated Learning and has published and edited numerous books, articles and journals.

Laurent Gajo has a PhD in linguistics and is Lecturer and Researcher at the Universities of Lausanne and Neuchâtel. His research fields include: bilingualism, second language learning and teaching, bilingual education, classroom interaction, language policy, migration. He has been a consultant for bilingual education in the Aosta Valley, Italy (since 1998); a member of the scientific committee 'Curriculum innovation', Thematic Network Project 2 of the European Language Council since 2000 as well as Associated Member of the scientific committee 'Teaching training and bilingual education', Thematic Network Project 1, European Language

Council from 1996-1999. In 1995-1996 he was a visiting researcher at the Ontario Institute for Studies in Education, Canada. In addition, he has been a researcher for a Swiss national project on the efficiency of the education system and has done other consulting and teacher training on bilingual education in Switzerland, and other parts of Europe. His ongoing research includes: development of content knowledge in the context of bilingual education; issues for non-linguistic disciplines; integrative bilingual teaching model connecting – in one and the same setting – content-oriented instruction with focus-on-form instruction.

Cecilia Serra is a Linguist, Lecturer and Researcher at the Universities of Neuchâtel and Bern (Switzerland). Her research interests include: second language acquisition, bilingual education, curriculum development and teacher training, classroom interaction, native/non native language communication and interaction, language policy, bilingual communication in migrant communities. She has consulted on various aspects of bilingual education in the Aosta Valley, Italy (since 1998); Chur, Switzerland (since 1999); and Zürich (since 1998) and in Bhutan, in October 1998. Her ongoing research in bilingual education covers: acquisition of content and of first and second language in bilingual education; improvement of an integrative bilingual teaching model connecting – in one and the same setting – content-oriented instruction with focus-on-form instruction.

Alex Housen studied Germanic Languages at the Vrije Universiteit Brussel and ESL/Applied Linguistics at UCLA before obtaining his PhD. from the Vrije Universiteit Brussels in 1995. Since then he has worked at the same university as a Research Fellow of the National Fund for Scientific Research (Flanders). His research interests include language acquisition, language teaching, bilingualism, bilingual education, and applied linguistics. He has been involved in research projects on processes and outcomes in bilingual education and second/foreign language programmes funded by the Ministry of Education of the Flemish Community, the European Science Foundation, the National Fund for Scientific Research (Flanders) and the Research Council of the Vrije Universiteit Brussel. He has worked as a consultant on language teaching and bilingual education for the Soros Foundation, the United Nations Development Programme and the Flemish Ministry of Education. His publications have appeared in various journals. He is co-editor of *Bilingualism – Beyond Basic Principles* (2002), *Opportunities and Challenges of Societal Bilingualism* (2002), *Current Issues in Instructed Second Language Learning* (forthcoming).

Gary M. Jones is a Senior Lecturer in the Department of English Language and Applied Linguistics at the University of Brunei Darussalam where he is also Deputy Dean of the Faculty of Arts and Social Sciences. His main research activity is the implementation of bilingual education in Brunei schools and the impact that this has had on the society. Related research activities and publications have included the role of gender in education and multiculturalism and language acquisition in bilingual communities. Prior to his present post he had worked in Sri Lanka, Germany, the United Arab Emirates and the United Kingdom.

Gao, Yihong was born in 1959. She obtained her M.A. in Linguistics from Durham University, Ed.M. in TESL from Boston University, and PhD. in Applied Linguistics from Peking University. Her major research interests lie in sociolinguistics (especially the social psychology of language learning and language use), and intercultural communication. She is the author of *Understanding and Transcending Linguistic and Cultural Differences, Foreign Language Learning: '1+1>2,'* co-author of *Culture and Foreign Language Teaching*, and is principal translator of B.L. Whorf's *Language, Thought and Reality* (Chinese edition). She is currently Professor of English and Linguistics at Peking University, and Vice Secretary General of the Chinese Association of Intercultural Communication.

Benjamin K. Tsou was born in Hong Kong and received his education in Shanghai, Singapore and Hong Kong before pursuing university studies in the US, where he obtained his M.A. (Linguistics) from Harvard University and PhD (Linguistics) from UC, Berkeley. His main research interests have been focused on language variation, at the macro- and micro-level, both quantitatively and qualitatively. He has taught in the US and Australia and has lectured extensively in other parts of the world. He is currently Professor of Linguistics and Asian Languages, and Director of the Language Information Sciences Research Centre of the City University of Hong Kong, where he worked in central administration for seven years.

Daniel W.C. So was born in Hong Kong. He received his Bachelor's and Master's degrees from Hong Kong University. Between 1979 and 1984, he studied at The University of Hawaii at Manoa on an East West Center grant and his doctoral dissertation was an eco-linguistic analysis of the differential selection of Chinese-medium and English-medium schools in the secondary sector of Hong Kong between 1949 and 1983. His current research interests are in the areas of language policy in education, profiles of biliterate and trilingual language learners and the vernacularisation of the linguistic standard in China between 1917 and 1955. He is currently associate professor at the Department of Chinese & Bilingual Studies of The Hong Kong Polytechnic University and leader of the programme B.A. (Hons) Language & Communication.

Shouhsin Teng received his postgraduate diploma in modern language teaching from Oxford University in 1967 and his PhD in linguistics in 1972 at the University of California, Berkeley. He held a teaching position as well as served as an administrator at the University of Massachusetts, Amherst from 1972 till 1995, when he returned to his native country to direct an M.A. programme in teaching Chinese as a second/foreign language. Since 1995, he has worked extensively and intensively on developing a pedagogical grammar of L2 Chinese.

Björn H. Jernudd is Chair Professor of Linguistics at the Hong Kong Baptist University. As of Easter 2002, he has the following in press: 'Development of national languages and management of English in East and Southeast Asia'; 'Cognition and language management'; 'Education reform and language selection in Hong Kong. Brief remarks by a linguist'; 'Managing languages at bilingual universities. Relationships between universities and their language environment'; 'Organised solutions to language problems: managing professional language in Hong Kong'; and 'Language planning on the eve of the 21st century'. Also in press are two papers of which he is the second author: 'Management of Chinese IT terminology' (first author Aman Chiu) and 'Terminological problems and terminology management for internet professionals in Hong Kong' (first author Charlotte To). He is also working on a monograph on language planning and language management organisations in Southeast and East Asia.

Mukul Saxena is a Senior Lecturer in the Department of English Language and Applied Linguistics at the University of Brunei Darussalam. Currently, he is involved in two multidisciplinary research projects on the languages and ethnic communities of Brunei and multilingual academic and non-academic literacies in Brunei. Before coming to Brunei he worked at York University, Lancaster University and the University College of Ripon & York St John in Britain. There, he taught and worked on research projects in the areas of language maintenance & shift, community-based multilingual literacies, bilingual classroom discourse and forensic linguistics.

Peter Sercombe is a Senior Lecturer in the School of Modern Languages at the University of Northumbria, UK, where he has just begun work. Previously, he worked in the Department of English Language and Applied Linguistics at the University of Brunei Darussalam for nine years. His main academic interests include language maintenance and shift, language & identity and the minority language of the Penans in Brunei (Borneo).

Rudi Janssens is a sociologist and is working as a researcher in the 'Centre for the Interdisciplinary Study of Brussels' at the Vrije Universiteit Brussel. He was formerly attached to the 'Centre for Statistics and Operational Research' and 'The Centre for Women's Studies' at the same university. He has published in Belgian and international journals and books on sociometry, the integration of Islamic minorities, gender aspects in education and on different aspects of the multilingual and multicultural situation of Brussels.

Els Witte studied history at the University of Ghent, receiving her doctorate in 1970. She has been a Professor at the Vrije Universiteit Brussel since 1974 (in the departments of Contemporary History, Mass Communication, Political Sciences) as well as Rector of the University from 1994-2000. Her offices and other interests include the following: Member of the board and secretary of the *Revue belge d'histoire contemporaine* since 1969; Director of the *Interdisciplinair Centrum voor de studie van Brussel* (Centre for the Interdisciplinary Study of Brussels); Dean of the Faculty of Arts (1983-1987); President of the board of Belgian Radio and Television (1988-1994); Member of the Belgian Royal Academy (since 1988); Member of the board of several associations of contemporary history and political sciences. Professor Witte is the author of several books and of some 100 articles on the Belgian political evolution and situation in the 19th and 20th centuries (parties and party-systems, parliament, government, the socialist and Flemish movements, etc.)

1. Bilingualism Is Not Enough! Plurilingual Repertoires for the Challenges of the 21st Century

Georges Lüdi
University of Basel

1. Monolingualism is curable

More than half of mankind is plurilingual and/or lives in multilingual settings. Plurilingualism and multilingualism are the normal case in most parts of the world; bilingualism must be seen as a minimal form of plurilingualism. In this sense, unilingualism can be defined as an exception. An issue of the European journal *Sociolinguistica* (No.11, 1997) uses 'Monolingualism is curable' as its title to highlight the fact that competence in only one language can result in a handicap.

Nevertheless, obstinate prejudices dominate public discussion about language diversity. Four such prejudices are briefly examined here.

Firstly, a monolingual view of the individual is widespread. At the end of the 19th century, a famous English professor could write, without being criticised, 'If it were possible for a child to live in two languages at once equally well, so much the worse. His intellectual and spiritual growth would not thereby be doubled, but halved. Unity of mind and character would have great difficulty in asserting itself in such circumstances.' (Laurie 1890: 15) Bilinguals were considered as potential traitors. In fact, anyone who belongs to two or more cultures was considered not entirely reliable because human beings should be monolingual and multilingualism weighs on mankind like a divine curse since the building of the tower of Babel (1st Moses 11: 6-7). However, towards the end of the previous millennium things changed considerably. Since the early eighties, specialists agree on a 'holistic' view of a bi- or plurilingual competence and of bi- or plurilingual persons respectively. The 'additive' conception of independent monolingual competences has been replaced by the

idea of an integrated bi- or plurilingual or polylectal competence
(Grosjean, 1985; Lüdi & Py, 1986; Titone, 1987; Siguan, 1987,
etc.). There is plenty of evidence that, in appropriate socio-
cultural conditions, plurilingual children are more creative, more
intelligent, more flexible in conversation and socially more
aware than monolingual children (Baker, 1996).

Secondly, monolingual representations of nations are at the
base of much resistance against plurilingual language policies.
As an example of this ideology we may quote a text of Phyllis
Schlafly published in the home page of the American site 'Town
Hall' under the title 'Bilingualism Is The Wrong Way To Go':
'For the last five years, Political Correctness has forced the
academic (and much of the political) world to pay homage to the
new sacred cows called multiculturalism and diversity. Those are
usually used as code words to challenge the assumption that
Western Civilisation is the basis of what we call the American
system, and to pretend that all cultures are equal and contributed
equally to the America we know.' As in the case of negative
stereotypes about individual bilingualism, the roots of this
attitude lie in two very ancient traditions represented, for
example, by the myth of Babel and by Antonio De Nebrija's
statement of 1492: *La lengua siempre es compañera del imperio.*
Both claim that persons and nations are ideally monolingual –
with a somewhat religious dimension (Goebl, 1989: 162ff.); they
can be traced back to the Renaissance and Greek philosophers
(Bronckart, 1988: 122) and developed into political maxims in
the period going from the French Revolution to World War I (e. g.
the concept of the *urwüchsige* Nation reflected in a common
language [Schulze, 1994]). Nations should coincide 'naturally'
with monolingual language territories. The massacres committed
in Ex-Yugoslavia in the fourth quarter of the twentieth century
are only one example of the perverse consequences of such an
ideology. In reality, most nation-states have always been and still
are plurilingual. Luxemburg, Singapore, Spain and Switzerland
are good examples of the possibility of founding national identity
on plurilingualism.

Thirdly, a mythical conception of bilingualism represents
another obstacle to a policy promoting bi- or plurilingualism.
Bloomfield (1933) defined bilingualism as 'native-like control of

two or more languages'. For Ducrot & Todorov 1972, an individual may be called bilingual if s/he masters two languages, both acquired as mother tongues; the bilingual speaks two languages 'perfectly well' (p. 83). Such a definition of bilingualism excludes most persons with competences in several languages. In order to cover the real phenomenon, a functional definition of plurilingualism is required: Any person will be called plurilingual if s/he uses regularly two or more linguistic varieties in his/her daily life and if s/he is able to switch from one to the other variety when it is necessary, independently of the balance between the competences in the varieties concerned, the modalities of their acquisition and their linguistic distances (Adapted from Lüdi & Py, 1986). Along with this definition, a migrant worker from Sicily in Zürich, having acquired enough Swiss German dialect for working purposes in addition to his original Sicilian dialect, is 'bilingual'. And so is a translator at the United Nations who developed her early childhood English-French bilingualism by systematic training. They represent two poles on a scale that covers all possible types of plurilingualism. The following communicative network of a French-speaking woman in Basel illustrates the way a plurilingual repertoire is exploited in daily life:

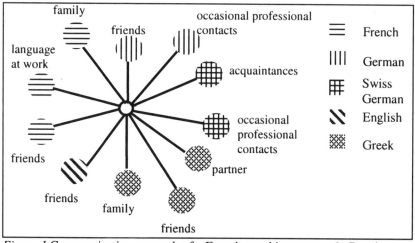

Figure 1 Communication network of a French-speaking woman in Basel

Her competencies are, of course, very unequal. For example, the written skills are much less developed in Greek and quasi non-existent in Swiss German, whereas her oral skills are much better in French and Greek than in all the other languages. This corresponds to the need for specialised competences in different languages as developed in the Common European Framework for language learning and teaching (Council of Europe, 2001). Competence scales ranging from elementary to near native (A1-C2) for each individual skill (listening, reading, interaction, continuous speech and writing) facilitate the representation of different profiles of plurilingual repertoires.

Finally, a diglossic future for the world is widely accepted in practice – if not explicitly sought through formal language policy, which refers to the trend towards English as dominant language for all international and intercommunity communication purposes. It would be taught as the only foreign or second language, local languages being restricted to local and internal communication. An immediate consequence of this trend is that lesser used languages would disappear and languages of wider diffusion – except English – would be reduced to 'lower' communicative functions and progressively lose certain domains such as that of scientific communication, education, media, etc.

2. A plea for educational policies favouring linguistic diversity

More and more specialists join the Italian philosopher Umberto Eco in fighting the obstinate search for 'unilingual' solutions to world wide communication by means of a 'universal language' and argue in favour of 're-evaluating Babel' (*Le Monde*, 7 Oct 1994). Similarly, most European countries and both the European Union and the Council of Europe have reacted vigorously against such prejudices. The 'European Charter for Regional and Minority Languages' of 1992 aims at maintaining and strengthening *all* the lesser used languages that are historically present on the European continent. Several normative texts like the 'White Paper on Education and Training. Teaching and Learning – Towards the Learning Society' of the European Union (European Commission, 1996), the 'Recommendation R(98)6' of the Council of Ministers of the Council of Europe (Council of

Europe, 1998) or the 'Recommendation 1383 (1998)' of the Parliamentary Assembly of the Council of Europe strongly argue in favour of functional plurilingualism in at least three languages (the local national language and two further European languages) as a goal for the educational systems. All Europeans should be able to communicate in three languages at the end of their education. More concretely, the Council of Ministers of the Council of Europe wants to 'promote widespread plurilingualism by encouraging all Europeans to achieve a degree of communicative ability in a number of languages' and 'by diversifying the languages on offer and setting objectives appropriate to each language' (Council of Europe, 1998). For the European Union 'proficiency in several Community languages and (inter)cultural competence are seen as indispensable for the free movement of people within the Union and for the development of understanding between the citizens of Europe. They are essential for the preservation and development of cultural wealth and traditions and are characteristic of European society' (European Commission, 1996).

There are at least four major arguments in favour of plurilingualism and diversity in foreign language learning and teaching:

a) Cultural heritage Language diversity is an important part of the 'inalienable cultural heritage' of Europe and the world. Thus, the protection of the world's languages, some of which are in immediate danger of extinction, contributes to the maintenance and development of the cultural wealth and traditions of mankind. Also according to the principles embodied in the United Nations International Covenant on Civil and Political Rights, and the spirit of the Council of Europe Convention for the Protection of Human Rights and Fundamental Freedoms, using a regional or minority language in private and public life is an inalienable right. Institutional multilingualism and individual plurilingualism are necessary conditions for achieving this goal.

b) Democratic citizenship When substantial groups in a population are unable, to a full or limited extent, to participate in mainstream economic or social life because of the language they speak, then the distribution of linguistic competences will clearly affect the social cohesion of the society. Individuals cannot indeed participate in the processes of society unless they have access to the different levels and kinds of discourse involved. Whether it is in terms of co-operation with others in a local community or in terms of voting in elections – or any other aspect of societal and community living – communication needs to be unimpeded by problems of access to the language and languages used. The global social, economic and political changes imply a new situation with respect to the opportunities all citizens must have for participation in formal and informal socio-political processes. The analogy with guarantees for minority languages within nation-states implies that protection and guarantees must be offered on an international level. Foreign language learning is thus the development of the capacity to play an active part in society, not just in the society of the nation-state. Access to foreign languages is thus an issue of human rights and democratic citizenship (cf. Byram & Ó Riagain, 1999).

c) **Economic reasons** The concept of the 'linguistic market' formulated by the French sociologist Pierre Bourdieu (1982) provides a framework for understanding the 'economic value' (in a broad sense) of plurilingual repertoires. Bourdieu speaks of a linguistic market in which linguistic competence (like any other cultural competence) functions as a capital resource for the individual. In a bilingual or plurilingual situation, the distribution of linguistic capital is related to and indexes the distribution of other forms of capital which together define the location of an individual within the social hierarchy. It is part of the 'practical competence' of speakers to know when, where, and how to speak one language rather than another in order to derive a 'profit' most advantageous to their interests. When an individual adopts a strategy with regard to the acquisition and use of a language, the profit that is realised may be symbolic or cultural, rather than simply economic. Nonetheless Bourdieu regards the latter as more fundamental, durable and influential. In short, competences in several languages represent a key qualification for professional life. The choice of the languages depends on the configuration of the local linguistic market. In the Swiss case for example, demolinguistic studies have shown the correlation between competences in several languages (mainly German, French and English) and the individuals' socio-professional status (Lüdi, Werlen & Franceschini et al., 1997). Similarly, studies in language economy provide evidence that good knowledge of three languages (again German, English and French) is correlated to higher salaries than bilingualism or unilingualism (Grin, 1997 & 1999) and that the society as a whole benefits from the plurilingual repertoires of its members.

d) Ecological reasons Finally, Skutnabb-Kangas (2000) argues convincingly that linguistic diversity is part of the world's functioning ecosystem, that each language provides a characteristic 'window on the world' and that the loss of a language and its corresponding culture represents a danger for the ecosystem of the earth which would be as serious as, if not more serious than, the dying out of a specific species of plants or animals.

3. The proposal for a holistic language education policy addressed to the Swiss Cantonal Ministers for Public Education in 1998

The ongoing effort towards a new language education policy for Switzerland provides a good example of how the challenge of plurilingualism can be met by an educational system.

Due to the federal system, there is no central Ministry of Education in Switzerland. The task of organising education lies basically in the hands of the cantons. The Federal Government provides only subsidiary regulation. In the past, the Conference of Cantonal Ministers for Public Education (EDK/CDIP) had issued a series of recommendations and guidelines concerning different aspects of foreign language teaching. Recently, certain cantons unilaterally manifested their intention to declare the learning of English compulsory at the lower level of secondary schools. This motivated the EDK/CDIP, in 1997, to mandate the elaboration of a concept for the teaching of foreign languages in compulsory schooling that should take into account the multilingualism of Switzerland.

An outline for such a general concept for language learning and teaching was presented in July 1998 (Lüdi et al., 1998). It is based on the following premises:

a) The ability to express trains of thoughts precisely, to argue in a differentiated way, and to communicate ideas using the medium of language is essential for cultural and political life as well as for the generation and dissemination of knowledge.

b) Linguistic and cultural diversity is deeply rooted in the history of Switzerland and Europe. It is part of the continent's identity and of the idea Swiss people have of their country. Its cultivation and maintenance is an explicit goal of Swiss (cf. article 70 in the Constitution) and European policies.

c) Due to numerous movements of migration, but also to the expansion of private tourism, Switzerland, historically quadrilingual, became multilingual.

d) The knowledge of neighbouring languages or partner languages not only permits cross-border communication, but also contributes to the development of mutual comprehension and an attitude of tolerance for other cultures and thus to peace.

e) As an additional professional qualification, proficiency in various languages is becoming more and more important in a world characterised by mobility and globalisation.

f) In terms of educational policy, the study of foreign languages has a central meaning as an element in education for citizenship.

g) During the compulsory school period, the foundations have to be laid so that each individual and the society as a whole can take on those challenges and meet them with success.

h) Building on their original monolingual or plurilingual competences, the repertoires of the pupils should be broadened in the direction of functional plurilingualism, within the framework of an integrated language pedagogy, and without any increase in the total load.

In summary, great importance is attributed to the development of the local language, the learning of additional national languages, the languages of neighbours and languages of larger diffusion because such efforts contribute to building a stable society, developing functional plurilingualism and creating access to a multicultural world. In order to realise these goals, the EDK/CDIP will issue a series of recommendations concerning language teaching and learning for the cantons. The form chosen is that of clear references regarding the number of foreign languages and the general objectives that should be achieved. This meets the requirements of a management oriented to efficiency.

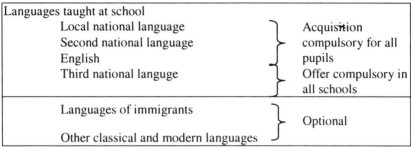

Figure 2 Languages Taught at School

The goals formulated are demanding and exceed in many ways the results previously obtained by the education system. (Figure 3)

At the same time, ways and means are described for enhancing the efficiency of language teaching in order to achieve these objectives:

(i)   Starting with second language learning at grade 2 or 3
(ii)   Meeting points guaranteeing coherence
(iii)   Integrated language pedagogy
(iv)   Teaching subjects through the media of foreign languages
(v)   Exchange pedagogy
(vi)   Diversity of teaching/learning methods
(vii)   Use of the European Language Portfolio for self-assessment.

It is obvious that a concept for language teaching can only be regarded as complete if it includes not only compulsory schooling but also the upper secondary level (general education and vocational training) and the tertiary level. This is especially true for the formulation of objectives. Only then will the offer of languages be coherent and transparent for the education system as a whole. Figure 2 shows the necessity of coordination in order to achieve vertical coherence throughout the education system – and between learning processes inside and outside the education system – by establishing goals for different levels and forms of learning within the same conceptual framework.

At the time of writing (March, 2001) the consultation process is still ongoing. A technical committee is preparing political recommendations and their realisation in the course of the next decade. Particular accents will lay on: (1) defining measurable levels of linguistic and cultural competence for both

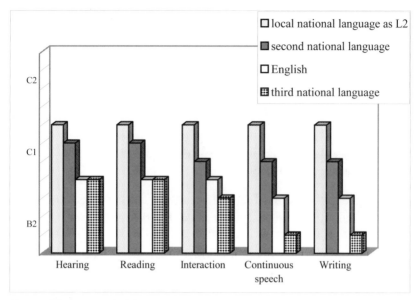

Figure 3 Language Achievements

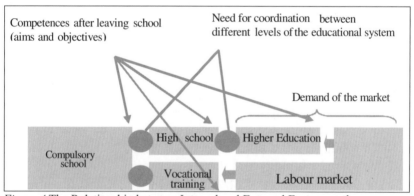

Figure 4 The Relationship between Internal and External Factors on the Education System

the local national language (as 'mother tongue') and the second national language, (2) the construction of suitable evaluation tools, (3) the development of elements and pedagogical means for teaching subjects through the medium of a foreign language and (4) the reform of the initial and on the job training for teachers (mainly for teachers of other disciplines or generalists required to teach foreign languages as subject and other subjects in foreign languages).

4. Further perspectives: Towards quality enhancement in language learning/teaching

Institutional measures optimising the context of language teaching are crucial, but not sufficient for improving the quality of language learning. There is an obvious reason in that: the learners, not the teachers, do the main work. All institutional measures will fail if they do not contribute to a significant change of the learning process itself. Wilhelm von Humboldt was certainly right in stating, back in the year 1836, that 'you cannot teach a language; you can only create favourable conditions for its spontaneous development in the mind'.

Much research has been conducted in applied linguistics on the conditions of successful language learning. A widely accepted constructionist view conceives (second) language learning as a process by which learners gradually reconstruct rules for speech they hear by formulating 'certain type of hypotheses about the language system being acquired, until the mismatch between what they are exposed to and what they produce is resolved' (Dulay & Burt, 1977: 97). From the UG-point of view, the learners' universal, innate knowledge, and the one that results from first language acquisition, entail a series of cognitive procedures by which they progressively construct the grammar of the new language. For the functional approach, acquisition is similarly maintained by the learner's continuous unconscious realisation of system internal incongruence, and/or mismatches between his temporary interlanguage system and the form/ function relation in the target language input.

There is, however, also much evidence that learning a language is a socially situated cognitive activity. This holds true for first as well as for second language acquisition. In other words, an important part of language acquisition takes place in interaction, in a dialectic alternation between self-structuration by the learner and other-structuration by more competent speakers (Py, 1996). As Bruner (1982, 1983 & 1985) stated, language acquisition is only partly made possible by the cognitive equipment of the child and in particular by the language acquisition device; the latter works properly only if the child can access data that have been organised for him by adults in the framework of a 'Language Acquisition Support System', comprising socio-affective relations, tutorship and other structuration. Like Py and others, Krafft/Dausendschön-Gay (1994) have transferred this view to second language learning. They speak of a 'Second Language Acquisition Support System' comprising all the above mentioned elements and, in addition, a set of 'interactive methods' that generates sequences particularly suited to the transmission and the acquisition of language faculties by the non-native speaker.

A research project conducted at Basel University aimed at answering the question Which degree language teaching, more precisely the forms of discourse used in the classroom, really favour these processes. The project was based on the assumption that the dynamics of interaction in the classroom contributes significantly to the success of language learning. The main result was that there are a multitude of forms of classroom interaction and all of them are not equally appropriate for language learning. The following piece of classroom discourse (Example one, page 14) illustrates a frequent form of dynamics in the classroom. The students are about 18 years old and are in the penultimate year of High School ('Gymnasium'). They have read a piece of French literature; the lesson aims at controlling their comprehension of the text.

In brief, the lesson is characterised by a mechanical, reproductive mode of interaction. As the teacher already knows the answers to her questions (often closed questions), there is no real communicative committment on the side of the students. The lesson is entirely dominated by the teacher who controls all the turn-taking without any major involvement of the students. The discourse consists of a series of initiative-response-evaluation sequences which are largely predictable. The responsability for the communication lies entirely in the hands of the teacher. Accordingly, the students' contributions are short, lexically poor and syntactically unelaborated.

A quantitative analysis shows significant differences in comparison to lessons conducted in a creative, interactive mode, where learners really want to say or know something (and the teacher is really interested in the answers to his/her open questions), where the organisation is unpredictable, leaving room for local negotiation between the teacher and the students and among the latter, where participants' roles are more variably distributed (the learners too may ask questions, evaluate, etc.) and where all participants share responsibility for the choice of topic, turn-taking, etc. In brief, students produce more elaborate and lexically richer utterances in the creative mode and the learning potential is significantly higher. Students perform better because they are fully challenged (see Lüdi, Pekarek & Saudan, 1999 and in particular Pekarek, 1999 for full results).

A second piece of research sheds more light on the above finding. It is about learners' usage of pieces of L1 (or any other language than the target one) when formulating utterances in L2. This usage differs from code-switching as practiced among competent bilinguals in its status more than in its form. We might call this well-known exolingual practice translinguistic wording and define it as a communicative strategy for getting oneself out of a predicament caused by limited lexical resources in L2. Translinguistic wording consists of the conscious use of single words or longer sequences of L1 (or in any other language likely to be understood by the native speaker of L2) as a form of lifebuoy. This technique is illustrated by Example Two (*Figure 6*) where the non-native speaker (NNS) is searching for the orthonym, proposes a German word which is then translated by one of the native speakers (NS) of French.

It has been mentioned earlier that interactive formats appear to facilitate the cognitive process of learning a second language. It has been shown that such interactive formats and collaborative formulation adopt characteristic patterns (Gülich, 1986; De Pietro, Matthey & Py, 1989). Typically, the learner utters an approximative formulation, the native speaker infers its meaning and proposes the orthonym, and the learner integrates the new lexical unit in his or her utterance (see Lüdi, 1994 for details). Shown in page 15 is a frequently quoted example of collaborative formulation involving a learner (a sixteen year old German girl) and a native speaker (the mother of the host family) who were brought together through a students' exchange.

P: je vous présente là un petit texte historique. veuillez bien XX ... de Pizarro qui était un des navigateurs (...) [tu présentes] un petit résumé. en tes propres paroles I present you here a short historical text please XX about Pizarro who was a great navigator (...) you make a short abstract with your own words	introduction, presentation of the task
E: eh un conquistateur espagnol est arrive en. Pérou avec ses hommes et des chevaux et après. après être euh a Spanish conqueror has arrived in Peru with his men and with horses and after ... after being	student starts answering and is blocked, presumably by a lexical problem
P: oui mmh Yeah	positive minimal feed-back
P: qui vivait là? who lived there	doesn't give the student time to search for words or to look for collaborative aid, but asks a precise question
E: des Incas Incas	correct one word answer
P: des indiens ou bien des incas. Indians or Incas	positive evaluation by affirmative reformulation of the answer (expected probably the more generic 'indienS')
P: dont le chef était ?[5s.] whose chief was	next question
E: [atahualpa]	next one word answer
P: oui ... Yes	minimal positive evaluation
P: puis qu'est-ce qui se passe? [4s.] les espagnols arrivent les indiens sont là ... on se rencontre Then what happens the Spaniards arrive the Indians are there they meet	next question after the student fails to answer, the teacher reminds the student of the fact
E: un combat A fight	next one word answer
P: un combat? A fight?	negative evaluation by repetition with a dubitative intonation
P: Pourquoi cela? Why that	doubled by a question
E: je ne sais pas I don't know	short answer
P: mais non. pas de combat But no. no fight	explicit negative evaluation

Figure 5 Classroom Interaction: Example One

NS1:	est-ce que les gens s'habillent de manière différente ici/
	do people dress in a different way here?
NNS:	moi je trouve plus . les filles surtout je trouve plus ehm
	oui . modernes . non ehm pas modernes . *gepflegt*
	I find more . especially the girls I find [them] more uhm
	yes . modern . no uhm not modern . (in German)
	well-groomed
NS2:	soignées/
	well-groomed?
NNS:	soignées oui
	well-groomed yes
NS1:	plus à la mode aussi
	more fashionalbe also
NNS:	aussi oui
	Also yes (corpus Saudan)

Figure 6 Classroom Interaction: Example Two

I	dans la ciél- .. äh dans la nuít- . il y a ähm des . (rit) tout petites
	lámpes+ dans la ciél/ à la nuít/
	in the sky... during the night... there are (laughs) tiny little lamps in
	the sky during the night (rising intonation marked by /)
	M mhm/ des étoíles/
	(positive minimal feedback) stars
I	ouí . des étoíles
	yes . stars ('Des tout petites lampes', 9:8. Corpus Bielefeld)

Figure 7 Classroom Interaction: Example Three

Examples Two and Three differ in the technique used for conveying approximately the intended meaning. However, the metaphorical 'tiny little lamps' and the translinguistic wording 'gepflegt' both provoke the same effect. The native speakers interpret them as a call for help, try to understand their meaning (which implies a minimal form of bilingualism in Example Two at least) and propose the correct word ('étoiles', 'soignées'), which is taken up by NSS. This represents an excellent learning occasion for the latter because the target word is delivered by the NS exactly at the moment where s/he wants really to say something, and therefore is communicatively committed (Pekarek, 1999). We might thus conceive this technique as a learning strategy. But it is far more than that. Tape recordings of conversations at work in multilingual settings, among persons with asymmetrical competences show that 'translinguistic wording' is a very efficient communicative strategy as well. In a creative, interactive mode of classroom discourse, students must take high risks in trying to formulate what they want to say, often whithout having acquired fully the appropriate language means. Thus, we might expect many occurrences of translinguistic wording. An appropriate reaction by the teacher (who is particularly challenged) and by the peers to this communicative strategy (it allows the speaker to be understood) and learning strategy (it entails a specific form of pedagogical sequences) will largely determine the efficiency of language learning (see Lüdi, 1999 for details).

Assessment of the results of language learning forms an integral part of education systems. But real quality enhancement in language learning and teaching presupposes much more than mere assessment of learners' results; it depends to an important part on precise knowledge of the types of verbal interaction that occur in the classroom, the risks learners are willing to assume, the appropriateness of the teachers' communicative strategies, etc. This cannot be done in a general way, independent from the specific setting. Which means research in classroom interaction is needed in every single setting and that the particular design of teacher training programmes, learning materials, etc. must be drawn from each specific setting separately. Examples like the ones shown in Figures 5-7 might point to the right direction for improving language teacher education and language learning classrooms.

2 Multilingual Education For The New Millennium

Fred Genesee

McGill University

The need to acquire two or more languages is not new. Historical documents indicate that individuals and whole communities around the world have been compelled to learn additional languages during the preceding two millennia for a variety of reasons – such as colonisation, trade, and intermarriage. We also know that promoting second language acquisition through education is itself not new or revolutionary and, indeed, we know that education through the medium of non-native languages was widespread during certain periods of history: for example, during the Roman Empire, education was available to colonies only through the medium of Latin, a non-indigenous language for many areas of the empire. This practice continued into modern times and was only slowly replaced by use of local languages for instructional purposes.

Notwithstanding historical patterns, we are facing growing needs to learn other languages and unprecedented reasons for doing so as we move into the new millennium (Tucker, 1998). While it is impossible to provide a thorough overview of the reasons that are motivating multilingualism here, it is worthwhile pointing out some of the most salient.

First, there is growing globalisation of business and commerce. During the last 10 to 15 years we have witnessed unprecedented internationalisation of industry and business. For example, in the automotive industry, head offices are located in one country (e.g., Japan), manufacture of automobiles takes place in another country (e.g., Brazil), and clients are in a third country (e.g., Canada). Even in North America, a relatively homogeneous linguistic community and trading block, we are challenged to learn other languages to remain competitive in markets such as Spanish-speaking Mexico and the French-speaking Quebec. While globalisation of the market place often provokes images of English domination, it also increases the demand to do business in local or regional languages.

Revolution in telecommunications has also created a need for proficiency in multiple languages. The Internet makes global communication available and easy, whether it be for personal, professional, commercial, or other reasons. On the one hand, this has created a particular need for proficiency in English, which is widespread on the Internet. On the other hand, as with globalisation of the economy, it also creates a need for proficiency in regional languages since Internet communication is not restricted to world languages. Indeed, the current domination of the Internet by English may give way to a much stronger presence of regional and local languages as e-commerce takes hold and begins to commit resources to communicating with local and regional markets.

Second, voluntary movement of people from country to country is taking place on an unprecedented scale. The economic reasons for this new development have already been mentioned; but, there are also educational, cultural, and strictly personal reasons.

Third, we are moving at the same time into a socio-political era when linguistic domination by 'big' languages of 'little' languages is becoming more difficult. Indigenous groups in a number of regions of the world are organising to preserve and promote their languages at the same time as they acquire other important national and regional languages: for example, Basque in the Basque Country; Mohawk in Canada; Hawaiian in the US.

Fourth and a final point with respect to the growing importance of English. While there is no doubt that English is growing in importance, there are reasons to believe that the situation will be more complex than the doomsayers predict and recent evidence suggests that the domination of English does not lead to the replacement of local languages and, moreover, it does not eradicate cultural differences (Wallraff, 2000). Recent statistics indicate that there are more Web sites in languages other than English (Global, 2000). The spread of English as a world language does not reduce the importance of knowing other languages – indeed, individuals and communities who know English AND other languages will have the real advantages (economic, political, etc.) in the future in comparison to those who know only English.

Case studies of trilingual education are presented in the next section that describe how three very different communities have responded to the need for multilingualism through innovative educational programming (see Cenoz & Genesee, 1998a, for other examples). Salient characteristics of the students, languages, instructional features, and goals of each programme are briefly presented. Finally, lessons that we have learnt from alternative forms of bilingual and multilingual education are discussed briefly. These lessons are drawn primarily from Canada's experience with immersion programmes and, therefore, may not apply unconditionally to other settings – indeed, one lesson we have learnt is that to be effective, bi- and multilingual forms of education must adapt to local or regional realities. This point will be illustrated in these three case studies.

CASE STUDIES in TRILINGUAL EDUCATION
I. HEBREW-FRENCH-ENGLISH IMMERSION
Location: Montreal, Quebec
For full details see: Genesee and Lambert (1983)
See Figure 1 (page 34) for a graphic summary of this programme.
The Students:
- From middle to upper middle class Jewish families who live in Montreal
- English is the dominant and, in most cases, the sole language of communication at home
- Exposure to French can occur through the media (TV, radio, newspapers) and in the community (stores, public events) – but is not necessarily frequent or regular
- Participation in the programme is voluntary
- Exposure to Hebrew is restricted in most cases to religious and cultural activities

The Languages:
- English: a majority, prestige language – spoken at home, in the community, and internationally
- French: a majority, prestige language – spoken in the community and internationally
- Hebrew: a minority language; not spoken at home except for religious and cultural activities (that occur periodically);

students and families may have exposure to Hebrew during visits to Israel
- English and French are cognate, Indo-European languages; Hebrew is Semitic, uses a different alphabet and is typologically distinct from English and French

Instructional Features:
- 30-32 hour school week (see Figure 1)
- French and Hebrew are taught through partial immersion from kindergarten onward
- English is taught using the core curriculum, beginning in grade 3 or 4
- Subject matter that is used to teach each language is specific to each language
- Teachers are native speakers of the respective languages

Motivational Features/Goals:
- To promote acquisition of oral and written proficiency in Quebec's official language (French) and in Canada's two official languages (English and French)
- To maintain and develop full proficiency in the students' L1 (English)
- To promote functional proficiency in the students' heritage language (Hebrew)
- To promote high standards in academic domains (mathematics and science, etc.)
- To cultivate cultural and religious knowledge of the students' Judaic heritage
- To expand students' understanding of the French culture while maintaining their knowledge of English Canadian culture

II. MOHAWK-ENGLISH-FRENCH IMMERSION
Location: Kahnewake, Quebec (near Montreal)
For full details see Jacobs and Cross (2001)
See Figure 2 (page 34) for a graphic summary
The Students:
- Members of an indigenous minority group – Mohawk
- Students come from working class to middle class families
- Students live in a community that is restricted to individuals with Mohawk background

- English is the dominant and often only language of communication in the home and community among students and their parents

The Languages:
- English: the primary (and often sole) language of communication in the home and community; English is spoken in the broader Quebec community (by 15% of the population) and throughout North America and worldwide
- Mohawk: spoken by some elders, but few parents; it is not spoken widely in the Mohawk community; there are few written forms of Mohawk (newspapers, books); some Mohawk on radio; the Mohawk language is at-risk with very few native speakers
- French: the dominant language in the province (in stores, on the street, in businesses, on TV, at the cinema, etc.); important for economic, job-related activities; not spoken frequently in the Mohawk community or at home
- English and French are cognate Indo-European languages; Mohawk is typologically different but uses the same alphabet as English and French
- Community language habits tend to be oral and are linked to Mohawk culture and language traditions

Instructional Features:
- Mohawk is taught initially using early total immersion approach
- Instruction and materials are culturally adapted to reflect unique Mohawk values and traditions
- Materials are all created locally
- Teachers are native or L2 speakers of Mohawk
- English is taught as an L1
- French is taught as L2 using non-immersion methods for one hour per day in grades 5 and 6

Motivational Features/Goals:
- To revitalize Mohawk and ensure its survival
- To promote functional proficiency in Mohawk for use as an every day language
- To instil Mohawk values and cultural traditions
- To maintain and promote full proficiency in L1 (English)
- To ensure functional proficiency in French (L3)
- To promote high levels of academic achievement

III. LADIN-ITALIAN-GERMAN

Location: northern Italy (south Tyrol)

For full details, see Egger and Lardschneider-McLean (2001)

See Figure 3 (page 35) for a graphic summary

The Students:

- Members of a linguistic minority that lives in five neighbouring valleys in south Tyrol, Italy
- From middle to upper middle class families
- Speak Ladin at home and in the local community
- Are exposed to Italian (state language) and German (language of tourism and business) on the street and in the media; higher education is available in Italian (and German)

The Languages:

- Ladin (L1): largely oral; related to Italian via Latin
- There are five dialects of Ladin which are dispersed over different valleys in the region
- Italian (L2): official state language; used regionally and nationally (oral and written) and available in all the media; important national language
- German (L3): former official language of the region when it was under Austrian control; not spoken as an L1 but spoken widely by tourists and by service-providers to tourists; some community members have strong identity with German culture for historical reasons
- Italian and Ladin are cognate Indo-European languages; German is non-cognate with Italian and Ladin

Instructional Features:

- Ladin is used as a 'vehicular' (i.e., ancillary) language to support instruction which is provided through Italian and German – use of Ladin in Classes 1 and 2 is primarily oral
- Language arts instruction is provided in Ladin starting in Class 3 for one to two hours per week
- No academic instruction is given in Ladin
- Italian is used as a medium of academic instruction (immersion); literacy is taught through Italian
- German is also used as medium of academic instruction; literacy is taught through Italian

- Both Italian and German are used equally for academic instruction beginning in Class 3 – so-called 'paritetic' system (parity system)
- Instruction in Italian and German follows traditional orientations

Motivational Features/Goals:

- To promote full proficiency in Italian and German (including literacy) because of their local, national, and international utility
- To respect the divergent socio-cultural orientations of the community – some members of the community are oriented to German while others are oriented to Italian
- To maintain high academic standards
- To promote understanding and appreciation of Italian, German, and Ladin cultural traditions

LESSONS LEARNT

These and other bi- and multilingual programmes have afforded us opportunities to learn much about the critical features of effective bi/multilingual programmes. I focus attention on lessons that pertain specifically to bi- and multilingual forms of education and leave aside for the moment important features of all successful education (e.g., the importance of appropriate and timely teacher education, appropriate and high quality instructional materials, systematic assessment, and so on) because the former are not always well understood in the education profession and, indeed, some of them are counterintuitive to many.

1. Integration of Language and Content

One of the truly great insights that has emerged from experiments with immersion education, in Canada and elsewhere, is that second, or third, language learning is most effective when it is integrated with meaningful and significant content (see Met, 1998, for a discussion of pedagogical issues concerning content-based foreign language instruction). This is also evident from scientific studies of first language acquisition (Wells, 1986). In school, this means integrating language instruction with academic instruction so that students are taught academic subjects through the medium of the target language, taking into account their language learning needs. The target second language(s) is also used for social interaction in class and elsewhere in the school. This approach is distinctive to Canadian immersion programmes and other forms of immersion that can now be found around the world (Johnson & Swain, 1997). Integration of language with academic instruction (especially in the case of young school-age children) takes advantage of young learners' natural language learning abilities because, in effect, it simulates the conditions that characterise first language acquisition. Integration of second language instruction with academic instruction has the added pedagogical benefit of efficiency – significant blocks of time do not need to be set aside for the sole purpose of direct L2 teaching (Genesee, 1987).

The immersion approach, however, does not mean that direct or formal language instruction is not useful; indeed, it is necessary if full proficiency in the L2 is to occur. In short, in the same way that we must provide formal language arts instruction in students' L1, we must also do it in the L2 in bilingual education programmes. However, research during the two decades in Canada suggests that simply integrating language and academic instruction does not necessarily optimise L2 acquisition (Genesee, 1991). There is evidence that a focus on the formal properties of the target language can enhance second language acquisition (e.g., see Lyster, 1994). There are a variety of ways in which this can be done – either during periods of academic instruction or by expanding the time devoted to formal language arts instruction.

I do not wish to suggest that the so-called immersion approach is the only way to implement multilingual education. Other methods can also be appropriate and effective, depending on one's goals and resources. For example, one may include foreign language instruction for limited periods of time each day – French is taught this way in the Mohawk programme; English is taught this way in the Ladin programme. However, if the objective is to promote high levels of functional proficiency in an L2 or L3, then some form of immersion is probably desirable (see Genesee, 1983, for a review of alternative forms of immersion). The Hebrew-French-English programme, described earlier, is an excellent example of how integration of language and academic content can be used to promote the development of three languages. Different content domains are taught in each language in that programme. In comparison, in the Mohawk programme, integration of language and content instruction is used to promote acquisition of the indigenous language and the students' L1 (English), but not their third language (French) – traditional second language techniques are used to teach French.

2. Additive Bilingualism/Multilingualism

To succeed in promoting multilingualism, it is not sufficient to simply integrate instruction in the L2 or L3 with academic instruction. It is essential that the programme also promote maintenance and development of the students' L1; that is to say, the programme must aim for additive multilingualism. It can be assumed that this is the case in most programmes intended for students from a majority language and cultural group. All three examples that I described include use of the L1 in some way. Promotion of the students' L1 is not always the case for programmes intended for students who come to school speaking a minority group language (e.g., Spanish speakers in the US or Turkish speakers in Belgium). Additive bilingualism is of particular concern in programmes for such students since special efforts to maintain and promote the students' L1 must be made otherwise proficiency in the L1 will be lost as the students acquire the second (or a third) language, leading to a situation of subtractive bilingualism. Use of languages that lack official status can be a highly political issue, as illustrated by recent events in the US where legislative measures have been taken to prohibit the use of languages other than English.

The beneficial educational effects of additive bilingualism are linked to both psycholinguistic and social psychological factors. Social psychologically, programmes that aim for additive bilingualism create supportive learning environments in which students acquire an L2 and even L3 and are also encouraged to maintain the language skills they bring to school and the cultural heritage that is a fundamental part of their social identities. Programmes that focus on the students' second or third language to the detriment of their L1 create subtractive learning environments in which students are expected to give up their L1 in order to learn a new language. Such programmes create pedagogical *double binds* for young learners. We know from many years of research that programmes that include the students' L1 are more successful at promoting competence in an L2 than programmes that do not (Genesee, 1987). As noted earlier, this is especially important in the case of minority language students, such as the Ladin-speaking students in Italy. Also, it is undoubtedly one of the reasons for the success of programmes for majority language students, such as French immersion for English-speaking Canadian students in Montreal.

Psycholinguistically, additive multilingual programmes take advantage of linguistic transfer (Cenoz & Genesee, 1998b). Transfer occurs when acquisition of one language facilitates acquisition of another language. This can occur either because specific features of the two languages are similar and, thus, acquired more easily, or because the learner acquires general learning strategies that facilitate the acquisition of additional languages. Research in the Basque Country shows that acquisition of English was enhanced in the case of students who were already bilingual (in Spanish and Basque) in comparison to students who were monolingual in Spanish only or Basque only (Cenoz & Valencia, 1994). Research on immersion programmes in Canada shows that native English-speaking students in total French immersion programmes need only one year in most cases to achieve parity in English development with other English-speaking students (Genesee, 1983). This short catch-up time is likely due to the transfer of critical skills from their L2 to their L1. Literacy skills are most likely to transfer. Evidence from Canada indicates further that transfer from French to English is enhanced the more advanced the students' French language skills are (Genesee, Holobow, Lambert & Chartrand, 1989). There is much we do not understand about transfer – for example, how extensive is it? And what transfers in the case of typologically distinct languages and/or languages with fundamentally distinct orthographies, such as Chinese or Japanese and English (see Bostwick, 2001, for an English-Japanese immersion programme in Japan). All three of the programmes that I described earlier are examples of additive multilingual education. The Ladin programme is somewhat controversial because although it teaches literacy in Ladin, it does not use Ladin for academic instruction. Arguably, Ladin is not treated equally with German and Italian. However, this is a model that the community supports and has found viable.

3. Age and SLA

Perhaps one of the most controversial issues in second language education is the question of age. It is widely believed that 'younger is better' when it comes to learning language, especially an L2. For educators, the issue is more complex since research evidence shows quite consistently that when it comes to learning second, or third, languages in school, older students often make faster progress than younger students. Let me illustrate this by reference to some Canadian immersion data. Evaluations of two-year (grade 7-8) late immersion programmes in comparison to early total immersion programmes indicates that late immersion students can achieve the same or almost the same levels of L2 proficiency as early immersion students even when the early immersion students have had two to three times more total exposure to 'French in school than the late immersion students (Genesee, 1981; see Figures 4A & 4B on pp. 35-36 for schematic representations of early and late immersion programmes in Canada). The advantage that older students have when it comes to L2 acquisition is not limited to immersion-type programmes since this has also been reported in evaluations of other forms of second language education (Burstall et al., 1974, in Britain, for example).

There are a number of reasons why older students can make such rapid progress in acquiring an L2 in school settings. First, older students have the benefit of a well-developed first language and, in particular, they have fully developed, or well developed, first language literacy skills. Literacy skills acquired in one language transfer readily to another language; this is true even for languages with different typologies and orthographies (Hebrew and English, for example). Older students may be faster L2 learners than younger students in school settings because language teaching and learning in school settings are generally abstract and context-reduced, to use Cummins's terminology (Cummins, 1981), and thus probably call on acquisitional strategies that are better developed in older learners. Finally, and in a related vein, we know that older students are generally faster learners than younger students no matter what the domain of learning because they are more cognitively mature. It is important to point out that younger learners are more likely to acquire native-like proficiency in the target language if given exposure to it in naturalistic settings outside school. The advantages that young language learners have in acquiring languages outside school probably result from language being highly contextualised, relatively concrete, and simplified. This is not the case for language use in the higher grade levels in school.

That older students can be effective L2 learners is a decided advantage when it comes to planning multilingual school programmes because it means that educators can introduce L3 instruction in the higher grades with considerable success. But, it might be questioned: can second or third languages be taught through a second language in higher grades without diminishing the students' academic achievement?   Studies in Canada on late immersion programmes which provide 80% of instruction through the medium of French (L2) in grades 7 and 8 have found that the participating students demonstrate the same levels of academic achievement as similar students who receive academic instruction through English in the same grades (see Figure 4B on page 36, and Genesee, 1981). This is true for below average, as well as average and above average students (Genesee, 1976 & 1987). Academic achievement was assessed in these studies using different kinds of tests: (1) national, standardised tests in mathematics and science, and (2) state high school examinations, and (3) local achievement tests.

4. Time and L2 Acquisition

Perhaps an equally controversial issue in discussions of L2 acquisition and bilingual education is the matter of time. It is often assumed that there is a direct link between the amount of exposure students have to an L2 in school and their achievement in the language – the notion of 'time on task'. Indeed, one of the reasons we begin instruction early (be it in second languages, mathematics, or other subject matter) is to provide more time for students to learn. Time is clearly important and often, although not always, students learn more when they have more exposure. This is true for second language learning as well – we know that students in total immersion programmes generally perform better on second language tests than students who have been in partial immersion programmes (see Figure 5). But, there are upper and lower limits to the importance of time. At the lower limits, variations in exposure to a second language probably make little difference – 20 versus 30 minutes per day, for example, is probably an unimportant difference. Likewise, at the upper limits, there may be diminishing returns on extended exposure. As noted earlier, late immersion students in some immersion programmes in Canada perform as well or almost as well as early total immersion students despite the fact that they have had significantly less exposure to their L2 (Genesee, 1981). Thus, time alone cannot always account for achievement differences in programme models. Another example that illustrates this point comes from research in Montreal that compared two groups of students, both in late immersion (Stevens, 1983). In one case, the students spent 80% of their school day immersed in French – all regular academic subjects were taught through the medium of French. The other group, in contrast, spent only half as much time – approximately 40% of their school day in French. Despite the time advantage of the first group, they did not score any higher than the second group on a variety of L2 measures. The explanation for the impressive performance of the students who received less exposure can be found in the pedagogical approach used in their programme. The half-day immersion students participated in a student-centred, activity-based programme that gave students certain choices about what they would study and how they would meet curricular objectives. In contrast, the other programme was characterised by a decidedly more teacher-centred approach where all students studied the same topics according to the same timeline. The lesson we learnt from this comparison is that time alone is not always the most significant predictor of L2 proficiency – the nature and quality of the programme and classroom instruction is equally, if not more, important.

Programmes that aim for multilingual competence must use time efficiently since students and teachers must cover the standard curriculum and two additional languages within the same number of school hours. Introduction of a third language can put substantial pressure on the schedule. It is noteworthy that two of the three programmes presented earlier – the Hebrew and the Ladin programmes – offer extended school weeks. The former has a 32-hour week and the latter a 37-hour week. Integrating language instruction with content instruction is one way in which time can be stretched effectively. Increasingly foreign language educators in North America are also using content-based approaches to teach foreign languages when there is insufficient time to simply add a second or third language to the curriculum. Content-based approaches that use academic material can be an effective way of teaching third languages in multilingual programmes since they allow educators to expand the amount of time committed to teaching languages without detracting from the time devoted to academic instruction.

5. Clearly Articulated Goals

Our investigations of time and language learning have taught us important lessons about the importance of clearly articulated goals (Cloud, Genesee & Hamayan, 2000; Met, 1998). Once again, the Canadian experiences with immersion programmes are relevant. In the beginning of the experiments with immersion in Canada, the language curriculum was determined largely by the needs of the academic curriculum since the rationale behind immersion is that students will learn those language and communication skills that are necessary to master academic material. In other words, students will learn the language of mathematics, science, and social studies as they do mathematics, science and social studies. Indeed, from the students' point of view, L2 or L3 learning in immersion often seems secondary or incidental to learning academic material since the language objectives are derived from and embedded in the academic curriculum. From the teachers' perspective, the primary focus of instructional attention is promoting mastery of the mathematics, science, and social studies objectives; the language skills that facilitate mastery of these objectives are taught as a means to achieving these ends.

While this approach is generally effective – more effective than any other method that we have tried (Genesee, 1987), it is not perfect. We now believe that it may be desirable to articulate the language objectives that are linked to specific content domains along side the content-area objectives in greater detail and in a more explicit manner than has been the case so far (see Snow, Met & Genesee, 1989, for a discussion of how such goal setting can be accomplished). Explicitly setting out language objectives in parallel with academic objectives is important so that teachers plan instructional activities that promote both academic and language objectives systematically. This does not mean that a focus on content should be abandoned; but rather there should be a more explicit identification of the language objectives to be taught and learnt. This approach ensures that teachers and students work on language development as well as academic development and that they do not leave language development to chance. If language objectives are systematically identified with content across grade levels, this approach also ensures that there will be a truly developmental focus to the curriculum (see Cloud, Genesee & Hamayan, 2000, Chapter 6, for how this can be done). Research in Canada suggests that there is not always continuous development of students' L2 skills and especially their grammatical competence from grade to grade (e.g., Adiv, 1980). This may result from the secondary and implicit focus on language development that tended to characterise the first generation of immersion programmes.

In this regard, Snow, Met and Genesee (1989) distinguish between content-obligatory and content-compatible language objectives. Content-obligatory language objectives are those aspects of language that are essential if students are to make normal progress in the academic domains. Each academic domain has its own set of language skills, and these include not only specialised vocabulary, but also specific grammatical and discourse/text patterns. It is these language objectives that must be articulated with academic objectives. Content-compatible language is not essential for communication about academic subjects. It includes language skills that can, however, be taught effectively through academic content – e.g., the names of different objects and the concepts 'bigger than', 'smaller than', 'the same size as' can be taught as part of a grade 2 social studies unit on 'farm animals'. Introducing content-compatible language during academic instruction allows teachers to stretch their students' language proficiency beyond that which is required of the prescribed academic curriculum. It also allows teachers to teach language skills that students will need at a later point in the curriculum when they become obligatory – for example, in a science lesson on 'flotation' later in the school year.

The important point here is that, as in all effective educational programmes, programmes that aim to promote multilingualism should have clearly articulated and developmentally appropriated sequences of language objectives if they are to optimise language learning within the time constraints they have (Genesee, 1994).

6. Parental Involvement

Finally, parents have a critical role to play if multilingual programmes are to be successful. In many communities, in fact, it is parents who are the chief advocates for innovative multilingual programmes. Multilingual programmes are complex and controversial, and parental support for the creation of such programmes is often crucial if fear, uncertainty, and inertia are to be overcome. This has been evident in virtually every bilingual or multilingual programme that I have worked with, be it in Canada, the US, Japan, Europe, or elsewhere.

It is important to involve parents not only at the outset, when a new programme is being discussed or planned; but also once a programme is running. Multilingual programmes, by definition, provide education that goes beyond what is normally offered in conventional schools. It is important that parents understand how the programme is different and what they can expect. Parents who are fully informed and consulted are likely to be more loyal and more supportive than parents who are not. As much as possible, parents should be informed about the progress their children are likely to make in the academic domains as well as in each language. In particular, in programmes that delay or reduce use of the L1 or that provide academic instruction through an L2 or L3, it is important to tell parents if their children's language or academic progress is going to be slowed down and for how long. L1 and academic development are generally the primary concerns of parents and, therefore, it is important that they be kept up to date as much as possible about these critical issues. Educating parents about a new multilingual programme is critical to ensure the long term effectiveness of the programme.

Parents of children in multilingual programmes are often concerned about their role with respect to language use at home, helping out with homework, school visits, etc. Successful programmes, thus, also make provisions to clarify parents' roles in each of these domains. There are ways that these concerns can be addressed. Parents also need to be informed of their obligations and responsibilities – the success and benefits of multilingual education result from long term commitment. Parents need to understand the short and long term benefits of the programme so that their decisions are well grounded.

It can be useful to create a parents' advisory committee to work with school authorities and teachers during both programme planning and implementation. Such a committee can provide a formal mechanism for dealing with controversial issues, for identifying sensitive concerns, or for responding to problems (see Chapter 9 in Cloud et al., 2000, for more examples of how to involve parents).

CONCLUSIONS

In the 1970's, the Canadian writer Marshall McLuhan coined the term 'the global village' to describe the evolution of communication among the peoples of the world as a result of newly emerging high-tech communication systems. McLuhan could not have been more prophetic; indeed, the global village is here. While technology-based communication has been receiving the lion's share of attention in this evolution, there is no doubt that face-to-face communication must also be considered. Both the challenges and rewards of global communication are enormous, and both demand that today's students be given expanded opportunities to acquire additional languages. We are very fortunate because we can take our inspiration from experiments that have been conducted in bilingual education during the last quarter century of the old millennium. I have attempted to show in this chapter that there is ample evidence that bi- and multilingual education, in a variety of forms, can and does work. We also know from current research that pre-school and school-age children are equally adept at acquiring two, or more, languages as one. That is to say, there is no neurocognitive limitation of any serious magnitude to dampen our enthusiasm for early multilingual education (Genesee, 2000).

Multilingual education programmes in the new millennium can be built using the lessons we have learnt from the many innovative and extensively evaluated bi- and multilingual forms of education that precede us. The future for multilingual education is challenging but very bright.

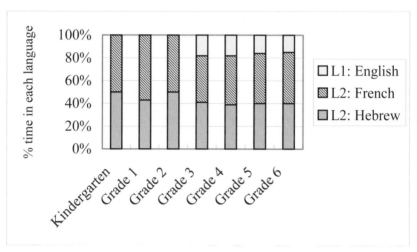

Figure 1 Hebrew-French-English Programme

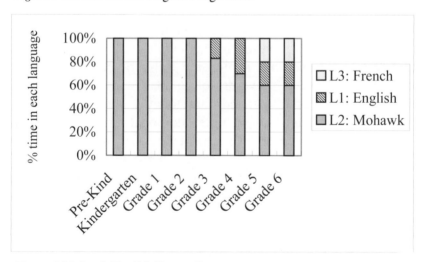

Figure 2 Mohawk-English-France Programme

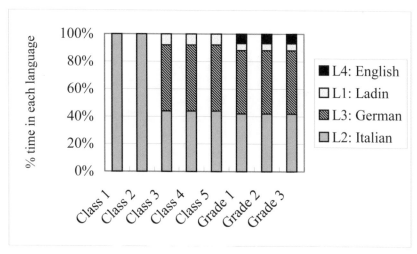

Figure 3 Italian-German-Ladin (English) Programme

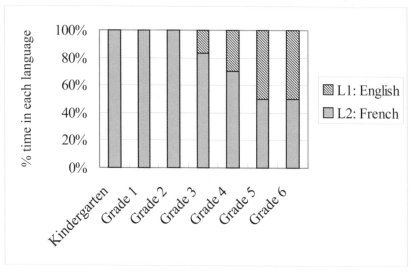

Figure 4A Early Total Immerison:Time in Each Language per Week

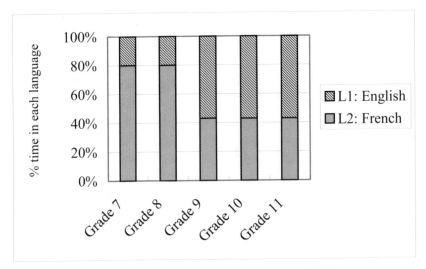

Figure 4B Two-year Late Immersion Programme: Time in Each Language per Week

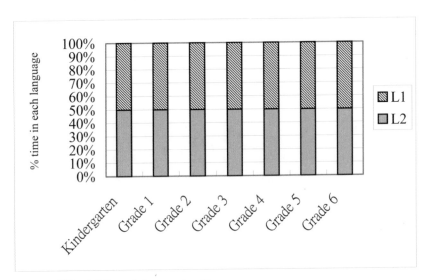

Figure 5 Partial French Immersion Program

3 Against All Odds: Lessons from Content and Language Integrated Learning in English Secondary Schools

Do Coyle
University of Nottingham

1. Monolingual myths: plurilingual potential – an introduction

We enter the 21st century with at least one certainty: that the world in which the next generation will grow up, learn, work and play will be very different from the one we know. Rapid technological, economic and social change over the past twenty years has created a world that is complex, inter-connected, interdependent. There are too many imponderables to allow a precise prediction of how it will look over the next two decades... nevertheless it is possible to identify the key trends likely to define the challenges and opportunities for the UK and thus the needs of the next generation. (Nuffield Language Inquiry, Final Report, 2000)

This paper focuses on the methodology of Content and Language Integrated Learning (CLIL) in mainstream comprehensive schools in England. During the early stages of piloting in the past ten years, small-scale results at classroom level have been very positive and CLIL is now 'quietly' appearing on the government agenda. The title of the paper – *Against all odds* – is chosen because the English language on a global scale is a force to be reckoned with – and since in the CLIL context the focus of attention is on using languages other than English. *Against all odds* that a form of 'additive bilingualism' by teaching subjects through the medium of a foreign language, like little acorns, is slowly beginning to grow and thus take effect. *Against all odds* that CLIL may significantly contribute to changing the moribund face of language learning in Britain.

I should like to begin by making three general observations. Firstly, that monolingual English speakers are disadvantaged in a world where those speaking English as a second language will shortly outnumber those speaking it as their first (Graddol, 1997). A hard lesson for English speakers is the understanding that we do not 'own' the language used in England – we use it along with millions of others. The so-called 'island mentality' has a reductive legacy, typified by the need for CILT (The Centre for Information on Language Teaching and Research, London) to promote the maxim '*monolingualism can be cured*'. One of the greatest paradoxes relative to this field is that Wales, Ireland and Scotland have their own languages, the heritage languages, in which their own medium-speaking schools and systems survive and thrive. Britain is not and never was a monolingual country. Yet this is silently ignored.

Secondly, as the phenomenon of 'Englishes' develops this is likely to bring about the decline in influence of the native-speaker of English, thus signalling a decline in the wholesale export of our language. The more traditional goal of using all four language skills in another language will undoubtedly be replaced by a wider, more acceptable reconceptualisation of communication needs in a technological oriented world.

Thirdly, foreign language or MFL (modern foreign language) learning in England is marginalised. Whilst the theoretical basis and wealth of pedagogic literature available in the ESOL field is more developed and extensive than that for teaching foreign languages, the two sides of the same coin rarely communicate. Moreover, for England to survive in a global economy, it is imperative to embrace plurilingualism and set English within the context of major world languages as shown in Table 1.

Table 1 **Number of First Language Speakers**

Chinese	1,113*
English	372
Hindi/Urdu	316
Spanish	304
Arabic	201
*In millions	

Source: Graddol, 1997: 8

It is easy to paint a depressing national picture with regard to English attitudes to 'foreignness' or 'otherness'. There is the highly politicised anti-European faction, whose voice is forever present in the tabloid and some broadsheet press. High profile racial incidents unleash xenophobic attitudes which sit uneasily with national realities, where our services and industries depend on a plurilingual and pluricultural workforce. It is of course a myth that England is monolingual although for many years the fact that bilingual children were treated as disadvantaged inconveniences was matched by a general disregard for the advantages which bilingual skills bring. According to a recent census (Baker & Eversley, 2000) 39 languages are spoken as first languages by school children in London alone; the BBC foreign languages Website logs 300,000 page hits per month and non English-speaking Internet users, it is estimated, will increase by 150% by 2005 leading to multiple language sites.

Whilst some of our European neighbours embrace plurilingual policies due to historical and sociocultural developments, the 1995 European White Paper's recommendation that all European citizens should have proficiency in three European languages, currently remains an unattainable goal for the English – especially since there does not exist a national Language Policy for putting macro strategies in place. The recent relatively successful government Literacy Strategy, introduced into the Primary and latterly early Secondary education sector targeting the raising of national standards of literacy, is in reality exclusive to English – in my view a wasted opportunity to reduce the concept of literacy to mother tongue usage. There is an anomaly in attempting to promote a plurilingual yet monoliterate generation. Little wonder then that Britain's linguistic capability lags behind that of its closest neighbours with low national standards in modern languages. Moreover, whilst diversification of language learning is a plurilingual requisite, the continued dominance of French as the major European language taught, is once again threatening the learning of German. Whilst Spanish is currently enjoying minor expansion, languages such as Italian, Russian and Japanese are fast disappearing from the school curriculum. Non-European languages and community languages such as

Gujerati, Punjabi and Arabic have low status and low profile, ignored by most government agencies.

In short, there is a national crisis in modern language teaching and learning: nine out of ten students stop foreign language learning at the age of 16, having started at 11; 'A' level candidates (18-year-olds taking the national subject examination at pre-university level) are decreasing by 9% per year; in 1998 only 6% of all 'A' levels were in one MFL, 2.5% in two. Moreover, the MFL National Curriculum (for 11 to 16-year-olds) introduced in 1990, failed to change attitudes and practice. Language learners are generally demotivated and disaffected. 'Linguistic' currency is devalued. This has resulted in teacher dissatisfaction, likened to 'gardening in a gale' (Hawkins, 1999) – especially given the introduction of performance-related pay and the burden of accountability in the form of examination results and National Curriculum standards. In general, classroom practice is typified by the familiar *'dead bodies, talking heads'* syndrome (Legutke & Thomas, 1996*)*. In short, the communicative legacy and related classroom discourse have succeeded in fostering communicative 'incompetence' (Donato, 1996), where students are told what to say based on textbook tests and examination syllabi. Little wonder then that students vote with their feet and the National Inspection OFSTED agency (the Office for Standards in Education) recently reported on low standards in MFL: *Progression from KS3 to 4* [from the third year of learning to the fourth] *is lower than in all other subjects...Pupils in KS4* [after four years] *are unable to express themselves in the target language in a wider range of contexts than in KS3* [after 3 years]. (OFSTED, 1996) Unless there is a significant reconceptualisation of the modern languages curriculum in our schools, then modern foreign language learning may well be in the balance – to revert to an 'option' reserved for an elite group of so-called linguists or to reinvent itself as a genuine entitlement for all learners embedded in a repertoire of flexible life skills (Coyle, 1999a).

2. Crisis: a catalyst for change

Perhaps the most crucial acknowledgement of the languages crisis was signified by the government's decision in 1998, to commission a national independent inquiry into the state of foreign languages in the UK. The Nuffield Language Inquiry (1998-9), led by Sir Trevor MacDonald, a high-profile BBC newsreader, reporting in 2000, shifted the debate into the public arena, and made a strong case for addressing the crisis in modern language teaching and learning:

> English alone will simply not do! The UK must shrug off its monolingual image. Capability in other languages – a much broader range than hitherto and in greater depth – is crucially important for a flourishing UK. The scale of what needs to be done has become ever more striking as our work has gone on. At the moment, by any reliable measure we are doing badly. We talk about communication but don't always communicate. Educational provision is fragmented, achievement poorly measured, continuity not very evident. In the language of our time, there is a lack of joined-up thinking.

The findings of the report were predictable and can be summarised as follows:

- English is not enough
- People are looking for leadership to improve the nation's capability in languages
- Young people from the UK are disadvantaged in the recruitment market
- The UK needs competence in many languages – not just French
- The government has no coherent approach to languages
- In spite of parental demand, there is still no UK-wide agenda for children to start languages early (in the UK, students begin their foreign language study at 11)
- Secondary school pupils lack motivation or direction
- Nine out of ten children stop learning languages at 16
- University language departments are closing, leaving the sector in deep crisis
- Adults are keen to learn languages but badly served by an impoverished system
- The UK desperately needs more language teachers

Of the twelve recommendations, I have selected seven which relate particularly to this paper:
- Designate languages a key skill
- Drive forward a national strategy
- Raise the profile of languages
- Improve arrangements in secondary schools
- Make languages a specified component of the 16-19 curriculum
- Establish a national standards framework for describing and accrediting language competence
- Co-ordinate initiatives linking technology and languages

In exposing the need for a national language strategy as well as a national standards framework for language competence, the inquiry advocates government-driven initiatives for the first time. If one considers that the principal drivers of change at the local level – such as teacher-led movements foregrounding diversity and flexibility, relevance, future life skills and ownership – must be matched by political will and policy at the national level, then a pathway for significant development begins to emerge.

I would argue too that the current crisis in MFL is a catalyst for change. Focusing on the class- room/local level, CLIL (the teaching of other subjects through the medium of French, Spanish or German) is one such grassroots movement which is gaining momentum and is thus set to contribute significantly to raising the profile of MFL in the school curriculum. Given the state of foreign language teaching in the UK, it is hardly surprising that the pioneers and advocates of CLIL are language teachers, unlike in many other European countries. Propelled by a need to change the image and use of language learning, CLIL is slowly developing in mainstream comprehensive schools. For many years there has been a handful of such schools focused on innovative delivery of the curriculum, either through establishing a bilingual section (there are about 20 such schools in England) or through less ambitious cross-curricular projects. All use the foreign language to learn and to communicate, ranging from the study of History and Geography in Spanish or French to GCSE level (the first national examination taken at 16+) to field visits and scientific studies led jointly by Humanities or Science and Languages Departments. However, despite their relative success, these were seen as 'marginal' curriculum projects until about five years ago.

Expansion was hampered by 'territorial threats' from subject specialists and their belief that a takeover by the language teachers would result in a 'dumbing down' of their subject – not only understandable in a country where teachers usually only have one specialism but in my view justifiable in the absence of collaborative pedagogical planning and curriculum delivery. The refusal of involvement by the Ministry which paid lip service to this success whilst 'sitting on the fence,' led to the withdrawal of permission by National Examinations Boards in the mid 1990s for subjects such as Geography, Business Studies and History to be taken through the medium of a language other than English – a decision perhaps partly based on the fear that allowing national examinations to take place in 'other languages' would in fact open the flood gates for community languages to gain a stronghold.

More recently however, the CLIL movement has become more strongly yet indirectly supported through the government creation of specialist state schools or colleges during the past six years (for technology, languages, sports, music, the arts) – one such category being 'Language Colleges' whose brief is to give MFL a high profile in order to justify the injection of increased funding. Many of these schools (currently over 100) are exploring CLIL in an attempt to be innovative, to deliver their development plans and fundamentally to motivate students and raise standards. The current rising interest in CLIL in England is also timely, since it coincides with a more rapid expansion of plurilingual education in mainland Europe and beyond.

I have spent some time setting the context for language learning and CLIL in England due to the complex nature of societal attitudes and government policy which shapes the models adopted. This echoes Baetens Beardsmore's (1993) sentiment that there is neither a single blueprint nor a single model which is 'for export'.

However, sharing lessons learnt is very much for pedagogical export. It is now therefore to the emergent processes of content and language integrated teaching and learning in England that I wish to turn. The urgent need to address modern languages problems in secondary schools has given rise to an ever growing movement of teachers at grassroots level who are willing to engage in reappraising classroom methodologies. The CLIL context forms a stimulating backdrop to these processes, which are set to play a significant role in promoting and improving the quality of learning through the integration of subject and language learning.

3. 'Mainstreaming' Content and Language Integrated Learning

I should therefore now like to consider CLIL in transition. Curriculum innovation in pioneering schools will remain on the margins of common practice unless the means to adapt and develop this practice is accessible to a wide range of schools – this process I call 'mainstreaming'. Analysing both the processes and the outcomes of current CLIL environments provides a useful foundation on which to build and a trigger for pedagogical expansion. From a language teacher perspective in England, recent results have shown that CLIL potentially:

- produces tangibly impressive results (language examinations taken at least one year early and /or excellent grades in foreign language assessments)
- increases learner motivation and confidence
- improves study skills and develops metalinguistic abilities
- improves attitudes (especially amongst boys)
- raises teacher and learner expectations
- encourages the use of language for verbal mediation
                (Ullmann, 1999; Coyle, 2000a, 1999c & 1994)

However, whilst these claims can be substantiated, CLIL *per se* is no guarantee of quality learning environments. In the English context, where CLIL is often taught by language teachers, subject teachers continue to express their concerns that linguistic gains are achieved at the expense of subject knowledge, skills and understanding. Whilst this tension is already well-documented and it is not my intention to re-open the debate in this paper, in terms of mainstreaming CLIL, the pedagogical issues which lie at the very core need to be addressed. I shall therefore present what I believe to be some of the fundamental principles upon which thriving CLIL learning communities can be built.

According to McGuiness (1999: 5), 'Changing content alone will not automatically lead to quality learning experiences. Standards can only be raised when attention is directed not only to what is to be learnt but on how children learn and how teachers intervene to achieve this.' During the past five years, in my work as a teacher educator in the field of CLIL, students, trainees and teachers are integral to the dynamic of conceptualising and reconceptualising what we collectively consider to be the fundamental principles upon which effective CLIL environments can be nurtured (Coyle, 2000a & b). These are dynamic and flexible, and can be summarised as follows:

- We use language for two purposes: to communicate and to learn
- All teachers are teachers of language (Bullock Report, 1975)
- CLIL (along with other forms of education) is ultimately concerned with improving the quality of learning experiences for young people
- One of the key CLIL concepts lies in the integration of language learning and subject learning
- Learner entitlement is also at the heart of the CLIL philosophy. CLIL is not the reserve of the most able and advanced linguists
- Since there are limited numbers of teachers with expertise in both a subject and a foreign language, then the CLIL environment must be able to function within our pool of human resources, i.e., we must turn our limitations to our advantage

According to Bruner (1999: 17), 'A choice of pedagogy inevitably communicates a conception of the learning process and the learner. Pedagogy is never innocent. It is a medium which carries its own message.' Making methodologies matter has been and remains a focus of CLIL teacher education in England. Our collaborative thinking has crystallised into the *4Cs curriculum* which is a practical organisational framework emanating from the defined set of fundamental principles for content and integrated learning. It is a tool, continually being developed and reconstructed by practitioners to assist in the planning, teaching and evaluation of CLIL learning environments.

4. Making methodologies matter: the 4Cs curriculum - a pedagogical tool

In outlining the framework, I hope to provide insights into the pedagogical issues which have become foregrounded and debated whilst moving forwards classroom practice. The four strands (content, communication, cognition and cultures) are used as a pedagogical measure to evaluate, change and improve the quality of learning. This brief overview may provide the reader with a stimulus for further discussion.

4.1 Content

According to Mohan (1986: 1), 'A language is a system which relates what is being talked about (content) and the means used to talk about it (expressions). Linguistic content is inseparable from linguistic expressions. In subject matter learning we overlook the role of language as a medium of learning. In language learning we overlook the fact that content is being communicated.' Perhaps one of most challenging questions for **language teachers** is to define the content of language learning, especially in the early to intermediate stages. Often the teaching syllabus is defined in terms of grammatical structures or linguistic functions and notions. The widespread acceptance of the communicative approach to language learning and the pragmatic appeal of predictable scenarios for future language use has, it seems, given way to an over emphasis on transactional scripts and role plays on the one hand and grammatical exercises and rote phrase learning on the other. Whilst language practice and production are essential to the language learning process, opportunities for using the language for the equally essential tasks of authentic communication and learning are limited. The need for such opportunities is succinctly recapitulated in Wiesemes (2000: 33), 'Even the best traditional communicative MFL lessons with a variety of activities cannot hide the fact that the teacher is basically playing the same old decontextualised tune over and over again – maybe s/he may have added a variety of special effects, but underneath the tune remains the same. If the community context is overwhelmingly monolingual and cannot offer the quality of exposure needed for successful MFL learning, the bilingual or multilingual tune should at least be played by the school.'

As long as the content of communication is defined in terms of topics which are facile and repetitive by comparison with the mother tongue primary curriculum, and contain little in terms of 'new' knowledge, then changing the 'code' (i.e., the language) but retaining the substance (i.e., the content) will not extend the use of the language to authentic communication and learning purposes. In the CLIL environment, however, the content of lessons is drawn from two potential sources – the subject itself and the language system. Teaching the comparative and superlatives of adjectives within the context of plotting the relative distances between planets in the solar system is very different from a typical language textbook approach which involves cartoon characters being shorter or taller than each other! (Coyle, 1994) As Mohan (1986: 13) observes, 'It is absurd to ignore the role of content in the language class, just as it is absurd to ignore the role of languages as a medium of learning in the content class. Every language teacher has to organise content material to support language learning and all language teachers have an interest in doing this more systematically.'

4.2 Communication

According to Allwright (1984: 169), 'Interaction is the process whereby everything that happens in the classroom gets to happen the way it does. Let us make the most of it.'

Perhaps one of the most challenging questions for **subject teachers** is to define the linguistic demands of their own discipline. The 1975 Bullock Report's claim that *all teachers are teachers of English*, is enjoying a revival in Primary schools due to the government's Literacy Strategy. Whether this will easily transfer to the secondary sector so that teachers of say Geography and Science look critically at English language needs within the Humanities or Science curriculum is in the balance. However in the CLIL environment, analysing subject content for linguistic demands is fundamental to the notion of integration at all levels. It is as relevant a consideration for those students with high level linguistic skills as it is for those with lower level skills if quality learning is at forefront. There is a focus on raising language awareness in both teachers and students as well as exploring appropriate strategies for 'scaffolding' student learning. To illustrate this I should like to quote two French teachers of Science after participating in a CLIL focus group (University of Nottingham, 1999):

This module has made me aware of the linguistic problems raised by teaching in a foreign language which I had not taken into consideration at all - it now seems obvious to me that although I am not an English teacher, I cannot afford to teach in English as I would in French.   (Teacher A, 1999)

When I planned this lesson, I set about my science objectives, then I considered what the students' needs were likely to be in terms of the language they would want to use and be familiar with. That's why I have emboldened the key words, given visual support throughout the worksheets and presented the statistical information in this grid.   (Teacher B, 1999)

Moreover, whilst communication skills are part of the language teacher's familiar repertoire, I would argue that 'speaking' (as defined by the 1999 National Curriculum for England and Wales) does not take the learners far enough. The CLIL classroom demands a level of talking, of interaction and dialogic activity which is different to that of the traditional language classroom. According to Van Lier (1996: 175) 'all in all, if we were to put quality in one word, it would have something to do with participability.' This notion is supported by Firth and Wagner (1997) who contend that an increased 'emic' (participant-relevant) sensitivity towards second language acquisition theory would place contextual and interactional dimensions at the core. Leith (2000: 12) who leads the national TALK project for foreign language learners makes this observation: 'Talking for real also requires learners to think deeply about how language fits together, with obvious benefits for all four language skills. Talkers generally have a richer pool of language and grammatical understanding upon which to draw. Most noticeably, boys become more motivated when they speak and bring their own humour and personalities into their language learning.'

And yet, enabling learners to talk – chat, banter, discuss, debate, summarise and synthesise – and interact meaningfully with each other, to engage with and in the language, requires a methodological shift in praxis. Some of the English CLIL teachers are actively experimenting in this area.

4.3 Cognition

Thinking skills and problem solving are currently receiving widespread acclaim in the UK as a means to involving students more effectively in the learning process. Moreover Nisbet's claim made in 1993 that no curriculum will be acceptable unless it includes the teaching of thinking has remained largely ignored. More recently CLIL teachers are beginning to grasp its relevance to their work. This is in sharp contrast to the reductive yet commonly held view that in order to motivate learners, language learning must be 'fun'. Within the CLIL environment, developing thinking skills is an integral element of the curriculum.

As Baker observes, 'The four basic language abilities are commonly regarded as speaking, listening, reading and writing. However, there are times when a person is not speaking, listening, reading or writing but is still using language...the language for thinking may be a fifth area of language competence...Cummins (1984) expresses this notion as cognitive competence in a language. That is the ability to use one or both languages for reasoning and deliberation.' (1996: 7)

Building on Baker's work that thinking could be considered as the fifth skill, CLIL teachers are encouraged to use an adaptation of the Cummins' matrix (1984) to audit the cognitive and linguistic demands they make on their learners. The plotting of classroom tasks in the appropriate quadrant gives rise to serious debate – for example regarding the pedagogic value of cognitively and linguistically undemanding activity. It also provides a clear overview of classroom activity which aims at motivating and nurturing learners through 'curriculum enrichment'.

Met (1998: 3) makes a strong case for using higher order thinking skills (such as analysing, synthesising, or predicting) to promote quality learning: 'Students need to communicate with the teacher, one another, or texts, in order to access or apply content. In so doing, the cognitive demand of task requires students to call upon their existing knowledge, concepts, skills and strategies. This strengthens the connections between the elements of language being practiced/ learnt and previous knowledge. As we have seen, research indicates that strengthening and making connections amongst concepts and knowledge increases learning and retention.'

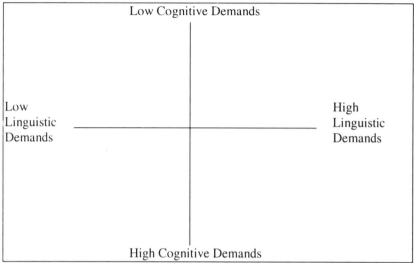

Figure 1 Adapted from Cummins 1984

McGuiness (1999) too claims that developing student thinking goes beyond an understanding of how students learn. She emphasises the role played by curricular design, availability of curricular materials, the nature of pedagogy, teachers' beliefs about learning and teaching as well as their professional development. In my view then, CLIL can and does respond to Leat's (1998) call for teachers to provide a rich learning environment in which learners have to think 'hard' – i.e., where 'cognitive conflict' is evident.

4.4 Cultures

The final strand of the 4 Cs curriculum focuses on the cultural opportunities which CLIL teaching and learning potentially affords. This for me represents an under-researched area. Not only does learning through another language facilitate the use of authentic materials, it enables wider interpretation and alternative perspectives to be brought into the learning frame. Notions such as 'otherness', citizenship, cultural identity and tolerance are forever present to be exploited for a deepening awareness of learner self.

Again, I should like to quote some CLIL teachers:

My conception of history teaching in English was limited to the simple translation of a typical French history lesson into

English which would be a good point of studying English sources in their original tongue... The outcome of it would have been (I thought) to enlarge the English vocabulary of the students on a specific topic.   (Teacher C, 1999)

The fact that our teaching methods are so different made us think about them – I'm pretty sure that I won't teach in the same way than before coming here because I now know some answers to the big question – how can we make students get involved in their learning, especially if it's difficult work.
                                        (Teacher D, 1999)

It was a powerful experience for me to see how 1066 and the Norman Invasion was presented in English textbooks...when I think about how we approach it.   (Teacher E, 1999)

4.5 Reconceptualising the curriculum

Through exploring the possible four complementary strands of a CLIL curriculum, I hope to have made a case for the powerful lead which reconceptualising classroom practice has had on the development of CLIL in England. Through an action inquiry approach, teachers are slowly experimenting with creating alternative learning environments which differ from their traditional language teaching classrooms, spurred on by some successes along the way. They are planning with colleagues in other departments. They are learning about how other subjects are taught. They are collaborating. They are engaging in pedagogic dialogue with other teachers and with their students. They are innovating. They are evaluating. They are questioning. They are risk-taking. But above all they are working towards creating more effective learning contexts – whether in History, German, Science or Geography-French, Business Studies-Spanish. The following quotation is significant:

I now know several ways to teach a specific historical or geographical subject through the medium of English, but I learnt much more about learning in general. (Teacher F, 1999)

5. Other factors influencing the expansion of content and integrated learning

As the numbers of teachers prepared to explore classroom methodologies has increased, then in parallel opportunities for pre- and in-service teacher education have also developed. The following examples illustrate the point.

5.1 Pre-service *BILD PGCE*

At pre-service level, the cascade effect of a small number of trainees per year being trained to teach CLIL in the secondary sector is now taking effect. Former trainees now in post are pioneering the introduction of CLIL in their schools (Coyle, 2000). The BILD PGCE (Bilingual Integration of Languages and Disciplines Post Graduate Certificate in Education, University of Nottingham, UK) training course:

• grants qualified teacher status to trainees
• targets both future language teachers and subject teachers
• is integrated within a one year teacher training course
• guarantees students teaching practice in a CLIL learning environment
• attracts small but consistent numbers
• is gaining recognition as its work cascades

5.2 In-service *SALT Project:* a significant landmark

This year-long national in-service course (SALT-subject and language teaching) funded by the French and Spanish Embassies and the Goethe Institut invited state comprehensive schools to select two teachers from each school (a subject teacher and a language teacher) to create CLIL modules for students in their third year of secondary education. The CLIL training offered included a residential course in countries where the target language is spoken, to provide opportunities for the subject teachers to improve their language skills and the collection of appropriate resources. The course promoted:

• collaboration between subject and language teachers each bringing respective expertise to create CLIL modules of work;
• a variety of schools to work through three foreign languages (French, German, Spanish) in four curricular areas (History, Geography, Science and Mathematics);
• exploitation of themes rooted in the regular curriculum, which were therefore not dependent on additional funding or delivery time (themes: mathematical inquiry, eating and digestion, water, Japan, natural hazards, hurricanes, civilians in war, the Second World War, the Cold War, Norman Conquest);
• targeting a wide range of learners in very different schools;
• modules planned using the 4Cs curriculum including the development of student thinking skills and learning strategies

Other significant examples include initiatives to offer Masters degrees in CLIL, European-funded professional development opportunities as well as the government-funded Teaching Observatory for CLIL training, where teachers can observe virtual CLIL lessons.

In sum, *against all odds* progress in implementing CLIL in England has so far relied on and benefited from a driving force at grassroots level which believes there are alternative methodologies which give rise to alternative ways of using and developing foreign language skills. This movement is propelled by a sense of professional ownership and reflection by the teachers and learners based on diversity of approach and differentiated objectives. Networks have grown, collaborative research projects have been set up and teacher supply, training and continued professional development is becoming more established. Some initiatives have been supported by universities and national agencies such as CILT, the Embassies, the Ministry and the City Technology Trust. The variety of learning communities involved is extensive, ranging from single sex selective schools to inner city action zones, from highly able students to those with learning difficulties, from native speaker teachers to those with limited language or subject knowledge, from school programmes of two or three years in duration to modules lasting two weeks.

6. *Against all odds* – towards 'joined-up' thinking

If you always do what you've always done, you'll always get what you've always got. If what you are doing is not working, do something else. (O'Connor & Seymour, 1990)

However, whilst teacher-led movements go some way to changing classroom practice, alone they are unlikely to permanently affect mainstream provision without wider support and policy implementation. To reiterate the message in the introduction to the Nuffield Enquiry: *Educational provision is fragmented, achievement poorly measured, continuity not very evident. In the language of our time, there is a lack of joined-up thinking.* (Nuffield Language Inquiry, 1998: 1) And yet how then might this 'joined-up' thinking be achieved?

The latest National Curriculum for England and Wales (Curriculum, 2000) is an inclusive curriculum which aims to provide effective learning opportunities for all pupils. With an emphasis on an entitlement to differentiated approaches to learning, the way lies open for a CLIL interpretation of the following statement printed in the final version:

> For pupils whose attainments significantly succeed the expected level of attainment...plan suitably challenging work... teachers may plan further differentiation by...work which draws on the content of different subjects.
>
> (Curriculum, 2000: 21)

Moreover, the MFL curriculum makes specific reference to links with other curricular areas in particular English (e.g. through grammar) and ICT (through presentation, communication and using resources to access information). Equally there is also a strong case to be made for linking MFL with History, Geography, Citizenship, Health Education and so on, which CLIL innovators must make strongly.

The Nuffield Inquiry in its final report made explicit recommendations that CLIL should be supported and developed. It cites the case of Hasland Hall comprehensive school as an example of good practice where 11-year-olds study Geography, ICT, History and PSE through the medium of French (without any prior understanding of the language). After one year, the teachers found that lower ability children who followed the bilingual programme performed better in mother tongue English than those who had not. Boys seemed to do especially well. Moreover, recommendation 7.8, suggests financial support for those schools prepared to create 'bilingual sections':

> Financial incentives should be made available for schools to introduce bilingual sections, in which a major part of the curriculum would be taught through the medium of a new language. Bilingual sections could be initiated independently or as part of a contract with a primary school making similar provision. Schools would provide classes in each year group, with children remaining in a bilingual class as they move up the school. Entry to bilingual classes where at least half the timetable would be taught through the medium of another language would be through parental choice. There should be arrangements also for public examinations at age 16 in bilingual forms for selected disciplines.
>
> (Nuffield Inquiry Final Report, 2000: 49)

Along with other Nuffield recommendations, previously reported in this paper such as greater diversity of provision in modern languages, more extensive use of ICT and the advancement of languages as a key skill, then there is a mood of cautious optimism which indicates that at the macro level CLIL is now on the government agenda. There is still some way to go – transforming the Nuffield recommendations into policy will take time; mainstreaming CLIL will have to subtly coincide with other government initiatives such as the Literacy Strategy and the drive to raise standards. There are many unresolved issues not least more extensive professional support and training, resources, public assessment and professional confidence that CLIL learning communities can benefit the widest range of students. But already, in the Effectiveness and Standards unit at the Ministry there is a team whose brief includes Nuffield implementation. Ultimately bringing together the micro and macro will make a difference.

> To include the world's diversity in a picture, a variety of lenses are needed. But it is not enough to inherit or be able to buy many lenses. An accomplished photographer also needs proper instruction: opportunities to use varied lenses to create multiple images and a balanced and focused vision, and to learn where to use one lens or the other, or both or all.
>
> (Skutnabb-Kangas, 1988: 224)

4 Content and Language Integrated Learning: An Evaluation of the German Approach

Dieter Wolff
University of Wuppertal

1. Introduction

Multilingualism has become a political goal, as well as a political necessity in Europe. In the Maastricht treaty the member states of the European Union (EU) have opted for the preservation of linguistic and cultural diversity in Europe. This decision was taken in the firm belief that a European union can only be achieved if this diversity is maintained. This approach to achieving unity via diversity may appear to be overtly idealistic, but there is also a clear political and economic necessity to promote multilingualism in Europe. Trade between the member states of the EU is growing every year, so-called *Euregios* are being developed across the borders of the member states, and exchanges among the inhabitants of the Union are becoming more and more frequent. Although in intercultural communication English is used as a *lingua franca*, it has become clear that the use of English as the only means of interaction has more negative than positive effects in such highly diversified linguistic contexts.

Multilingualism has been identified as a political necessity in Europe, but this consensus has not yet induced member states to make the efforts necessary to attain this goal. Although educationists and language teaching specialists have understood that our present approach to learning and teaching foreign languages – which Baker (1993) ironically but appropriately characterises as 'drip-feed education' – will never lead to multilingualism in Europe, there is disagreement about the best way to develop linguistic proficiency in several languages at a level of competence higher than what is attained nowadays in traditional language teaching and learning. A number of so-called post-communicative approaches are under discussion: task-based and process-oriented language teaching and learner autonomy are among the most frequently discussed models.

One model which is becoming very popular all over Europe is Content and Language Integrated Learning, or CLIL. This approach has also been called Bilingual Content Teaching, Bilingual Subject Teaching or Content-Based Language Teaching. The term CLIL is now the one most commonly used, however, especially since a definition has been found which is acceptable to all dealing with this new approach:

> Content and Language Integrated Learning (CLIL) is a generic term and refers to any educational situation in which an additional language, and therefore not the most widely used language of the environment, is used for the teaching and learning of subjects other than the language itself.

This definition of CLIL was developed by a group of language and content teaching specialists from various European universities for a research project in which different models of content and language integrated teaching and learning in Europe are being analysed (cf. www.clilcompendium.com). In the context of this project, which was financed by the EU, questionnaires were sent to more than 1800 CLIL schools all over Europe in order to find out more about their individual approaches to CLIL. During the analysis of the data – the final results were published in the so-called CLIL compendium in mid June 2001 – it became clear that CLIL approaches vary considerably in different European countries and that this variation is a result of, among other things, the educational and linguistic background of each specific country. It is taken that the definition of CLIL which was developed on the basis of these questionnaires is very general; but it can integrate all CLIL approaches practised in Europe. It cannot, however, take into account the individual features of each single approach developed in one particular country.

In this paper I will describe and evaluate one approach to CLIL which was developed in Germany. I will first draw a picture of the German approach, its linguistic and educational background and the way CLIL is integrated in the German school system. I will then talk about CLIL pedagogy in Germany. I will look at CLIL curricula, selection of students, language and content teaching methodology, materials for CLIL, students' assessment, teacher training and research on CLIL. Part four of my paper is devoted to new methodological issues related to CLIL. Two questions will be focused upon: the pedagogical potential of CLIL and the need for a CLIL methodology. I will argue that it is the learning environment created by the integration of content and language in these classrooms, which is highly beneficial both for the language learning process and the understanding of the content subject. I will also argue that teachers have not succeeded in using the full learning potential of this new learning environment and that a specific CLIL methodology will have to be developed. In my concluding remarks I will argue that CLIL, as practised in Germany, but also in a number of other countries, would benefit immensely if it were integrated methodologically into an approach defined by principles of learner autonomy and if this approach made more use of the resources and the tool functions of the New Technologies.

2. The German approach to Content and Language Integrated Learning

In this part I will draw a picture of the German approach and its main characteristics. I will begin by giving a brief overview of the linguistic and educational background and will then show in which way CLIL is integrated into the German school system.

2.1 Linguistic and educational background

In theory, the Federal Republic of Germany is a monolingual country. The official majority language is German, a language which is also spoken in Austria and parts of Switzerland and is thus the most widely used native language in the European Union. Besides German there are two minority languages officially recognised in the constitution, Danish and Sorbic; the first is spoken in the Danish-German border region in the north of Schleswig-Holstein, and the second – a Slavic language – is spoken by a small ethnic community in a rural area in Brandenburg. Apart from these two minority languages, which do not really play any significant role in the country's linguistic profile, there are languages spoken by large groups of migrants and immigrants: Turkish, Serbo-Croatian, Greek, and Italian are among the most widely spread.

Although these languages are tolerated in Germany, they have no official status. But their speakers, by the sheer force of their numbers, have much influence on political decisions with respect to language policy and therefore the development of multilingualism as well.

It is important to note also that Germany is a federal republic, which means, in terms of educational policy, that the fifteen states of the confederation each have their own educational system which can differ considerably from those of the others, sometimes even to such an extent that children have difficulties in moving from one state system to another.

As far as language teaching is concerned the structure of the German education system is rather traditional. Until now foreign language teaching starts at grade five at the age of ten, when children move from primary to secondary school. The first language is usually English; some more traditional *Gymnasien* might still offer Latin as a first language, and in the regions bordering France, French can be the first language. In grade seven, when children are twelve years old, a second foreign language is introduced, either French, English or Latin (depending on the first language the child has chosen). In grade nine a third non-obligatory language is introduced: this can be French, Spanish, Russian or even Latin. Languages are taught three to four periods (of 45 minutes) a week. It is important to mention at this stage that most German states have recently decided to introduce a first foreign language in primary school. From 2003 onwards children in Germany will begin learning English in the third grade, at the age of eight. This decision will have consequences for CLIL as well.

One last point is important in the context of this paper. In Germany, secondary school teachers do not teach one subject only: to become a state school teacher one is required to be able to teach two subjects. Many students combine two languages (English and French); others will study English and German. But quite a number of prospective teachers study a language and a content subject, for example English and Geography or French and History. These are the teachers who are of interest to our CLIL classes.

2.2 CLIL in the German school system

History of CLIL in Germany: In Germany Content and Language Integrated Learning has a fairly long tradition. It was not an innovation of any government agency or ministry of education. Instead it partly grew out of the European School model as an approach to promoting foreign language competence. Its success is to a large extent also due to the development of the so-called Franco-German schools in the late 1960s and early 1970s. These schools were founded after the French-German friendship treaty had been signed in the early 1960s. The number of secondary schools practising CLIL was very small in the beginning. In most of them French was used as the language of instruction. In the early 1970s a few schools began to introduce English, but, on the whole, this approach was regarded as fairly idiosyncratic until the middle of the 1980s when the number of children dramatically decreased and more and more schools offered CLIL as an option to attract students. To date, more than 300 schools in Germany have optional CLIL branches with almost eighty of them using French as the language of instruction (cf. Table 1).

Organisation of CLIL in the German school system: CLIL in Germany is usually organised according to the following pattern. When children begin their secondary education at the age of ten, they have the choice to opt for a CLIL education. They do not enter a CLIL class right away, however, but during the first two years they take part in a preparatory language course in the CLIL language of the school. Usually this preparatory course consists of two to three additional language lessons per week, in which the students are expected to develop a higher degree of general language competence, but also some basic English for Special Purposes (ESP) proficiency in the content subjects.

In grade seven, at the age of twelve, content education in a foreign language begins. The most favoured content subjects are history and geography; politics is also a favourite, but even content subjects like biology, sports or religious instruction are taught in a foreign language. As in normal classes, content subjects are taught two hours a week so that together with the regular language courses learners are exposed to the foreign language six to seven hours a week (cf. Table 2).

Table 1 **CLIL schools in Germany (cf. Thuermann 2000)**

Stage	English	French	Other languages	Total
Baden-Wuerttemberg	5	6	0	11
Bayern	26	5	2	33
Berlin	2	2	0	4
Brandenburg	1	0	1	2
Bremen	10	0	0	10
Hamburg	5	1	0	6
Hessen	14	6	0	20
Niedersachsen	29	1	2	32
Nordrhein-Westfalen	90	24	9	123
Rheinland-Pfalz	20	16	0	36
Saarland	0	11	0	11
Sachsen	0	2	0	2
Sachsen-Anhalt	2	0	0	2
Schleswig-Holstein	9	0	0	9
Thueringen	3	3	0	6
	216	77	14	307

In grade nine a second content subject is introduced, which is taught in the same foreign language. At grade eleven in some schools a third content subject is introduced for students who continue their schooling to obtain their final degree, the Abitur (cf. Figure 1).

The languages of instruction in CLIL classes are mostly English and French. Other lesser-used languages are Italian, Spanish, Russian or Polish. It is important to underline that when a school in Germany has opted for CLIL, content teaching, unlike in other European countries, usually takes place in only one foreign language. Nevertheless, other foreign languages may be taught at the same school.

Table 2 also shows that CLIL languages and content subjects are related to each other. For example, history is proportionately more often taught through French, geography more often through English. This has something to do with the choices students make when they acquire their teaching diploma. French and history is a more common combination than English and history; English and geography is a more common combination than French and geography. The schools are free to choose the language of instruction; in general, they can select their content

Table 2 **Content Subjects in CLIL classes (cf. Thuermann 2000)**

Subjects	Grade 7	Grade 8	Grade 9	Grade 10	Total
Geography	E=61,24%*	E=46,30%	E=36,84%	E=24,48%	E=41,77%
	F=66,00%	F=54,87%	F=36,51%	F=15,00%	F=42,75%
History	E=21,91%*	E=27,31%	E=37,72%	E=39,58%	E=26,54%
	F=16,00%	F=20,96%	F=57,14%	F=41,66%	F=40,00%
Politics	E= 0,56%	E=14,81%	E= 7,89%	E=20,31%	E=11,06%
	---	F=17,74%	---	F=18,33%	F= 8,63%
Social science	E= 3,37%	E= 2,78%	E= 5,70%	E= 6,25%	E= 4,55%
	F= 4,00%	F= 3,22%	F= 3,18%	F=18,33%	F= 6,67%
Biology	E= 2,81%	E=3,24%	E= 4,82%	E= 4,17%	E= 3,81%
Sports	E= 5,62%	E= 2,78%	E= 2,19%	E= 1,56%	E= 2,95%
	F= 4,00%	---	---	---	F= 0,78%
Economics	E= 2,81%	E= 2,31%	E= 2,19%	E= 1,56%	E= 2,21%
	---	---	---	F= 3,33%	F= 0,78%
Music	E= 0,56%	---	E= 0,88%	E= 0,52%	E= 0,49%
	---	F= 1,61%	F= 1,59%	F= 1,66%	F= 1,18%
Physics	0	0	E= 0,88%	E= 1,04%	E= 0,49%
Art	E= 0,56%	E= 0,46%	E= 0,44%	---	E= 0,37%
	F= 2,00%	F= 1,61%	F= 1,59%	F= 1,66%	F= 1,57%
Religious instruction	0	0	E= 0,44%	E= 1,04%	E= 0,25%
Cultural learning	E= 0,56%	0	0	0	E= 0,12%
	F= 8,00%	---	---	---	F= 1,57%
					En =1,056
					Fn = 225

Key: E = English, F = French

*The percentages refer to the number of students learning a specific content subject in a specific grade in one of the two languages. For example, 61,24% of the students with English as the language of instruction are taught geography in grade seven, whereas only 21,91% are taught history.

Grade				
Grade 5	**Pre-course**			
Grade 6				
Grade 7		**First content**		
Grade 8		**subject**		
Grade 9			**Second**	
Grade 10			**content**	
Grade 11			**subject**	**(Third**
Grade 12				**content**
Grade 13				**subject)**

Figure 1 Introduction of content subject in secondary school

subjects from a set of six to eight. Of course, with respect to the language and the content subjects, their choice depends on the availability of the teachers concerned at the school.

At the end of their schooling, students who have successfully gone through a CLIL branch obtain the same degree as students who have been taught in their mother tongue. Students whose language of instruction is French are given an additional diploma which allows them to register at any university in France without having to pass a language test.

Motives for introducing CLIL: I have mentioned already that until now schools in Germany have been free to open a CLIL branch. In the past ministerial permission was given when the school could prove that a sufficient number of qualified language and content subject teachers were available and that there were enough students interested in taking a CLIL course. Ministries usually gave financial support to such schools or provided them with an additional teaching post. This situation has changed now, as is explained below, but it is still interesting to look at the motives a school has in opening a CLIL branch.

Table 3 lists the main reasons schools gave when they were asked why they introduced CLIL. The data are from a questionnaire which was sent to all CLIL schools in Germany by one of the ministries of education.

When looking at the data statistically we can see that four reasons given for the introduction of CLIL at a specific school are equally important. Most schools believe that CLIL branches develop a higher degree of intercultural understanding in the European context and a higher competence for the European job market; they also believe that students having studied in a CLIL branch have better chances at university and in professional life. Teachers and school administrators also believe that within a CLIL branch it is easier to develop general language competence, communicative competence and intercultural competence. When analysing these motives for the introduction of CLIL it can be seen that they are either pragmatic or language-focused. Schools believe that it is the foreign language which is promoted through CLIL; and a good knowledge of the foreign language will help students to get better jobs both in Germany and in Europe. The fact that specific content subjects are taught through a foreign language and the consequences of this for content-subject learning do not seem to play a role (neither negatively nor positively) in the decision to introduce a CLIL branch.

Table 3 **Reasons for introducing CLIL (cf. Thuermann 2000)**

Main reasons for introducing CLIL	English	French	Total in %
Higher competence for Europe	15	6	15,97
Better chances for students at university and in professional life	16	6	15,28
Communicative competence, general language competence	16	6	15,28
Intercultural competence	12	4	11,11
CLIL as an educational innovation	5	4	6,25
Suitable location (language border)	5	3	5,56
Foreign language as a world language	8	0	5,56
Development of cultural knowledge	3	3	4,17
Development of ESP competence	5	0	3,47
Development of bilingualism	3	2	3,47
Better understanding of the partner country	0	4	2,78
Ability and readiness for mobility	4	0	2,78
Possibility to move to other schools	3	0	2,08
Learning across the curriculum	3	0	2,08
Double diploma	0	3	2,08
Advantages in competition with other schools	1	0	0,69
Promotion of girls	1	0	0,69
Education for multilingualism	0	1	0,69
	100	44	144=100%

Although only four schools mention 'better understanding of the partner country' as a reason, it is interesting to note that all of them use French as the CLIL language, the partner country thus being France. The answers make clear that France is still seen as a partner country which can be understood as a cultural unit, whereas English is related to so many different countries with so many different cultures that understanding these cultures does not seem possible. It seems likely that teachers and school administrators relate English to some kind of multinationalism which cannot be identified culturally any more: students learn French as a language related to the French culture, whereas English is learnt as an international language no longer related to any culture.

Future plans: I have mentioned that until now the processes involved in installing a CLIL branch at a German secondary school were quite simple. This situation has changed recently due to lack of state funding. Instead, ministries of education all over Germany propose a new model for CLIL which is based on a so-called modular principle. The modular approach is expected to introduce elements of Content and Language Integrated Learning into all secondary schools. Teachers who are both language and content teachers are expected to do part of their content teaching in the foreign language. They are expected to develop specific teaching sequences (projects) dealing with a topic which lends itself to being taught in a foreign language, for example a project on the French revolution in French, or on early industrialisation in England in English. Ideally, in content teaching teachers would switch between the mother tongue and the foreign language several times during a school year. Of course the modular approach cannot be compared with 'traditional' CLIL. Neither is there any linguistic preparation for the CLIL course nor do learners develop a specific register for the content subject in the foreign language. The results of modular CLIL with respect to language proficiency will not be as good as the results of traditional CLIL. On the other hand, modular CLIL is probably more efficient than traditional language teaching as it bridges the gap for all students between language learning on the one hand and content learning on the other. Modular CLIL is a particularly interesting model for vocational training.

3. CLIL pedagogy in Germany

In what follows I would like to discuss in more detail some pedagogical aspects of the CLIL model, beginning with more structural aspects and ending with some remarks on teacher training and research on CLIL.

3.1 Curricula

The state of the art with respect to curricular development varies among the fifteen states of the Federal Republic. In many states no specific curricula for CLIL exist; teachers do what they think is best within the general CLIL framework. On the other hand, in Northrhine-Westphalia, the largest state, specific curricula have been devised for all subjects which can be chosen as content subjects for CLIL. Although these curricula, in general, closely resemble the corresponding mother tongue curricula, they are different in that they focus, for example, more on contents which are important for the target language culture. One principle is inherent in all content subject curricula: at the end of their school career students having gone through a CLIL branch must have the same knowledge of the content subject as those who have studied it through their mother tongue.

3.2 Selection of students

As mentioned earlier, students have to choose at the age of ten whether they want to enter a CLIL class at the beginning of grade seven. This choice depends on a number of factors: for example, there must be a CLIL school in the vicinity of where they reside, and their primary school teachers are asked to evaluate the child's chances of success in a CLIL class. But, in general, any child can enter a CLIL branch without having to pass an exam or go through an interview. Although this seems to be a highly democratic procedure with respect to the selection of students, it should be made clear that secondary schools try to form CLIL classes with only the most gifted children or at least what they believe to be the most gifted. Demographic analyses of CLIL classes also show that the number of migrant children is fairly low and that children of well-to-do parents are in the majority. In a way CLIL classes seem to have taken the place of classes which started with Latin as a first language and which were the prestige classes in a school.

3.3 Language teaching and learning methodology

Mainstream foreign language teaching in Germany, as in the rest of Europe, is based on the so-called communicative approach, a language-teaching model which was introduced in the early 1970s in the context of new developments in linguistics, sociolinguistics and philosophy (i.e., speech act theory and pragmatics). Neither from a theoretical nor from a practical perspective does communicative language teaching present itself, however, as one homogeneous approach. There are many different varieties, ranging from radical theoretical approaches representing the 'pure doctrine' to more traditional approaches which try to maintain older concepts and to relate them to fundamental principles of the communicative approach. In German schools a fairly conventional type of communicative language teaching prevails; it is still highly dependent on audiolingual and cognitive principles, but also includes elements of communication. Most teachers have developed their own eclectic approach which includes both interaction between teachers and students – not so much among students – but also heavily relies on grammar teaching, rule learning and conventional ways of vocabulary work. Unfortunately, this traditional way of dealing with language is also typical of the German CLIL classroom.

3.4 Content teaching and learning methodology

The way content subjects are taught in German classrooms is no less traditional. In general, all teaching and learning is textbook-centred, i.e., textbook materials are the only materials used in the classroom, with the exception of the occasional video film. It can be observed, however, that content teaching in CLIL classes is beginning to undergo major changes which have something to do with the different learning environment. Since there are no content subject textbooks in the foreign language, teachers have to develop their own materials. There are no ready-made dictionaries available which contain the technical vocabulary of the content subjects, so teachers and pupils have to compile their own vocabulary lists. In a way, the CLIL learning environment seems to lead to new ways of looking at methodology in the content classroom, and this interest in methodology seems to be higher on the content than on the language side.

3.5 Materials

Materials are a delicate and controversial issue in the German CLIL approach. Many CLIL teachers complain that there are no materials available. Although some resources have been developed by schoolbook editors – mainly small collections of texts focusing on one specific topic (for example on deserts or the rain forest in geography) – most editors are not really interested in producing materials on a large-scale basis, the market being too small and too diversified. Other teachers adapt materials from the target language country, using for example French history or English geography books. Problems arise because the target language textbooks do not reflect the German curriculum, and because, at least in the beginning, the texts are too difficult for German learners. A third group of teachers are looking for their own materials, making use of all kinds of sources: the Internet, television, radio, and print media, etc. Often materials development is an issue which is taken care of by the pedagogical institutes of the different states. The data bases prepared by some of the institutes show that in the near future sufficient resources will be available on the Internet for most content subjects and the major languages.

3.6 Students' assessment

Within the general framework of the German educational system, in which frequent learner assessment plays an important role, the evaluation of the students' progress both in the content subject and in the foreign language is quite problematic. The question arises whether students should be assessed according to their linguistic achievements or to their results in the content subject. There can be no doubt that this question is important also in conventional language teaching: many teachers are confronted almost daily with the problem in which way an essay should be assessed: an essay may be brilliant from a language point of view but poor content-wise. But in CLIL the consequences reach further because two different school subjects are involved at the same time. Should a student whose English or French is good but whose knowledge in the content subject is less than average get a better mark in the content subject because he or she can express himself of herself more fluently than another student whose content knowledge is better than that of the first student, but whose linguistic competence is less developed? In general, within the German CLIL framework content knowledge should decide on the student's assessment in the content subject, and linguistic proficiency in the language subject. But very often it is difficult to separate the two competencies. The assessment issue has not been solved in the present context. It can only be solved if the approach to assessment in general is changed.

3.7 Teacher training

CLIL as an innovative educational concept can only be put into practice on a larger scale if there is a sufficient number of teachers who can teach content subjects through a foreign language, i.e., who are not only qualified subject and foreign language teachers but who are also familiar with CLIL as a content and language integrated approach to learning. In Germany we have not gone very far yet in CLIL teacher training although the demand for teachers for our CLIL branches is fairly high. Until recently there has neither been any pre-service nor any in-service training. Most CLIL teachers learn the CLIL-specific aspects of their profession in the field, i.e., while they are teaching in CLIL classes. Now some German universities (including my own) offer an additional pre-service teacher training programme for students who want to qualify as CLIL teachers. Our programme consists of a module in bilingualism and bilingual education, a course on English or French for specific purposes, a course on learning strategies and a course on materials development. It also includes a module of six weeks in a CLIL school and a three months' stay at a school in the target language country. Some in-service teacher training centres now also offer specific training seminars for future CLIL teachers.

3.8 Research on CLIL

The existing research on CLIL in Germany is mainly classroom or action research. Although this research is important as it sheds light on the difficulties teachers have, a more sophisticated research programme will have to be developed to find out more about CLIL and the way it works in the German context. From a language teaching perspective, one important question should be what distinguishes the linguistic development of a student learning a foreign language in a CLIL context from a student in a traditional classroom. Although a number of researchers are dealing with this question, they focus mainly on structural and lexical aspects of language: learners are compared in terms of lexical richness and structural complexity. What we would need, however, is research on the overall language proficiency of both learner types. This cannot be analysed on the basis of lexis and grammar, but necessitates a much more sophisticated research programme. A research project which we have started to work on in Wuppertal is concerned with the question in what way the representation of content changes in an individual if content is learnt through another language.

4. New methodological issues

As I have tried to show in describing the German approach to CLIL, mainstream methodology is fairly traditional both with respect to the content and the language teaching component. Some CLIL experts – most of them language teaching specialists – have, however, raised a number of methodological issues in recent years in order to overcome the shortcomings inherent in the German model. These issues centre around two points: the critical reflection of the pedagogical potential of CLIL and the development of a CLIL methodology. I would like to deal with these two issues in more detail now.

4.1 Reflecting on the pedagogical potential of CLIL

Adherents of CLIL in Germany have always been convinced that their learners develop a higher competence in the foreign language because they are exposed to it for longer periods of time than in conventional language teaching. They also believe that using the foreign language as a working language in a content subject is more authentic than using it to talk about the traditional topics of a foreign language classroom, i.e., Peter and Betty, their pets, their father's job, their leisure time activities, going to a cinema or to the disco, etc. According to CLIL specialists it is not only the interaction which becomes authentic in the CLIL classroom; subject-specific materials (maps, graphs, and pictures, etc.) which are used in the classroom are more authentic than foreign language textbooks, in which topics are dealt with in a rather naive and superficial way. So, according to adherents of CLIL, this approach is superior to conventional language teaching because of its higher degree of authenticity and its higher frequency of exposure.

These advantages, which are purely language-oriented, should not be underestimated, but there are a number of additional features in CLIL which, if integrated more consistently into the classroom, will make this approach a more powerful instrument, not just for the promotion of language competence. It is important to see that through CLIL a learning environment is created in which modern pedagogical theories can be applied much more easily. I can discuss only a few aspects here (cf. also Wolff, 1997).

The learning environment created through CLIL lends itself much better to the use of learning techniques and strategies. The student will learn to use strategies of hypothesis building and hypothesis testing in the content subject and will transfer them to his language learning process. Learners will, for example, be introduced to analytic strategies in the interpretation of maps and will also use them in language learning. They will work with subject-specific vocabulary and thus increase their vocabulary learning potential. Learning techniques and strategies are the most important tools for the autonomous learner. Although their potential in the CLIL classroom is beginning to be recognised, they have not yet found their adequate position.

Another pedagogical principle which can be integrated much better into the learning environment of the CLIL classroom is to make the acquisition of skills and knowledge – which can be used in real life – a central issue in all classroom activities. The knowledge passed on in schools should not be different from real life or action knowledge. What must be avoided in CLIL classes is to teach factual historical or geographical knowledge: this knowledge will not really involve learners and will not, either language- or content-wise, induce them to make processing efforts.

This principle leads to another equally important principle. A CLIL classroom offers an environment for explorative learning which cannot be found in a conventional classroom. Exploring the content subject and experimenting with specific aspects are natural activities in a CLIL classroom. Discovery learning and project work are much easier to embed into such a learning environment than into a conventional classroom.

4.2 Developing a CLIL methodology

We should first ask the question whether CLIL really needs a methodology of its own. Although many teachers and teacher trainers do not believe that a specific CLIL methodology is necessary, a number of more innovative advocates of CLIL (cf. Thuermann, 1999) defend the necessity of such a methodology. The methodological discussion centres around three general issues: receptive processing, language production and autonomy.

It has become clear that reading, and thus reading skills, are of great importance in the CLIL classroom. Most of the acquisitional processes are related to language comprehension: learners work with documents and other sources in order to acquire content subject knowledge, and they have to develop the strategies necessary to process information. Although reading strategies play an important role in all foreign language learning contexts, in CLIL they decide on the student's success or failure. A specific CLIL methodology must take this issue into account; reading strategies must play an important part both in the preparatory classes, and in the learning process in the CLIL classroom. But in CLIL receptive processing does not only mean reading texts; content subject work also includes working with graphs, tables, maps, and charts, etc. Here specific processing strategies are necessary as well, which will help learners to process the information contained in these materials.

Although language production is a less neglected issue in the traditional language classroom, it has to be looked upon in a new way in the context of CLIL. Classroom discourse, for example, plays a much more important role in the CLIL classroom (cf. Thuermann, 1999). Discourse necessary for the CLIL classroom can be analysed as consisting of two sets of skills: one more general functional set valid for all content subjects and consisting of the following speech acts or text formats,

identify – classify/define – describe – explain – conclude/argue – evaluate,

and one more specific set which differs according to content subjects or groups of subjects,

defining – classifying – making inductions/stating laws – describing states and processes – working with graphs, diagrams, and tables, etc. – interpreting – writing reports.

In order to develop these skills, students need language support – words and phrases for classroom discourse, etc.

In this context it should also be mentioned that terminological aspects have lost their overwhelming importance in the discussion of CLIL methodology. Especially in the early CLIL years teachers believed that content teaching could only work if students had the precise terminology in the foreign language at

their disposal; nowadays it has become clear that the terminological inventory of a content subject can be differentiated into
more general and more specific terms. As Krechel (1996) put it,
in CLIL one should begin by providing more general content
subject-oriented vocabulary and should then slowly move
towards more and more specific vocabulary (the French term
l'inondation belongs to the more general technical vocabulary of
geography and can also be found in general French, whereas the
term *le surpaturage* is a highly specific one used only when
discussing questions of agriculture in geography).

Not much needs to be said here about the third issue,
autonomy. CLIL methodologists in Germany have recognised the
importance of autonomy in all learning and thus also in language
and content learning (cf. Wolff, 1994). They suggest raising
learners' awareness of their own learning and language learning
processes. To develop autonomy, they propose to promote general
study and learning skills so that learners can work independently
in the classroom. Autonomy can be more easily realised in a
learning environment such as the one provided by CLIL.

5. Concluding remarks

Like all approaches to CLIL, the German model shows
specific features which distinguish it from all the other CLIL
models. As I indicated already these features have something to
do with the German linguistic and educational context. In a
country in which learners normally have very little contact with
the target languages outside school, it is understandable that
immersion-type approaches to CLIL – as found in bilingual or
multilingual countries – were not introduced. Although a number
of researchers – among others Wode (1995) – have pleaded for
immersion CLIL in the German context, it has become clear that
Canadian, Australian or American immersion programmes –
even if they work in these countries – cannot simply be
transferred into the European context, especially not in a
monolingual country. German CLIL, which like immersion relies
on exposure, but also on a systematic methodological approach
to language and content, seems to be the most suitable approach
to develop multilingualism in the linguistic context in which
Germany is situated.

Like a number of other approaches, CLIL in Germany aims at additive bilingualism. In this it is different from maintenance or transitional CLIL programmes. It should be kept in mind, however, that in German CLIL programmes great emphasis is laid on integration of language and content. CLIL is not simply a means to an end, in that CLIL students are exposed to the foreign language more frequently than others and thus develop a higher competence in this language. The new perspective on content which students develop when they learn it through another language is equally important. In our research project in Wuppertal, where we compare students of history who study this content subject in their native language, German, to those who study it in French, we are able to show that the way the latter deal with historical problems is much more extensive, more far-reaching and multi-perspectival.

To sum up: CLIL as practised in Germany but also in a number of other countries seems to be a very convincing approach to promoting higher language proficiency and a better understanding of content. However, it would benefit enormously if it were integrated methodologically into an approach defined by the principles of learner autonomy and if it did make better use of the resources and the tool functions of the New Technologies. But this is another topic.

5 Bilingual Teaching: Connecting Language and Concepts in Mathematics

Laurent Gajo and Cecilia Serra
Universities of Bern, Lausanne and Neuchâtel

1. Introduction

Current studies in second language acquisition as well as those on bilingual education are putting greater emphasis on classroom-oriented research that examines acquisition processes. In addition, greater attention is paid to the role that content-oriented instruction and code-oriented instruction play in teaching bilingual or immersion classes.

In this contribution, we argue for an integrative bilingual teaching model connecting – in one and the same setting – content-oriented instruction with focus-on-form instruction. More significantly, we assume that focus-on-form instruction not only refers to occasional shifting to linguistic code features triggered by perceived problems with content comprehension or production (Long & Robinson, 1998), but also entails a focus on the linguistic structures (in both L1 and L2) needed to get the content meaning across. We then consider the issues of the learning of non-linguistic disciplines in the context of bilingual education.

In our ongoing research and consultancy work in developing bilingual teaching at the Secondary School level in the Aosta Valley (Italy), we have developed an integrative bilingual teaching model for several disciplines, notably mathematics.

2. Three stages of bilingual education

In the recent history of bilingual education research and pedagogy, three different stages can be identified (Gajo, 2000), where each stage places different emphasis on the major questions underlying any new programme or experimentation:
a) The L1-problem: will L1 develop normally despite an important amount of instruction time being conducted in L2?
b) The L2-problem: will L2 really develop better if an important amount of instruction time is conducted in it?

c) The subject-problem (school knowledge): does L2 complicate the subject learning and 'brake' progress in the curriculum subject?

d) The socio-psychological problem: is bilingual education appropriate for any student profile? Could socio-psychological difficulties be reinforced through bilingual education?

Research has variably addressed these questions, but in the early stages it tended to merely produce findings answering questions (a), (c) and (d) in the affirmative and question (b) in very strong positive terms. Bilingual education was in fact developed in order to improve L2 teaching and learning. The most important question was therefore about L2 proficiency. Researchers were expected to demonstrate that instruction through a second language benefited L2 proficiency development without hampering first language development and the learning of content subjects.

Canadian research in French immersion particularly stressed that instruction through a second language did not cause any 'collateral' damage. At the same time, however, certain scepticism about the kind of L2 proficiency developed in such programmes was emerging. It was often found that students from these programmes could easily communicate, but their morpho-syntactic errors tended to fossilise. In the late 1980's and 1990's, a large part of research was devoted to this problem (cf. Swain, 1996; Lyster & Ranta, 1997). Bilingual education was effective for communication, but L2 acquisition was found to require improvement. This new research focus is the definitive feature of the second stage of bilingual education research. The latest trend appears in the third stage, where researchers cope with question (c) and try to ascertain whether bilingual education will provide added value in the form of greater L2 proficiency in addition to subject knowledge (cf. Gajo & Serra, 2000). The question can be reformulated as follows:

- Is subject matter better learnt through bilingual education?
- What is the impact of bilingual education on subject teaching and learning?

This question is fundamental, not only for learning issues, but also for educational policies. Bilingual education must have the support of and commitment from subject teachers, who 'lend' their discipline for language goals. They have to develop new methods of teaching their subject. Language and subject must take advantage of each other, for more general educational progress. Therefore, research has to focus on subject oriented results of learning.

Stage	Emblematic designation*	Didactic orientation	Communication competence	Data processing techniques
1st	Immersion	Language	Strategic	Experimental/ Quantitative (product-oriented)
2nd	Content and Language Integrated Learning (CLIL)	Language	Morpho-syntactic ('grammatical')	Experimental/ Quantitative (product-oriented)
3rd	'Enseignement d'une Matière par l'Intégration d'une Langue Etrangère' (EMILE)	Subject	Discursive	Ethnographic/ Qualitative (process-oriented)

Figure 1 The Three Stages of Bilingual Education Research
*Umbrella term: 'bilingual education'

These stages are not to be considered in a chronological perspective, since their definitive features are present in one form or the other in all bilingual education experiments conducted today and these experiments also have variable focus on language and non-language teaching. However, 2nd or 3rd stage models can often be found in regions that have experimented with bilingual education for a long time (cf. §3).

Starting from the second stage, the major research focus is on content and language integration. However, the functions and modes of this integration vary considerably, and there is a lack of reflection on the concept of integration itself. In the second stage, integration has to serve language goals and L2 pedagogy. The challenge is to put more linguistic knowledge in the non-linguistic curriculum, to combine the teaching of an L2 with teaching through an L2. In the third stage, content and language integration must be an asset for the discipline and needs an analysis from the perspective of non-language pedagogy. There is a need for an integrated pedagogy.

The terminology adopted at the European level implicitly reflects the change of perspective from the second to the third stage. In our view, the new French acronym EMILE[1] (proposed by Baetens Beardsmore, 1999) is not only an equivalent for CLIL, but also a cue for a reorientation in bilingual education research.

All three stages pay attention to the development of communicative skills. However, we can observe variability in the focus on the different components of communicative competence. The first stage underlines the major importance of strategic competence for managing conversation in a L2. The second stage aims to avoid fossilisation by improving L2 knowledge and accuracy, thus limiting the need for strategic competence. Bilingual education has to provide students with a more correct language than could be learnt on the street. The third stage aims to determine the specific links between linguistic knowledge and non-linguistic knowledge, in order to address, on the one hand, specific subject matter problems and to develop, on the other hand, the awareness of 'new' language components or units. These components belong to discourse organisation (pragmatic) and often are not mastered even in the L1. The third stage proposes a close articulation between negotiation of form and negotiation of meaning, which are often considered as separate skills.

With regard to the methods used to analyse data, we note a dominating use of experimental/quantitative methodology. The goal is generally to evaluate bilingual programmes and to serve political objectives. Input and output variables are identified and tested through experimental tasks. The lack of ethnographic/ qualitative studies was stressed in the late 1980's. This methodology, notably through interaction analysis, allows for a description of the processes underlying bilingual education and is necessary to understand how language and content can be integrated. Third-stage bilingual education research particularly needs to be conducted by qualitative methods, which produce the kind of findings that usually provide teachers with concrete and efficient tools for pedagogic action.

---

[1]   The acronym stands for Enseignement d'une Matière Intégrée à une Langue Étrangère.

3. The Aosta Valley

The Aosta Valley is a region of North-Western Italy, bordering Switzerland (to the north) and France (to the west). To the east and south it borders the Italian region of Piedmont, of which it formed a part until 1948 when it became an autonomous region with a special status. In the last century, large numbers of people moved down to the valley floor and towards nearby Piedmont causing depopulation of the mountain areas. After the Second World War, internal Italian migration – and more recently external migration – has been recorded towards the valley floor and the major resort areas, where tourism has now almost supplanted the original mountain agriculture.

The official languages of the region are Italian and French, considered as having equal status in education and administration. Most of the local population still use 'patois', a dialect of Franco-Provençal origin, while only one valley uses a Walser dialect, a variety of German. The internal and external migrant people use Italian and/or share other language varieties. In everyday life, the weight of Italian and French is unequal. Italian is the national language and as such holds a strong position, whereas French is less widely shared among the local population, mainly for historical and political reasons. Public and private use of French was forbidden by the Fascists in 1922 and was only reintroduced in 1948, when the Valley became an autonomous region. Hence, one of the targets of bilingual education is to restore the use of French as an everyday language and to promote bilingualism by means of the compulsory education system.

4. Implementing bilingual education in secondary school

In 1984, bilingual instruction was implemented in kinder-garten (age: 3-5), followed by primary school (grades 1-5) in 1988. At both levels, French and Italian were given an equal number of teaching hours and both languages were used for teaching all subject areas. In 1994, after three years of teacher training and bilingual experimental teaching, bilingual teaching was officially introduced at the secondary level (grades 6-9).

At first, bilingual teaching mainly consisted of projects grouping together different subject areas (e.g., history, history of art, and environment) dealing with one common, major theme. The alternate use of Italian or French was intended to develop macro-alternating sequences, allowing the use of the one or the other language in different learning activities. The target was to shift from the first to the second stage of bilingual education, in that more linguistic knowledge had to be put in the subject teaching, to combine the teaching of an L2 with the teaching through an L2. However, this first explorative approach led to several questions ranging from the negotiation of meaning in a communicative bilingual situation, to the learning of subject knowledge, or the implementation of integrated pedagogy. Particularly, it questioned the legitimacy of learners' code alternations (i.e., intra-sentential code-switching), the choice of L1 and L2 documents to implement the curriculum, the use of French to develop concepts, and the integration of language teaching.

Accordingly, a research programme 'Disciplines et bilinguisme', then 'Projeter l'alternance', was started in 1995 to implement a bilingual curriculum in mathematics, history and artistic education, with the help of experts in subject methodology and in linguistics.[2] From 1995 to 1999 the programme involved nine schools, 10 teachers of mathematics, 14 of history, 12 of artistic education and about 350 pupils. From 1997 onwards teachers of French joined the team, in order to integrate their teaching into the subject activities. So far, two teachers (a language teacher and a subject teacher) can teach a lesson together. This allows for a better integration of language and content, and for effective teacher co-operation.

Working hand in hand with the experts in subject methodology and the teachers, we first focused on the role of L1 (Italian) and L2 (French) in learners' activities to develop cognitive capacities, such as deducing, inferring, tracing and categorising information, in order to gain knowledge from documents written in two languages. At this stage, it appeared that learner's difficulties mostly concerned language processing, in L1 as well, which could be improved by an integrated use of both languages.

---

[2]   The authors have been in charge of the programme since 1996.

By that, we mean the reciprocal focus on both languages to build a common, negotiated meaning through interaction. The negotiation of meaning through the use of both languages induces deep processing, as it enables learners to establish links between unfamiliar items in the input and their previous knowledge.

We then considered the bringing together of everyday and instructional language. Language awareness – in the form of metatalk – is one of the principal ways of mediating learning, including language learning, in situations ranging from the metalinguistic use of L1 and L2, to the interconnection of subject and everyday language in L1 and L2. The next move was to focus on the linguistic structure of the subject discourse, i.e., the linguistic structures that are used to carry out a mathematical demonstration, the definition of a theorem or the properties of a geometric form. We wished to determine the specific links between linguistic knowledge and non-linguistic knowledge, in order to address, on the one hand, specific subject-matter problems and to develop, on the other hand, the awareness of 'new' linguistic components or units. At this stage, we shifted to the third stage model, by proposing a close articulation between negotiation of form and negotiation of meaning, as an interface of languages and subject contents.

5. The integrative bilingual teaching model: An example taken from mathematics

The proposed integrative bilingual teaching model is based on four assumptions:

a) *Any content or linguistic knowledge built up in the classroom is mainly elaborated through verbal interaction. Negotiation of meaning and of form promotes deep processing of the input.*

This assumption has to be considered in both a general and particular way. Generally, it is now assumed that bilingualism and bilingual education lead to metalinguistic and cognitive development, by enhancing both the awareness and the analytic orientation to the formal and semantic aspects of language (cf. Cummins & Swain, 1986; Ellis, 1999, for an extended review). In particular, research on class interaction shows that even in bilingual classrooms, the pupils' metalinguistic awareness is often not taken into proper account by the teacher, in that the attention paid to pupils' target language use is mostly directed to improving their linguistic knowledge. On the other hand, focusing on content more than on grammar improves content knowledge but does not necessarily enhance language production skills. As Snow, Met and Genesee (1989) point out, 'It is unlikely that the desired levels of second or foreign language proficiency will emerge simply from the teaching of content through a second or a foreign language. The specification of language-learning objectives must be undertaken with deliberate, systematic planning of the language and content curricula' (1989: 204).

When observing bilingual classroom interactions, we focused on conversational sequences where meaning was negotiated by using L2 and/or L1. The trigger elements might be code-switchings, hesitations, unachieved (i.e., unfinished) sentences or words, hypothesis testing formulations, and clarification questions, etc. The teachers' repair usually consisted of a short resolution of the emerging problem, followed sometimes by pupils' response. From a conversational point of view, these 'side' sequences repair breakdown in any communication (Schegloff, Jefferson & Sacks, 1977), and as such they are used in bilingual classroom interactions as well. Many studies have investigated how repair sequences involving L2 learners – particularly intermediate learners – facilitate acquisition, and more generally, how interaction plays a major part in creating the conditions in which language acquisition (L1 and L2) can take place. (Ellis, 1999; Serra, 1999 a/b; Gajo & Mondada, 2000). Besides, the use of curricular materials in L1 and L2 provides a meaningful context and increases opportunities for output, particularly in drawing attention to form-function links (Swain, 1998).

In view of such observations, we suggested that the spontaneous use of conversational routines had to be expanded into broader sequences, producing a dual focus on form and meaning, and bringing learners to recognise consciously the relationship between meaning, forms, and function in a highly context-sensitive situation. We then provided a conceptual framework for the integration of languages and content mostly based upon the explicit and controlled use of language alternation (L1/L2) as a metalinguistic device, allowing reformulations in both L1 and L2. Reformulating enables the processing of curricular materials, in that the opportunity to negotiate meaning provides learners with the time they need to attend to form while processing the message content. Accordingly, teachers and learners should make use of reformulation in different ways such as using synonyms or analysing words in a variety of content-bound contexts, giving attention to the derivational or inflectional morphology of words in context and focusing on elements of 'grammar' relevant to meaning.

By means of such metalinguistic devices, which often take the form of metatalk, i.e., talking about language without using metalinguistic terminology, teachers and learners were enabled to carry out a reciprocal regulation of their linguistic and cognitive activities. Teachers (subject and language teachers) would re-formulate their speech according to the linguistic elements structuring the processing of new information by pupils. Pupils' reformulations would make evident how they integrate the new information into the old. Negotiation of meaning and of form, through explicit metalinguistic activities, became the key concept of our integrative bilingual model.

b) *Curricular materials mainly use everyday language. A general or particular weakness in processing everyday language – in L2 and in L1 – may lead learners to misinterpret meaning or key concepts. On the teachers' side, it may lead to underestimating the linguistic origin of problems encountered by learners in curricular tasks.*

Bilingual instruction uses curricular materials that ask for attention to meaning and to form; grammar is not isolated from meaning or context. However, 'attention to form' is a key concept not equally shared by language teachers and by subject teachers. For the first, particularly for L2 teachers, attention to form is typically understood to focus on the grammar regularities of the linguistic code features of the L2. In this case, knowledge can be gained through oral and written activities, similar to the curricular approach taken by Day and Shapson (1991), who attempted to maximise both student interaction and task-natural opportunities to use the conditional in L2 French immersion.

For mathematics teachers, attention to form is a way of checking whether language correctly translates mathematical reasoning. Even if mathematics teaching is increasingly making use of learners' factual knowledge, several phases of pro- ceduralisation will then restructure factual knowledge into a more usable cognitive format. Verbal accuracy is mainly achieved through output, when learners test hypotheses that attract feedback leading them to reprocess meaning through more appropriate linguistic forms. In mathematics, the focus is generally put on higher organisational principles or conventions governing language use beyond the sentence level (e.g., discourse rules, pragmatic awareness, and strategic competence, etc.) (cf. §5c). However, verbal accuracy demands focus on every language level, on morphology and simple syntactic structures which are often neither per- ceptually nor communicatively salient in everyday language. In mathematics, the search for accuracy has to attract learners' attention to form with attention to meaning, rather than isolating attention to meaning as a separate component (Lyster, 1994). The example shown in Figure 2 is illustrative.

| S1 | les côtés ne sont pas égaux
the sides are not equal |
| T2 | il n'y a pas de côtés égaux .. alors . quindi . tous les côtés sont différents
(change in intonation) there is no equal sides .. therefore (in French and repeated in Italian) *all sides are different* |

Figure 2 Student-Teacher interaction *vis-à-vis* attention to form & meaning

In the above example, the pupil (S1) comes to the conclusion of a geometry problem. His reasoning is coherent, the sentence is well formed and the use of the French negation (*ne .. pas*) is mastered. However, the teacher (T1) reformulates (i.e., recasts) it, stressing that at this stage the whole sentence, and not a single constituent, should be negated. Then the teacher brings the pupil's reasoning to the logical end, by adding a generalisation linked to the previous sentence by an adverb through code- alternating in French and Italian. The alternation highlights another sensitive point, i.e., the choice of the right connective that has to be used to signal the conclusion. The teacher's reformu- lation focuses both on content and linguistic accuracy, thus showing their meaningful interconnection. Further, it attracts the pupil's attention to sensitive points, such as the use of a presentative form (*il n'y a*), and the function of negation patterns and adverbial forms (cf. §5c).

In a general way, any discourse can make use of argumentative conclusions, followed or not by generalisations. But whereas everyday discourse or subject discourse, e.g., history or the environment, tolerate approximations or progressive reformulations, mathematical reasoning mostly operates within a minimal context, thus asking for an exact mapping of meaning and form. To students, indeed, mathematics constitutes an excellent instrument for testing the relevant use of linguistic forms that are mostly used in variation in other contexts.

As illustrated by the example in Figure 2, the teacher uses code-alternation. By doing that, he is following our suggestion to make use of language alternation as a metalinguistic device, allowing reformulations in both L1 and L2. This suggestion came up after observing an initial immersive stage, evidencing the difficulties encountered by students in understanding mathematics items or complex structures either in L1 or in L2. We made clear that the direction of the code alternation was not relevant, i.e., switching to Italian was not more helpful than switching to French, but when the form in focus was embedded in one language, it was to be followed by a reformulation in the other language. It is, indeed, the code alternation itself that produces an important carrier for the meaning in focus, as in Figure 3:

T1	dunque congruenti . c'est un mot un peu plus élégant qu'on utilise en géométrie où ça veut dire égal mais on ne l'utilise pas en arithmétique *(in Italian) well congruent . (in French) is a more elegant word we use in geometry where it means equal but we don't use it in arithmetic*
S1	come simmetrico *(question in Italian) like symmetrical*
T2	no che combaciano come le mani eh (fa il gesto) *(in Italian) no it means fit together like hands do euh (makes the gesture)*

Figure 3 Student-Teacher interaction *vis-à-vis* code alternation as carrier for the meaning in focus

In Figure 3, the teacher's (T1) reformulation of the Italian item *congruenti* into French *égal* leads to a meaningful simplification, since the latter is a common word, close to Italian *uguale*. This step brings the pupil (S1) to recognise the link between meaning and form and then to negotiate the teacher's reformulation in order to integrate the new information into his existing knowledge. The teacher's clarification (T2) is then achieved by a gesture making the concepts in focus more transparent.

Code alternated reformulations are taken into account by pupils as well. For instance, when they have to cope with similar words or syntactic structures in Italian and in French, which may provide them with a distorted sample of the target discourse, they are invited to negotiate meaning, or they spontaneously do it, making cognitive comparisons and using code alternation as a metalinguistic device. Thus, they gain both linguistic control and subject knowledge.

More generally, meaning negotiation and recasts are embedded in broader reformulation activities providing negative evidence and opportunities for modified output. Long (1996: 413) defines negative evidence as input that provides 'direct or indirect evidence of what is grammatical'. By using explicit metalinguistic devices, such as code alternation, the search for 'grammaticality' involves both the subject language and the everyday language (in L1 and L2) used to reformulate, in order to 'construct' or 'reconstruct' the intended meaning. As the border between subject language and everyday language is not easy to draw or even not often relevant, learners have access to an enlarged input and have opportunities for modified output providing further evidence of the need for restructuring their interlanguage.

Finally, we asked the teachers to alternate subject sub-activities (oral and written) using L1 or L2, each of them being a required element to build up the whole activity. Under these conditions, including the use of the metalinguistic devices discussed above, the macro – and micro – alternating use of L1 and L2 is improving the pupils' grip on both languages and subject content.

c) *Instructional language in any subject area has its own organisation, based upon a specific utilisation of natural language.*

This assumption develops one previous point further, i.e., the use of the subject language.

As stated, mathematics discourse makes use of higher organisational principles or conventions governing language beyond the sentence level (e.g., discourse rules, pragmatic awareness, and strategic competence, etc.). However, by observing pupils in monolingual or bilingual classrooms we came to the conclusion that they were almost unable to produce, sometimes even to understand, complex structures either in L1 or in L2. Although teachers take for granted that pupils master their native language, we observed that they encountered difficulties in processing discourse rules, e.g., aspect, modality, argumentative patterns, and indirect speech constraints. Many difficulties arise from the interconnection between everyday and instructional language, both sharing the same discourse forms but having particular usage conventions that even for mathematics teachers – let alone for pupils – are difficult to grasp. Mathematics teachers use these conventions in very specific contexts like formulas. As for pupils, they are taught conventions and discourse rules only in L1 curriculum at grade nine, while L2 teaching mainly deals with raising communicative abilities, i.e., to make learners' language fluent, possibly accurate, but in no case complex. Bilingual teaching, on the other hand, pushes teachers and learners to cope with complex text types, based on documents in two languages, in order to build up knowledge by deducing, inferring, tracing and categorising information.

Accordingly, the next step was to draw language and mathematics teachers' attention to such linguistic features, by using examples of ordinary tasks, usually performed at grade seven. As the example in Figure 4 (page 89) shows, an ordinary geometry gap-filling task requires knowledge both in geometry and in language. The inherent cognitive activity cannot be achieved if the linguistic tools are not equally developed in everyday and instructional language.

In the example provided in Figure 4, the problem solving activity is structured by the argumentative progression of the verbal formulation. It therefore leads to a sub-task of processing and organising the linguistic information. But the sub-task may be hindered if some ambiguities are not solved first, e.g.,
Re: Ambiguity of syntactic constraints:

At (2), *in modo che la semi-retta MN si sovrapponga*, the use of the subjunctive mode suggests a possibility (the phenomenon may happen or not), while the next use of the indicative mode *il punto P si sovrappone* indicates a certitude (the phenomenon happens). Actually, the subjunctive mode depends on the syntactic constraint provided by the use of the connective *in modo che*. The two propositions are therefore equivalent, and the conveyed meaning is certitude in both cases.

Re: Ambiguity of adverbial connectives:

At (5) *dunque* and *quindi* are used in everyday language as synonyms and signal a conclusion. However, in mathematics the former (*dunque*) signals the intermediate conclusion of an argumentation, while the latter (*quindi*) signals the final conclusion.

The use of metalinguistic devices, such as code alternation, raised the awareness of such linguistic constraints, mainly when teachers and students were testing the language paradigm to find equivalent forms, meaning and function in both L1 and L2. When a geometry task, close to Figure 4, was worked out in a bilingual classroom, teachers and students negotiated the functional opposition of *dunque vs quindi* throughout the search for equivalent French forms. The resulting string of adverbs *donc/par conséquent/en conséquence* was then tested again to verify whether the close Italian adverbial form 'di conseguenza' had the same function as Italian *quindi* or not.

Once code-alternation has been internalised as a metalinguistic practice, it becomes easier to shift to intralanguage negotiation of form without losing pupils' attention, mainly when the form in question is crucial to convey meaning, as French example in Figure 5 illustrates.

In the example shown in Figure 5, the teacher's clarification question is aiming at verifying whether the pupil's (S1) appropriate definition is conveying the presupposition driven by the adverbial *au moins* automatically, i.e., like a formula, or not. The same question is also drawing attention, in an implicit way, on the function of the article *les* as a generalisation marker. Even if the pupil's answer (S2) displays the correct understanding of these language functions, the teacher's reformulation (T3) makes it more explicit for the whole class.

1. Dobbiamo dimostrare che i due triangoli sono congruenti, ossia che esiste un movimento rigido che li fa ...
   (in Italian) We have to demonstrate that the two triangles are congruent, namely that there exists a rigid movement that makes them...
2. Siccome l'angolo M è congruente...esiste un movimento che fa coincidere il secondo con il primo, <u>in modo che</u> la semi-retta MN <u>si sovrapponga</u> ... e che la semi-retta MP <u>si sovrapponga</u>...
   Since the angle M is congruent..., there exists a movement which makes the second coincide with the first, so that the half straight-line MN is superimposed on... and that the half straight-line MP is superimposed on...
3. Siccome il lato MN è congruente... questo stesso movimento fa coincidere N...
   Because the side MN is congruent..., this same movement makes N to coincide with ...
4. Analogamente, poiché il lato MP è congruente..., il punto P <u>si sovrappone</u> ... e il lato NP va a coincidere ...
   By analogy, since the side MP is congruent..., the point P is superimposed on ... , the side NP is going to coincide with ...
5. <u>Dunque,</u> il movimento che ha fatto coincidere i due angoli congruenti A e M, fa coincidere anche...dei triangoli dati. Possiamo <u>quindi</u> concludere ...
   Therefore, the movement that made the two congruent angles A and M to coincide, makes as well...of the given triangles to coincide. We can therefore conclude that ...

Figure 4 An Example of Problem Solving Activity

S1   le trapèze a au moins deux côtés parallèles
     the trapezium has at least two parallel sides
T1   il y a une différence entre 'au moins deux côtés' et 'les côtés parallèles'
     (question) *is there any difference between 'at least two sides' and 'the parallel sides'*
S2   oui deux ou plus
     yes two or more
T3   juste . au moins veut dire qu'il faut que deux côtés soient . parallèles
     right . at least means that two sides have to be parallel

Figure 5 Example of Intralanguage Negotiation of Form

At this stage, the negotiation of meaning helps mainly to enhance the output in subject language. In addition, the use of L2 has an instrumental function, close to the use of L1 in a 'normal' mathematics lesson. It should be noticed, however, that this teacher (like all teachers of the bilingual teaching programme) is now able to focus on higher organisational forms involving either subject or everyday language meaning.

d)   *The scaffolding of basic cognitive operations, such as selecting information, making connections, mapping, and problem solving operations, etc., is implemented by focusing on the language structures (in L1 and in L2) that organise or underlie them.*

As it has often been stated in second language acquisition studies, mainly when interaction is the focus, 'cognitive development arises interpsychologically through concrete social situations. It is facilitated when learners have the opportunity to interact with a more experienced person who can guide, support and shape their actions (i.e., scaffold their attempt to perform new functions) (Ellis, 1999: 224). In our perspective, scaffolding covers a wider scope, i.e., focusing both on second language and curricular learning through oral and written activities. As shown above, language awareness – in the form of metatalk – is one of the principal ways of mediating learning, including language learning, in situations ranging from the metalinguistic use of L1 and L2, to the interconnection of subject and everyday language in L1 and L2.

The more teachers and learners explored this way, the more it became evident that the next move in scaffolding had to focus on the linguistic structures of the subject discourse, i.e., the linguistic structures used for a mathematical demonstration, the definition of a theorem or the properties of a geometric form. This stage was carried through the collaborative assistance of language teachers who helped mathematics teachers to identify the linguistic structure underlying subject discourse and provide them with some 'linguistic' methods of investigation. On their part, L1 and L2 language teachers implemented the linguistic structures underlying different subject discourse types through meaningful oral and written activities in their teaching lessons. Discourse types, e.g., argumentation, description, asserting, and categorisation activities, etc., are commonly shared by any subject discourse, even if every subject uses them in a more specific or conventional way.

The scaffolding of cognitive operations by way of discourse structures enhances language comprehension, and strengthens reflective thinking as well as cognitive skills (Gajo & Serra, 1999). This finding embraces Swain's concept of enhanced input (1985 & 1998), in the sense that discourse types, more than texts, become salient and fully understood through explicit teaching and negotiation of form. Focus on discourse types also increases opportunities for output, in that it notably triggers the meta-linguistic function and metatalk. By encouraging teachers and learners to use metatalk as a pedagogical means for noticing, for formulating hypothesis on situated meaning and for solving cognitive problems, we were aiming at triggering metacognitive strategies, i.e., the conscious reflection of how to process the instructional information. This is opposite to Lyster's findings in Canadian immersion classrooms (1994), where as a matter of pedagogical principle, when meaning is paramount, for example, in a history or mathematics lesson, many immersion teachers consider error correction and attention to form to be inappropriate.

At this stage, instead, meaning is carried out by a linguistic work on the very logical and discursive operations that underlie mathematical reasoning. Teachers and learners negotiate the features of mathematical forms by defining their linguistic properties, in metalinguistic discourse sequences that investigate how language contributes to shape and to distinguish forms and properties. The alternation of L1 and L2 is used in a functional manner, more to provide bilingual talking routines (Martin-Jones, 1990; Lüdi, 1991) than to repair local lexical gaps. The focus is

S1	la définition ce sont les propriétés caractéristique de la figure. euh . les propriétés
	the definition is the characteristic properties of the figure . hmh . the properties
T1	comment vous faites pour reconnaître une définition. j'espère que tu as un critère
	how can you recognise a definition. I hope you have a standard
S2	parce qu'il dit 'il est' eh 'être'
	because it says 'it is' euh 'to be'
T2	voilà . en français et en italien c'est la même chose . c'est le verbe être . Marco a dit le trapèze a des angles et coetera c'est le verbe avoir . alors c'est des propriétés . alors vous cherchez le verbe être vous trouvez la définition . la définition . cherchez le verbe être .. les propriétés . le verbe avoir .
	OK . in French and in Italian it is the same . it is the verb to be . Marco said the trapezium has angles and so on . it is the verb to have so they are properties . then you look for the verb to be and you find the definition . the definition . look for the verb to be .. the properties. the verb to have .

Figure 6 Example of resolving mathematical problems by means of focus on form

on the formal features of L1 and L2 that define the internal properties of mathematical objects. Examples shown in Figures 6, 7 and 8 show how teachers and pupils involved in mathematical problems find a meaningful solution by means of focus on form.

In the example in Figure 6, the teacher and two pupils oppose the definition to the properties of any geometric form by means of the opposition between the verbs *être* (to be) and *avoir* (to have).

S1	je je non ho capito li les côtés. Euh
	I I(Italian) *didn't understand the* (French) *the sides*
T1	alors le théorème vous le prenez pour quelque chose de VRAI primo . alors tu n'as pas compris le théorème . alors dans le théorème on commence toujours avec si .. in italiano è
	well first you take the theorem for TRUE . now you didn't understand the theorem . well the theorem always starts with if .. in Italian is
S2	se
	(Italian) *if*
T3	ensuite alors c'è questo . questo e quest'altro allora succede questo o quest'altro . si puntini puntini alors puntini puntini . beh si puntini c'est la condition
	then there is (Italian) *this . this and that . then it happens this or that . if so and so* (French) *then so and so . well if so and so* (French) *is the condition*

Figure 7 Example of resolving mathematical problems by means of focus on form

T1	alors quelle est la consigne . la domanda da 500 punti
	then (question) *what is the instruction .* (Italian) *the 500 points question*
S1	si il y a ça .. alors ... ça . hmm
	if there is this .. then .. that . mhm
T2	alors en utilisant ce théorème on peut réécrire la définition dans une autre manière peut-être en enlevant quelque chose qui n'est plus indispensable ou bien ajouter quelque chose. capito hmm et je répète quelque chose veut dire quelques phrases. cette phrase n'est plus indispensable parce qu'elle veut dire la même chose. on prend le théorème. si la première phrase est vraie alors on peut enlever le reste
	well using this theorem we can rewrite the definiton in another way maybe dropping something no more indispensable or adding something else . right mhm I tell it again something means sentences . this sentence is no more indispensable because it means the same . we take the theorem . if the first sentence is true we can drop the rest

Figure 8 Example of resolving mathematical problems by means of focus on form

In the example in Figure 7, the teacher (T3) generalises the logico-discursive conditions of the theorem definition by explicitly focusing on the linguistic formula, and by avoiding inserting any situated content in her formulation.

Finally in the example in Figure 8, the teacher reformulates her talk (T2) to stress that if the geometric definition of a form requires redundant geometric properties to be dropped, this can be achieved through language use by an equal dropping of redundant sentences.

6. Conclusion

At the end of the school year 1998/1999, a group of mathematics teachers assessed 39 pupils at grade eight, comparing a bilingual class to a monolingual one. The pupils' performances were measured against the following standards:

In a general way, the results were considered positive for bilingual pupils and average for monolinguals. For standard one, where 'knowledge' indicates the capacity of reproducing a wide range of mathematical knowledge, the monolingual pupils were better than bilinguals; for standard two, the rate of good and sufficient bilingual pupils was higher than in monolinguals (87% vs 79%); for standards 3 and 4, the percentage of better pupils was higher among bilinguals than among monolinguals. Accordingly, monolingual and bilingual pupils developed different ways of

Table 1 Performance of Pupils in Monolingual & Bilingual Classes in Maths

STANDARDS	BILINGUAL PUPILS			MONOLINGUAL PUPILS		
	Good	*sufficient*	*negative*	*good*	*sufficient*	*Negative*
1.knowledge	56.4%*	28.2%	15.4%	90%	10%	Ø
2.find elements and apply rules	54%	33%	12%	67%	12.5%	20.5%
3.work out structured problems	67%	5%	28%	7.6%	18%	74.4%
4.comprehension and use of subject language	61.5%	5.2%	33.3%	7.6%	38.6%	53.8%
*100% = 39 pupils						

processing subject knowledge: the strength of monolinguals being informational knowledge; while for bilinguals it is operational knowledge. More generally, informational knowledge refers to the capacity to memorise knowledge, i.e., 'knowing that'; while operational knowledge refers to the ability to transfer and apply knowledge to new situations, i.e., 'knowing how'.

In 1999, all bilingual pupils at grade nine were assessed by a University psycho-pedagogic team from the IUFM Versailles (University Teacher Training Centre, France), external to the bilingual development programme team (Assuied & Ragot, 2000). The pupils' cognitive capacities were both assessed in L1 and L2, by means of nine written tasks, aiming at sorting out and categorising information and argumentation. The assessment answered the following questions:

- Can pupils process information in L1 and in L2 alike?
- To what extent has the utilisation of language resources influence on the performance of the tasks?
- Is the construction of concepts, i.e., abstract thinking, generalising, defining, logical processing of data, and put at stake by the use of L2?

The final report gave positive answers to all questions, showing how bilingual pupils equally developed such cognitive capacities in L1 and L2. The report concludes that focusing on subject language structures in L2 even helped pupils to strengthen reflective thinking and cognitive skills.

Both assessments match our observations and give a positive feedback to our way of integrating L1 and L2 in a bilingual curriculum by way of interaction. As was shown, bilingual interaction focuses on higher processing levels and organi-sational principles in language that are closer to the subject knowledge, by pushing teachers and learners to use metatalk as a communicative and pedagogical means for noticing, for formulating hypothesis on situated meaning and for solving cognitive problems. It was then stressed how focus on linguistic structures underlying discourse types increases opportunities for output, in that it notably triggers the conscious reflection on processing instructional information. Thus, the interaction itself often becomes the object of learning, as it combines both L1 and L2 and subject matter.

To the objection that this way of teaching mainly works with intermediate and advanced learners of L2, it can be answered that one of the authors (C. Serra) is implementing the same method at the primary level with L2 absolute beginners and is meeting equally positive outcomes (Serra, 2001).

In our opinion, difficulties arise at the didactic level, mainly because teachers are not trained to integrate L1 and L2 languages or language and subject teaching. The research in linguistics and in pedagogy should provide more instruments to develop teaching methods focusing on cognitive skills and on subject content. In this sense, bilingualism gives teachers and pupils excellent tools to work on the construction of subject knowledge. Further, it helps in developing problem solving strategies at any level of language learning, thus supporting constructivist and interactionist procedures of teaching and learning.

6 Second Language Achievement in the European School System of Multilingual Education.

Alex Housen
Vrije Universiteit Brussel
Fund for Scientific Research – Flanders

1. Introduction

In the past three decades, bilingual and multilingual education have inspired a torrent of books, monographs and articles. Most of these publications have been devoted to Canadian-style immersion. Other models and contexts have received far less attention. One such model is the European School (ES) model which has been in operation for nearly 50 years and is currently implemented in 12 schools located in six member states of the European Union.[1] Over the years the European School system has gained a solid reputation as a successful model of multilingual and multicultural education and of language teaching in particular. The growing interest in the European Schools as a source of inspiration for developing multilingual education and language teaching programmes elsewhere (cf. EEC, 1990; Skutnabb-Kangas, 1995) justifies highlighting the available research on the process of language learning in these schools and the lessons that can be drawn for language acquisition in varied contexts. The following section presents necessary background information about the European School model. Sections Three to Five survey research on the process of second/foreign language learning in the European Schools carried out at the Vrije Universiteit Brussel. Section Six considers some wider implications of this research for second language education and bilingual education.

---

[1]   One school in Luxembourg (Grand Duchy of Luxembourgh), Varese (Italy), Bergen (the Netherlands), Culham (UK), Alicante (Spain), Frankfurt, Karlsruhe and Munich (Germany), Mol (Belgium), and three schools in Brussels (Belgium).

2. The European Schools as Multilingual Hubs

European Schools (ESs) are primarily intended for children of European Union officials though others, including migrant children, also attend. About 17,000 pupils are currently enrolled, representing over fifty nationalities and over thirty different language backgrounds. Each European School consists of several first language sections, collectively covering eleven of the European Union's official languages (i.e., Danish, Dutch, English, Finnish, French, German, Greek, Italian, Portuguese, Spanish, Swedish). All schools and all language sections follow the same curriculum which leads to the *European Baccalaureate*, a special diploma which provides access to universities worldwide.

European Schools are multilingual and multicultural, not only in terms of their pupil population, but also in their organisation, ethos and goals. These goals include the promotion of (a) high levels of scholastic and intellectual development, (b) intercultural understanding and a pluralistic identity, and (c) high levels of functional proficiency in at least two languages. These two languages are, in principle, the child's home language plus a language of wider currency, namely French, English or German, the three working languages of the European Schools.

The goals the European Schools set out to achieve are by no means self-evident and require a carefully designed educational programme, probably the most complex in existence. The programme comprises three cycles: kindergarten, primary school (Years 1-5) and secondary school (Years 6-12). Pupils receive their basic education in one of the eleven different first language (L1) sections and are all taught a second language (L2) – either English, French or German – from the first year of primary school onwards. The L2 is first taught as a subject but from Year Three of primary school onwards it is increasingly used as a medium of instruction for other school subjects. In Years 7 to 9 in secondary school all pupils are further taught a third language (L3) which they may continue as an elective in Years 10 to 12.[1] In addition to

---

[1] Second language (L2) and third language (L3) are respectively the first and second foreign languages studied by pupils as part of their curriculum. A pupil's L2 and/or L3 can either be a 'second language' (i.e., spoken in the wider environment of the school) or a 'foreign language' (not spoken in the wider environment).

formal classroom contact, European School pupils have the possibility to use their target languages (TLs) as a vehicular language with peers from other first language backgrounds (including native speakers of the target language) in both curricular and extra-curricular activities, though this depends on the individual pupil, the specific school and the specific language involved, which may, yet need not be, the *lingua franca* of the school or wider community. (For more details on the European School model, see Baetens Beardsmore, 1993 & 1995).

3 Previous research on language learning in the European Schools.

In a series of studies conducted in the 1980s, Baetens Beardsmore and his colleagues measured global levels of L2 and L3 achievement in the European Schools of Brussels and Mol (Belgium) and compared these with the outcomes obtained in other multilingual programmes. Using standardised tests developed in Canada, Baetens Beardsmore & Swain (1985) and Lebrun & Baetens Beardsmore (1991) found that levels of French-L2 achievement of 13-year-old pupils in the European Schools in Brussels were comparable to those of 13-year-olds in Canadian French immersion and in the system of trilingual education in the Grand Duchy of Luxembourg (see Table 1, adapted from Baetens Beardsmore, 1993: 110).

Another (unpublished) study (Verstrepen, 1986) compared achievement in French-L2 and French-L3 among 13 and 14 year olds in one of the European School in Brussels, while yet another (unpublished) study (Devolder, 1989) cross-linguistically compared English-L2 and French-L2 achievement among 13-year-olds in the European School of Mol, (where neither English nor French is part of the wider, out-of-school environment).

Collectively, the findings of these studies indicated that global levels of French and English proficiency attained in the European Schools were comparable to those attained in other models of multilingual education and superior to the levels of achievement that are normally observed in mainstream foreign language programmes, though exact levels would vary depending on the availability of the target language in the wider, out-of-school context.

Table 1 **French-L2 Achievement scores for European School, Grand Duchy of Luxembourg and Canadian Immersion pupils**

	ES Brussels (N = 80)	Canadian Immersion (N = 80)	Luxembourg (N = 179)
L2 in wider context	+	-	+
Total class contact	1325	4450	1450
Written comprehension (Max. = 22)	15.6	14.6	15.26
Auditory comprehension (Max. =22)	17.7	14.9	14.84
Cloze test (Max. = 44)	21.95	19.9	21.3
Total (Max. = 88)	55.25	49.4	51.4

Explanations for these findings pointed to the complex interplay of both curricular and extra-curricular factors as the determinant of the 'manifest success' (Baetens Beardsmore, 1993: 110) of the ES model: the carefully engineered structure of the programme with its teaching of languages and other subjects in the target languages, and its regular juxtaposition of different language groups, creates daily possibilities for communication, both inside and outside the classroom (Housen & Baetens Beardsmore, 1987). The pupils' perceived pertinence for learning languages and their self-motivated use of the target language in the classroom and in peer-group interaction emerged as major contributory factors to the acknowledged success of language teaching in the European Schools (Baetens Beardsmore & Kohls, 1988; Baetens Beardsmore, 1993).

4 Recent research on language learning in the European Schools.

4.1 Rationale

These earlier studies on language learning in the European Schools leave unanswered a number of important questions. They provide empirical information on levels of language proficiency at the middle stages of education (ages 13-14) but not on the early and final stages, nor on the development of language proficiency over time. They also provide no information on patterns of variation between individual pupils, groups of pupils, or between the different European Schools. Such information is important. We may expect the range of variation in the European Schools to be wider than in the average immersion context because the European Schools cater for a more heterogeneous population which is more diverse, both in terms of L1 backgrounds and in terms of L2 proficiency (which may range from the absolute beginner to the near-native speaker). Also, the sociolinguistic status of the target languages and the extracurricular input and output conditions vary considerably from school to school. Although previous studies have suggested that these factors have an impact on linguistic outcomes, the extent of this impact is still unknown.

Moreover, these early studies do not provide direct evidence as to ES pupils' ability to perform in their target language in a communicative setting, especially their ability to produce grammatically and lexically precise self-sustained discourse – an ability which many immersion pupils have been shown to lack (Swain, 1985; Hammerly, 1991).

It was to obtain information of this kind that a new series of studies was initiated. Results from the first two studies are available and will be reported here. Both studies, referred to here as Study A and Study B, investigate the development of lexical and grammatical competence by ES pupils learning English as their L2.

4.2 Methodological Procedures

A total of 145 pupils participated in the two studies, involving four different L1 backgrounds (Dutch, French, Greek, Italian), five age/Year levels, and three different European Schools (Brussels, Varese, Culham).

In both studies English-L2 speech data were collected in standardised oral interviews, each lasting for about 30 to 120 minutes (depending on the pupil) and consisting of both informal free conversation and semi-guided speech tasks designed to elicit a wide variety of grammatical and lexical forms. Pupils were asked to talk about past experiences and future plans, to describe pictures, retell films they had seen, and retell three picture stories involving a variety of characters and actions. One of the picture stories is the Frog Story, which has been used in various other studies on L1 and L2 acquisition (e.g., Berman & Slobin, 1994).

The interviews were audio-taped and transcribed and coded in CHAT format (MacWhinney, 1995).

In addition to these speech data, a sample of 23 ESL lessons in the European Schools of Brussels and Varese were observed with the help of the COLT observation scheme (Spada & Fröhlich, 1995) to investigate various parameters of classroom interaction and instruction such as the relative communicative orientation of the language lessons, proportion and type of teacher and pupil talk and the proportion of L2 and L1 usage and code-switching by teachers and pupils.

The following sections discuss the specific objectives and research designs of each of the two studies separately.

4.2.1 Study A

This cross-sectional study examined levels of English-L2 proficiency among Italian speaking pupils in the primary cycle of three different European Schools: Varese, Brussels and Culham.[2] For purposes of comparison, similar data were obtained from native English pupils and from Italian pupils in traditional English-Foreign Language (EFL) classes in two Italian main-stream schools near Bologna (Italy). Table 2 summarises the distribution of the pupils who participated in this study.

Table 2 **Informants of Study A (L1-Italian, L2-English)**

Grade Level:	2	3	4	5	Total
Context:					
Foreign Language (Bologna, Italy)	---	---	---	24	24
ES Varese (Italy)	---	20	4	---	24
ES Brussels (Belgium)	---	13	---	---	13
ES Culham (UK)	3	8	4	1	16
Native speakers	---	---	10	---	10

The principal aim was to identify similarities and differences in L2 learning as a function of varying extracurricular context. To this end the L1 and L2 of the pupils were held constant, as were curricular variables such as type and amount of formal class

[2]   This study was undertaken within the framework of the Project "The Teaching and Learning of Foreign Languages in European Primary Schools", an activity funded by the European Science Foundation. The data were collected and processed with the help of Gabriele Pallotti, Astrid Kern, Isabelle Castro Moore, Franscesca Gallutto, Evangelia Moussouri, Areti Sougari, Annie Pottolia and Cecile Sabatier.

contact with the L2 (in principle, all the Italian pupils had had 250 hours of formal classroom contact with English). The main difference between the three schools are the role and status of the L1 and the L2 outside the classroom. The Italian pupils in Year Three at the European School in Varese receive English instruction very much like in mainstream Italian schools, the differences being that the English teachers in the ES are native speakers and that the pupils have the opportunity to hear English occasionally being used by their English-speaking peers and teachers on the playground or when attending other classes. In addition, the Varese pupils 'know' that English will be used as a medium of instruction in secondary school in general content classes such as History and Geography. This could render the learning of English more pertinent for them than for their peers in mainstream Italian schools. For the rest, the presence of Italian is strongly felt in the European School in Varese. It very much functions as a *lingua franca* among pupils and staff members from different language backgrounds.

The main difference between the European Schools in Varese and Brussels is that the Italian pupils in Brussels cannot normally use their first language for communication in the out-of-school context, or in interactions in the school with peers from other first language backgrounds (French being the *lingua franca* in the Brussels schools). This could make the learning of English seem more pertinent to the Italian pupils in Brussels than to the Italian pupils in Varese.

Finally, in the context of the Culham school, Italian plays no significant role outside the Italian section itself, English being the dominant language inside and outside the school.

The central research question investigated in Study A was whether the pupils in these three different contexts had developed different attitudes and motivations for learning English and, if so, whether this was reflected in the rate and outcome of the language learning process.

4.2.2 Study B

The objective of Study B was to describe the route, rate and outcome of the L2 learning process and identify commonalities and differences across pupils from different L1 backgrounds in the same multilingual educational context. A total of 92 pupils from the French, Dutch and Greek L1 sections in the European Schools in Brussels participated.

Twelve of the 92 pupils (six for L1 French, six for L1 Dutch) were studied longitudinally over a period of three years (Years 3-5) and were interviewed on five occasions at five-month intervals. The remaining 80 pupils were sampled from Years 3, 5, 7, 9 and 11 (roughly corresponding to the ages of 9, 11, 13, 15, and 17 respectively). They were interviewed on one occasion only.

Similar interviews were conducted with ten native speakers (NSs) from the English section of the European School in Brussels (five each from Years 5 and 7) to provide baseline data.

Table 3 shows the distribution of the pupils in this study, together with an estimation of the accumulated amount of formal class contact with English at the end of each of the five Years levels involved.

In principle, all pupils in this study learn English under the same curricular conditions. They are together in the same English-L2 classrooms and attend the same English-L2 medium classes. They receive the same classroom input and expectations about their linguistic progress are also the same. However, the three L1 groups are not the same in terms of the extra-curricular conditions of their language learning experience. French being the *lingua franca* in the European Schools of Brussels and in the wider, out-of-school context, it was hypothesised that the French-speaking pupils perceive the learning of English as less pertinent to their immediate communicative needs than the Greek and Dutch pupils. The Dutch pupils in turn were predicted to perceive the learning of English as slightly less pertinent than the Greek pupils because Dutch, in contrast to Greek, is one of the official languages in the bilingual city of Brussels, although its presence in daily life is not strongly felt. In addition, the three L1 groups also differ in the degree of typological proximity between their respective L1 and the target language, Dutch being the closest to English, followed by French and then Greek. Previous research suggests that this factor, too, can have a considerable impact on levels of L2 achievement in education contexts (Ringbom, 1987).

Table 3 **Sample of ES pupils in Study B**

	Cross-sectional					Longitudinal	Total (N=102)
Year Level	grade 3	grade 5	grade 7	grade 9	grade 11	grade 3-5	---
Age	9	11	13	15	17	9-11	---
L2 class contact hrs	(250)	(370)	(1045)	(2095)	(2670)	(250-370)	---
L1-Dutch	6	6	6	6	6	6	36
L1-French	6	6	6	6	6	6	36
L1-Greek	4	4	4	4	4	---	20
L1-English	---	5	5	---	---	---	10

The aim of this study, then, was to investigate the variable effect of these two factors, immediate pertinence and typological relatedness, on the route, rate and outcome of the second language learning process. Immediate pertinence predicts that the Greek pupils will learn more and faster than the Dutch pupils who in turn will outperform the French pupils; Typological proximity predicts a learning advantage for the Dutch learners, followed by the French pupils and then the Greek pupils.

4.3 Analytic procedures

In both studies, the interviews were analysed quantitatively and qualitatively to assess the pupils' control of linguistic features of English and to determine similarities and differences in the route, rate and ultimate level of attainment between the different groups.

Two sets of quantitative indices were used to assess levels of linguistic proficiency in English. The first set taps the pupils' lexical proficiency and consists of three measures of lexical richness: the Guiraud Index, the Verb Suppliance Ratio, and Number of Verb Types. The Guiraud Index is an improved version of the traditional type/token ratio and is calculated by dividing the number of lemmas in a given text by the square root of the number of tokens. The Verb Suppliance Ratio is the proportion between the number of verb tokens and the sum of the number of verb tokens and noun tokens in a given extract of speech. Number of Verb Types is the number of phonologically distinct verb types in a given text. Justification for using this rather simple measure comes from previous studies on first and second language acquisition which found verb type number to be a reliable diagnostic for both lexical and more general linguistic development (cf. Clark, 1995; Bloom, 1981).

The scores obtained for the three separate lexical measures were standardised and averaged, yielding a Global Lexical Richness Score.

The second set of indices relates to the pupils' morpho-syntactic proficiency and consists of an indicator of morphological richness, the Morphological Variation Score, a measure of morpho-syntactic accuracy, the Target-Like Usage Score, and one measure of syntactic complexity, the Complex Syntax Score. The Morphological Variation Score was computed for the verb and noun system. It expresses the ratio of all inflected verb and noun forms to the total number of verb and noun forms in a given speech extract. The Target-like Usage score is the ratio of the number of accurate uses of a given morphological feature to the sum of all its uses and its omissions in obligatory contexts. It was calculated for 10 different grammatical functors (e.g., 3rd person singular present tense -s, regular and irregular plurals, regular and irregular past tense inflections). Finally, the Complex Syntax Score is the ratio of subordinated clauses to the total number of clauses in a speech extract. Different types of subordinated clauses were weighted differently according to their linguistic and psycholinguistic complexity (e.g., adverbial clauses were given a weight of one, relative clauses a weight of 3 or 4 depending on the degree of embedding in the matrix sentence).

Here, too, a Global Grammatical Development Score was obtained by standardising and averaging over the scores of the three grammatical indices.

All measures were computed for each L2 learner and native speaker of English on the basis of equal stretches of speech. For the purpose of presentation and comparability, the raw scores obtained by the native speaker comparison groups were taken as a benchmark and the raw scores of the ES pupils were expressed as a percentage score relative to the native speaker scores (which equal 100%).

Although these linguistic measures have all been previously established as reliable and valid proficiency diagnostics (for the lexical measures, see Broeder et al., 1993; Dietrich, 1990; Sato, 1990. For the grammatical measures, see Kesckes & Papp, 2000; Sato, 1990; Pica, 1984; Reilley et al., 1998), none of them are unproblematic, either in their computation or interpretation. But they suited our particular goal of providing a baseline against which the various pupils and groups could be compared.

The following section presents the findings that emerged from the two studies, focusing on both general trends and patterns of variation in the domains of lexical and morpho-syntactic development.

4.4 Findings

4.4.1 Lexical Development

4.4.1.1 Study A

The relative vocabulary size of the ES pupils and its development over time across different Year levels are first considered. The figures in Table 4 show the mean scores obtained by the Italian pupils in the primary sections of the European Schools of Varese, Brussels and Culham and those of the two comparison groups in study A (i.e., Italian pupils in a mainstream EFL programme in Bologna and native English pupils). As can be seen, the measures all point towards the same trend. The lowest lexical richness scores are obtained by the traditional EFL pupils and the scores increase from Varese to Brussels to Culham, in that order. As expected, the native speakers obtain the highest scores. Somewhat surprisingly, the Bologna EFL pupils appear on average to do almost as well as the pupils in the European School of Varese. In fact, on the Verb Suppliance Ratio they even outperform the Varese pupils. Although the scores of the Brussels pupils are consistently higher than those of the Varese and Bologna pupils, the differences are slight. Analysis of variance (ANOVA) revealed no significant difference between the scores of these three groups. The differences in scores between these three groups and the Culham group are significant ($p=.0001$), however, as are the differences between the Culham pupils and the natives speakers ($p=.0003$).

Table 4 **English-L2 Lexical Richness Scores of Italian pupils in three ESs and a traditional EFL programme (in % relative to native speaker scores)**

	Bologna (EFL)	ES-Varese	ES-Brussels	ES-Culham	Natives
Verb Type Number	26	30	33	71	100
Guiraud Index	34	41	44	73	100
Verb Suppliance Ratio	66	60	68	84	100
Global Lexical Index	42	44	48	76	100

A qualitative analysis of the lexical items used in one of the speech tasks – the telling of the Frog story – illustrate these quantitative trends.

The Bologna, Varese and Brussels pupils have at their disposal a very restricted vocabulary to tell the frog story. It consists of the following nouns: *boy(s), frog, dog, water, house, tree, child/children, forest* and *animal*.

The Culham pupils use, in addition to the above, more specific nouns such as *deer, bees, rock, window, hole, nest, lake* and *pond*. The native speakers use all of these and, in addition, terms like *beehive, branches, antlers, mole, rodent, weasel, windowsill*.

The Bologna, Varese and Brussels pupils produced hardly any adverbs (except for occasionally *then* and *there*) but the Culham pupils had a slightly richer adverbial repertoire with items such as *very, anymore*, and *again*. These were also the adverbs frequently used by the native speakers, who in addition used a few less frequently used adverbs such as *frantically* and *gradually*. The five groups did not vary much in terms of the use of adjectives. Except for *big, happy* and *little*, few adjectives were used by the five groups. The Culham pupils and the native speakers sometimes used adjectives which the other groups never used, such as *silly, stupid, naughty, angry, wet, scared*.

The greatest difference was observed in the number of different verbs used, as shown by the Verb Type Number scores in Table 4. Of all the various measures computed, *Verb Type Number* emerges as the most straightforward indicator of lexical richness, for our purposes and for our specific data. The verb repertoire of the Bologna, Varese and Brussels pupils is still very restricted, in some cases consisting of five to ten verbs only. The most commonly used verbs are *be, have, look, come* and *go*, which are regularly overextended to denote a wide variety of states, perceptions, sensations and actions. Other 'early' lexical verbs include *eat, sleep, say* and *run*. The following extracts are from the Frog Story retellings.[3]

VI32:   it is uh... and uh look... and look... &f forest.
INV: uhuh and then?
VI32:   And then dogs is coming .
        boys is sssh.
        and look... and look two frogs... and six little frogs.
        and is uh and the dog is uh +...

The Culham pupils have a much richer verbal repertoire, including verbs such as *wake up, push, fall, climb, escape, shout, search, hold, start, see* and *hear*. These allow for greater fluency and detail of expression.

CI41:   once upon a time there was a boy and a frog and a dog.
        the boy had a... had a frog.
        the dog and boy went to sleep.
        and the frog came out [c] +...
        and escaped.
        the boy woke up and the dog +...
        and they &s &s saw [c] +...
        +, that the frog was not there anymore.
        and... the boy dressed up.

Verbs absent from the repertoire of the Culham pupils but part of the native speakers' lexicon include *sniff, lick, chase, bark, decide, scream, yell, check, bother, disturb, touch, knock down, grab, throw*.

NS41:   then the little boy checked... in in a little hole in the ground.
        and the dog was... in the in... was bothering the beehive.

---

[3]   Learner identification codes consist of 4 characters: the first character indicates the school or context (B = Brussels, C = Culham, V = Varese), the second character indicates L1 background (F = French, D = Dutch, G = Greek, I = Italian), the third indicates Year level (1-5 = primary, 6-11 = secondary), and the last number is a personal number and may consist of one or two digits. The longitudinal learners are indicated by three initials, followed by an F or D indicating their L1 and a number from 1 to 5 indicating the interview session (e.g., EMAD4).

then a a squirrel came out of the little out of the hole
[c]+...
and... and bited [%err] the little boy.
then the dog # knocked the little... the the the
beehive down.

In sum, the results of the analyses presented here reflect the similarity between the Bologna, Varese and Brussels contexts in terms of rate and outcome of lexical learning. Whatever advantage the European School pupils in Varese and Brussels have in terms of better input and output opportunities for learning English, this does not pay off in faster lexical growth during the first three years of primary school. This contrasts with the European School in Culham, where the overall presence of the target language has resulted in a richer and more varied vocabulary.

4.4.1.2 Study B

The lexical development over time within the *same* educational context is considered in this section. Table 5 presents the Global Lexical Richness scores of the Greek, Dutch and French-speaking pupils in the European Schools of Brussels.[4]

Table 5 **Development of the English-L2 Global Lexical Richness Scores of French, Greek and Dutch-speaking pupils in the ES in Brussels (in % relative to native speaker scores)**

Year:	3	5	7	9	11
French-L1	41.6	43.9	74.0	79.9	88.0
Greek-L1	45.9	50.0	75.5	83.0	90.0
Dutch-L1	60.8	70.6	84.0	88.0	94.4
Mean	49.4	54.9	77.8	83.6	90.8

The following trends can be discerned. First, the Dutch pupils consistently obtain the highest scores, followed by the Greek pupils and then the French-speaking pupils. However, the differences between the French and Greek pupils are slight and not significant (with $p > .05$). (It is noted in passing that the scores of the Year 3 French and Greek pupils are comparable to those of the Year 3

---

[4]   As in the study of the Italian pupils, the various measures (Guirault Index, Verb Type Number, Verb Suppliance Ratio) all pointed in the same direction. To avoid redundancy, only the composite Global Lexical Index Score is presented here.

Italian pupils in the ES-Brussels in Study A). The Dutch pupils significantly outperform the Greek and French pupils, at least in the early grades (at $p \leq .001$). With time, the difference between the Dutch-speaking pupils and the French and Greek pupils gradually decreases. By Year Nine, the differences between the Greek and the Dutch pupils are no longer significant ($p=.078$), and by Year 11 there are no more significant differences between any of the three L1 groups on these measures of lexical richness. Moreover, by Year 11 all three L1 groups closely approximate the scores of the native speaker control group (whose score equals 100%) and in the case of the Greek and the Dutch pupils the difference with the native speakers scores is no longer significant. Also it has to be noted that the Greek and French pupils make minimal progress in the course of primary schooling (Years 3 to 5) but demonstrate a lexical 'spurt' in the first two years of secondary school (Years 6 and 7). Whereas the Dutch pupils' progress is fairly gradual and steady over time. From Year Seven onwards, the lexical development of the Greek and French pupils seems to proceed again at a slower pace.

These results indicate the considerable range of variation in lexical development that exists among pupils in the same L2 classroom in the European Schools, particularly in the early phases of education, where the Dutch pupils have at their disposal a far richer vocabulary than the French and Greek pupils. In the course of secondary education, however, these differences are somehow levelled out so that by the end of secondary education all ES pupils attain comparable levels of lexical proficiency which approximate those of native speakers.[5]

These findings invite several interpretations and explanations which will be discussed after the presentation of the results of the analyses of the ES pupils' morpho-syntactic development.

---

[5]   This finding should be interpreted with caution. Recall that the scores presented here are based on pupils' performance on a series of everyday speech tasks which do not require an extensive or specialised lexicon. More refined measures of lexical richness and a wider range of tasks are needed to determine exactly how close the English-L2 pupils' vocabulary approximates that of native speakers.

4.4.2 Grammatical Development

Research on second language acquisition has shown that in contrast to lexical development, grammatical growth in second language learning is typically a late and slow process which follows a clear developmental pattern (e.g., Perdue, 1993; Sato, 1990; Wode, 1981). There is evidence indicating that the European School learners, too, pass through a number of general stages in their acquisition of L2 grammar, and this regardless of their L1 background. This is particularly evident in the domains of inflectional morphology, negation, interrogation, word order and subordination strategies (Housen, 1995, 1997 & 2000, forthcoming; Housen & Pallotti, forthcoming). Many of the developmental features demonstrated by the ES pupils are generally characteristic of L2 learners everywhere (e.g., formal under- and overextensions such as *he go, two frog, teached, childrens*) and are probably the result of universal mechanisms of language acquisition. However, more important for the purposes of this paper is the observation that while the ES pupils progress from one stage to another, they do not do so at an equal pace, nor do they all attain the same level of grammatical attainment. This is clearly borne out by the results of the quantitative analyses.

4.4.2.1 Study A

Table 6 displays the scores on the measures of grammatical proficiency obtained by the Italian-speaking primary school pupils in the three European Schools of Varese, Brussels and Culham and in the mainstream EFL context of the Bologna schools. The general trend that emerges is familiar from the discussion of the lexical scores in the previous section: the EFL pupils in Bologna have the lowest scores, followed by the ES pupils in Varese, Brussels and Culham, in that order. Again, the native speaker comparison group has the highest scores. Although the same general trend appears for these grammatical measures as for the lexical measures, some differences can be noted as well.

Table 6 **Grammatical proficiency scores of Italian pupils in three ESs and a traditional EFL programme (in % relative to native speaker scores)**

	Bologna (EFL)	ES-Varese	ES-Brussels	ES-Culham	Natives
Morphological Variation	15	22	27	75	100
Morphological Accuracy	31	54	57	91	100
Syntactic Complexity	10	20	18	67	100
Global Grammatical Index	19	32	34	78	100

The Morphological Variation Ratio expresses the extent to which the pupils use morphologically inflected verb and noun forms rather than unmarked base forms. In absolute terms, the Bologna group is the morphologically least advanced group (15%), followed by the Varese group (22%), the Brussels group (27%) and the Culham group (75%). The differences between the Bologna, Varese and Brussels pupils are not significant ($p=.201$). The difference between the scores of the Culham group and the other three groups is highly significant ($p=.00001$). The difference between the Culham and the Native Speaker criterion group is also significant (at $p=.0069$). In other words, the Culham learners produce a morphologically richer English than the other L2 learners investigated but it is still not as rich as that of comparable native English speakers.

Note that the Morphological Variation Ratio is a fairly crude measure of morphological proficiency. It does not reliably reflect the full range of different morphological forms in a learner's data set nor does it take into account the accuracy of use of forms. The latter aspect is captured by the Target-Like Usage Score, the measure used here to assess morphological accuracy. The results for this measure show a similar pattern: the Bologna pupils are the least accurate in their morphological production (31%), the Culham pupils the most accurate (91%), and the Varese (54%) and Brussels (57%) pupils are somewhere in between. Two observations can be made here. First, this time the difference between the Bologna group on the one hand and the Varese and Brussels groups on the other hand is significant (at respectively $p=.0011$ and $p=.0008$). In other words, although their morphological repertoire may not be significantly richer than that of the Bologna pupils, the Varese and Brussels ES pupils use whatever morphological forms they have more accurately than their peers in a traditional EFL context. Second, the Culham group not only reaches a significantly higher score than the other three groups but it also appears to have reached target-like levels of morphological accuracy with a mean score just above the criterion level (conventionally set at 90%).

The third measure, the Syntactic Complexity Score, reflects the proportion and type of subordinate clauses which the pupils produced. The syntactically most complex speech is produced by the Culham pupils (67%), the simplest by the Bologna pupils (10%). The scores of the Varese and Brussels pupils are roughly the same, although this time the Varese group (20%) slightly outperforms the Brussels group (18%). The difference is not significant, however, nor is the difference with the Bologna pupils. Only the scores of the Culham pupils are significantly higher than those of the other three groups (though still significantly lower than those of the native speaker comparisons). Syntactic structures used by the Culham pupils but not or far less used by the Bologna, Varese and Brussels pupils include passive clauses, relative clauses and participial complement clauses, as illustrated in the examples below.

CI34:   and here the dog's being chased by the bees.

CI35:   the dog [c] who is always playing [c] barks at the bees.

CI41:   there was a bird [c] coming out of the tree.

The native speakers used basically the same repertoire of syntactic devices as the Culham pupils but they used them more frequently. One clause type only attested in the native speaker data but not in the learner data are cleft and pseudo-cleft constructions (e.g., *What he didn't know was [c] that a mole was living there*).

The Global Grammatical Index Scores in Table 6 summarise the relevant grammatical trends discussed above: The pupils in the ESs of Varese, Brussels and Culham significantly outperform the Bologna pupils (at $p \leq .005$). The difference between the Varese and Bologna pupils indicates that the curricular component of the ES context makes a significant contribution to the development of grammatical competence. Whatever differentiates the Varese and Brussels contexts, it does not seem to affect grammatical development in the first three years of primary school because the Italian pupils in these two schools attain comparable levels of proficiency. Finally, although the Culham pupils still perform significantly lower than the native speaker controls ($p \leq .0001$) they significantly outperform their Varese and Brussels counterparts ($p \leq .0001$). This points to the effect of the extracurricular context which promotes the development of grammatical L2-competence in the ES in Culham.

4.4.2.2 Study B

This section examines the findings of Study B about the rate and outcomes in the development of grammatical proficiency over time by pupils from different L1 backgrounds who are in the same ES context and in the same L2-medium classrooms. Tables 7 to 10 present the relevant scores of the Greek, Dutch and French-speaking pupils in the European Schools of Brussels. The general trends that emerge from these tables echo those observed for lexical development, with a few noticeable differences and specifications.

Table 7 Development of Morphological Variation in the English-L2 speech of French, Greek and Dutch-speaking pupils in the ES in Brussels (in % relative to native speaker scores)

Year:	3	5	7	9	11
French-L1	18.4	23.9	51.2	71.0	82.2
Greek-L1	22.2	35.9	59.7	69.4	84.2
Dutch-L1	34.7	46.3	73.7	87.4	91.2
Mean	25.1	35.4	61.5	75.9	85.9

Table 8 Development of Morphological Accuracy in the English-L2 speech of French, Greek and Dutch-speaking pupils in the ES in Brussels (in % relative to native speaker scores)

Year:	3	5	7	9	11
French-L1	31.8	34.7	56.1	64.4	83.8
Greek-L1	30.9	40.5	59.4	67.5	85.2
Dutch-L1	40.6	46.5	77.6	84.4	93.2
Mean	34.4	40.6	64.4	72.1	87.4

Table 9 Development of Syntactic Complexity in the English-L2 speech of French, Greek and Dutch-speaking pupils in the ES in Brussels (in % relative to native speaker scores)

Year:	3	5	7	9	11
French-L1	12.5	17.9	43.2	56.4	67.8
Greek-L1	15.6	25.5	46.7	57.5	74.2
Dutch-L1	32.6	40.1	67.4	79.4	81.5
Mean	20.2	27.8	52.4	64.4	74.5

Table 10 **Global Grammatical Index scores of French, Greek and Dutch-speaking pupils in the ES in Brussels (in % relative to native speaker scores)**

Year:	3	5	7	9	11
French-L1	20.9	25.5	50.2	63.9	77.9
Greek-L1	22.9	34.0	55.3	64.8	81.2
Dutch-L1	36.0	44.3	72.9	83.7	88.6
Mean	26.6	34.6	59.4	70.8	82.6

It is first observed that all grammatical proficiency scores steadily and significantly increase as schooling proceeds. The mean Global Grammatical Index score at Year 11 amounts to 82.6%. This is still significantly ($p \leq .0001$) below the score of the native comparison group (who represent 100%), and more so than the Year 11 mean Global Lexical Index score (which was 90.8%). This seems to suggest that the rate and ultimate levels of grammatical development in the European School system are lower than the rate and outcome of lexical development.

As in the case of lexical richness, the grammatical scores of the Greek and French pupils are comparable. The Greek pupils usually perform somewhat better than the French pupils but not significantly so. The Dutch groups consistently and significantly outperform the French and Greek groups, especially on the Grammatical Accuracy and Syntactic Complexity measures. As in the case of the development of lexical proficiency, a developmental spurt can be observed between the 5th and the 7th Year, coinciding with the transition from primary to secondary school. This time, however, a similar pattern can be observed in the data of the Dutch pupils as well. In fact, this grammatical spurt is even more pronounced for the Dutch than for the Greek and French pupils (with respectively 28.6, 21.3 and 24.7 percentage points difference between the Year 5 and Year 7 Global Grammatical Index scores). In fact, the superiority of the Dutch pupils is more pronounced on the whole in the grammatical than in the lexical domain (with an average of 12.4 percentage points difference between the Dutch *vs* the Greek and French pupils in the lexical domain as opposed to an average 15.4 percentage points difference in the grammatical domain).

Furthermore, whereas the lexical gap between the Dutch pupils and the French and Greek pupils gradually narrows with time, the grammatical gap in the grammatical scores further widens. In Years 7 and 9, the average difference between the Dutch pupils and the Greek and French pupils amounts to 20 percentage points. And although the Greek and French pupils somewhat make up for their arrears in the final years of secondary school, their Year 11 scores are still some 10 percentage points behind those of their Dutch-speaking peers (as opposed to a five percentage point difference for the lexical measures).

Clearly then, the Dutch pupils in the ES in Brussels make more and faster progress in their grammatical development than the Greek and French pupils.

4.4.3 Within-group variability

In this section a somewhat different instance of developmental variation observed in Study A is presented. The mean scores obtained by the group of Italian pupils in the ES of Varese show high standard deviations, indicating great within-group variability. In an attempt to account for this variability, the data of the Varese Year Three pupils were reanalysed. The results of the reanalyses showed that this variation is correlated with the specific English L2-class to which the Varese pupils belong. The 20 Year Three pupils from Varese came from three different ESL classes, each taught by a different teacher. Tables 11 and 12 show the average scores of these three classes. Examination of these two tables reveals that the Class 1 pupils perform consistently below the pupils in Class 2 and Class 3. The differences are not always significant but suggestive nevertheless.[6]

Table 11 **Lexical Richness Scores of Italian pupils in three ESL classes in Year 3 of the European School in Varese (in % relative to native speaker scores)**

	Class 1 N=7	Class 2 N=6	Class 3 N=7	Average N=20
Verb Type Number	25	32	30	29
Guiraud Index	34	43	41	39
Verb Suppliance Ratio	53	60	61	58
Global Lexical Score	37	45	44	42

---

[6]   The average scores in the last column of Tables 11 and 12 do not add up to the scores of the Varese pupils in Tables 4 and 6. This is because the figures in Tables 11 and 12 are based on the 20 grade 3 pupils in the Varese school only; the scores in Tables 4 and 6 are based on 24 pupils (20 grade 3 plus 4 grade 4 pupils).

Table 12 **Grammatical proficiency scores of Italian pupils in three ESL classes in Year 3 of the European School in Varese (in % relative to native speaker scores)**

	Class 1 N=7	Class 2 N=6	Class 3 N=7	Average N=20
Morphological Variation	17	23	21	20
Morphological Accuracy	44	53	56	51
Syntactic Complexity	12	26	23	20
Global Grammatical Score	24	34	33	31

Analysis of the patterns of classroom interactions in Class 1 and Class 2 using the COLT observation scheme further indicates that there is one potentially relevant difference between these classes and their respective teachers.[7] Whereas the English teacher in Class 2 used the L2 consistently and never spoke Italian, the teacher in Class 1 frequently switched from English to Italian, mainly for translation and classroom-managerial purposes. An average of 28 switches per lesson were counted in Class 1 and the use of the L1 made up almost 20% of all teacher discourse.

Again, the differences between the scores of the three classes are not always statistically significant and the sample of lessons observed is too small to draw any firm conclusions, but the findings are suggestive nevertheless, pointing to an adverse relation between use of the L1 (or non-use of the L2) during the ESL lessons and the levels of L2 proficiency attained.

5. Summary and discussion

The two studies of the English-L2 speech production in the European School system presented here reveal a number of patterns in the process of second language development. These are summarised and discussed below.

5.1 Study A

The first study compared levels of L2 achievement in the early phases of schooling (Year Three of primary school) in the ES model across three different schools (Varese, Brussels, Culham) which differ in the role and status of the L1 (Italian) and L2 (English) inside and outside the school context and thus,

---

[7]   No lessons were observed in Class 3.

it was hypothesised, in the rate and outcome in the initial stages of L2 development. Native English speakers and Italian pupils in a traditional English-Foreign-Language programme (in Bologna) served as comparisons. The main findings are the following:

a) The Bologna EFL pupils and the Varese and Brussels ES pupils have attained comparable levels of productive lexical proficiency.

This finding suggests that whatever distinguishes the L2 learning experience in the European Schools of Varese and Brussels from that in a traditional EFL programme, it does not lead to faster lexical growth, at least not in the short term (i.e., after three years or roughly 250 hours of classroom contact with English).

b) The grammatical skills of the Varese and Brussels ES pupils are superior to those of the Bologna Foreign-Language pupils.

This finding suggests that the European School experience has an early positive effect on the development of *grammatical* proficiency in the L2, relative to the traditional Foreign Language learning experience. It is not clear, however, which factor or set of factors in the ES experience is responsible for this advantage but it is probably related to the curricular rather than to the extra-curricular component given that the Bologna and Varese contexts are comparable in terms of their extra-curricular components.

It is not clear either why this factor (or set of factors) affects the development of grammatical proficiency but not the development of lexical proficiency.

c) The Varese and the Brussels ES pupils attain comparable levels of lexical and grammatical competence.

This suggests that the difference in sociolinguistic status of the Italian pupils' L1 in the European Schools of Varese and Brussels does not affect linguistic development in the first three years of primary school.

Differences in the status of the *L2*, however, are clearly felt. This is shown by the scores of the Culham pupils discussed in (d).

d) The pupils in the ES Culham have developed a more elaborate and more accurate vocabulary and grammar in English than the pupils in the ESs in Varese and Brussels.

This is not a very surprising finding. The role of the target language as a *lingua franca* inside and outside the school provides the Culham pupils with additional input and output opportunities and probably creates a more fertile socio-psychological climate for language learning as well. What is somewhat more striking is the magnitude of these effects: the Culham pupils outperform the pupils in Brussels and Varese by some 30 percentage points in the lexical domain and nearly 50 percentage points in the grammatical domain. This also suggests that the impact of these extracurricular variables is more strongly felt in grammar than in lexical development.

e) Pupils in the ES of Varese whose ESL teacher frequently uses the L1 (Italian) during English lessons demonstrate lower levels of lexical and grammatical proficiency than pupils whose teachers consistently use the L2.

This finding is still quite tentative but, if confirmed, points to the importance of using the L2 consistently in designated L2-medium classes, at least in contexts where additional, extra-curricular L2-input sources are lacking.

5.2 Study B

Study B compared patterns of lexical and grammatical L2 development by Dutch, French, and Greek-speaking pupils across five different Year levels in the European School of Brussels. Native English-speaking pupils served as comparisons. The three first languages considered here differ in their status as vehicular languages inside and outside the Brussels school and in their typological proximity to the target language. It was hypothesised that these factors differentially affect L2 learning outcomes in this particular learning context. The findings can be summarised as follows:

f) ES pupils from different L1 backgrounds vary considerably in the rate and outcome of both lexical and grammatical L2 development, in spite of the fact that they sit together in same L2-language and L2-medium classes in the European Schools. The Dutch pupils dispose, in general, of a much richer vocabulary and a more elaborate and accurate grammar than the French and Greek pupils, who are very much comparable in these respects.

g) This variation is most extensive in the early phases of education (i.e., primary school). The Greek and French pupils manage to catch up with the Dutch pupils in the course of secondary schooling as far as lexical growth is concerned. By

Year 11 all pupils have comparable levels of lexical achievement, which approximate those of native speaker peers.

h) All three L1 groups also make significant progress in the domain of grammatical development but here the Dutch pupils maintain their lead until the end of secondary schooling.

Typological proximity between the L1 and the L2 emerges as the most likely factor to account for the observed differences between the Dutch versus the French and Greek pupils in the ES-Brussels. The existence of many cognate and near-cognate forms in English and Dutch gives the Dutch-speaking learners a considerable headstart by opening gateways into the lexical system of the target language as well as into some of its morphological subsystems (e.g., pronouns, auxiliaries). Although the Greek pupils in the ES in Brussels were predicted to perceive the learning of English as the most pertinent to their immediate communicative needs, this has apparently not resulted in a significantly faster learning of English than the French pupils, who were predicted to perceive the learning of English as the least pertinent to their needs.

i) Different structural domains of language develop relatively independently from each other. The rate of lexical L2 development in the European School system is faster and its ultimate outcome closer to native-like levels than the rate and outcome of grammatical (esp. morphological) development.

This finding corroborates the observation of other studies concerning the developmental primacy of lexis over grammar in language learning (e.g., Sato, 1990; Perdue, 1993). Many factors can account for the early and fast development of lexical expressions and the late and generally slow development of grammatical markings (see Housen, 2000), including (a) the primacy of associative (lexical) processing over rule-based (grammatical) processing, (b) the relative markedness of morphology versus lexis (cf. the semantic and morphotactic opaqueness of grammatical morphemes versus the more stable nature of lexical morphemes), and (c) the greater communicative load of lexical morphemes than of grammatical morphemes. Finally there are the typical communicative pressures on L2 learners which push them to seek immediate and simple *lexical* solutions to their immediate communicative needs rather than slow and complex grammatical ones (Perdue, 1993).

j)   Although L2 progress in the ES system is on the whole a gradual and incremental process, there are certain periods of extensive change. In both the lexical and grammatical domain, a developmental spurt can be observed between the 5th and the 7th Year. This spurt is more outspoken in grammar learning than in lexical learning.

The timing of this spurt is probably not coincidental. It coincides with the transition from primary to secondary school. This transition is marked by two curricular developments.

The first is the increased use in secondary school of the L2 as a medium of instruction in content lessons such as History and Geography. This has a dual effect. First, it considerably increases the amount of input and output opportunities for L2 learning. Research on Canadian immersion (Swain, 1985) has particularly emphasised the importance of comprehensible output in this respect. The role of comprehensible output is to provide opportunities for generating meaningful, coherent, appropriate and precise L2-discourse, moving the learner from a purely semantic-pragmatic analysis of the L2 to a structural analysis (Swain, 1985: 25). Our classroom observations in the European Schools of Brussels and Varese indicate that, in general, there is little opportunity during L2 lessons in primary school to produce sustained discourse to promote morpho-syntactic processing in the L2, given the emphasis on the early promotion of receptive skills in the L2. This is in contrast to the L2-medium content classes in secondary school where pupils *are* regularly required to produce such self-generated continuous oral and written discourse, thus heightening their awareness of lexical and grammatical forms of the language.

Use of the L2 as a medium in content classes not only increases input and output opportunities for L2 learning but it also renders the learning of the L2 more pertinent to the pupils' immediate communicative and academic needs, thus creating a more favourable psychological disposition to learn the L2. Research on the role of motivational factors in language learning has shown that it is important for learners to perceive the learning of a second language as pertinent to their needs and goals, preferably to their immediate social and/or communicative needs and goals rather than to some long-term instrumental ones. This will lead them to invest more effort and sustain longer in making the effort required for successful language learning. Using the L2 as a medium for teaching academic content matter is one proved way of rendering the L2-learning task pertinent.

The second development that marks the transition from primary to secondary education is the increase in analytic, form-focused instruction in the L2-subject classes. This type of instruction is rare or absent in L2-subject classes in primary school, where foci are on the L2 as a means for language play and for exchanging meaning and content. Previous research (Swain, 1985; Harley, 1993; Hammerly, 1991) suggests that while mere comprehensible input and output may be sufficient for attaining high levels of general receptive proficiency and productive fluency in L2, an awareness of structure and form may be necessary for attaining high levels of lexical precision and, especially, grammatical accuracy in L2 production, particularly in situations where sufficient output conditions cannot be guaranteed; that is, situations where use of the L2 is restricted to the school or even the classroom setting (the case of English in the ESs in Brussels and Varese). To this end, analytic L2 instruction is needed which focuses on linguistic form and usage. Such instruction is an important component of the L2 curriculum in the secondary school in the ES system. This analytic work can take many forms, depending on the individual teacher. It may range from explicit metalinguistic explanation, grammar rule presentation, structure repetition and error correction, to more implicit strategies for drawing pupils' attention to the formal properties of the target language (e.g., highlighting occurrences of particular verb or noun endings in a text and allowing the pupils to formulate their own rules). Whatever the type of analytic instruction chosen, the sharp increase in lexical and grammatical proficiency observed over the first two years of secondary school in the ES suggests that it is effective. It seems reasonable to assume that this component, together with the general concern with accuracy, precision and appropriateness that marks all L2-lessons in the European School (Baetens Beardsmore, 1995), contributes to the high levels of linguistic accuracy and precision attained by ES pupils at the end of secondary school.

5.3 Conclusion

The two studies presented in this paper show three things. First, they provide empirical evidence for what can be considered as one of the greatest achievements of the ES model, namely European School pupils' ability to produce their own independent grammatically accurate and lexically precise sustained discourse in an L2, even in contexts where additional, out-of-school support for L2 learning is absent. This is in contrast to many early total Canadian immersion pupils, who even by the end of secondary education continue to reveal striking grammatical inaccuracies in their speaking and writing (Swain, 1985; Hammerly, 1991). Importantly, attainment of these high levels of L2 proficiency in the ES does not seem to occur at the expense of proficiency in the L1. The ES experience can thus be said to lead to additive bilingualism.

Secondly, these findings also show that learning a second language cannot be taken for granted even in favourable contexts such as the European Schools where the second language concerned is as prestigious and ubiquitous as English. The high levels of achievement are attained at the end of secondary schooling only. They are the outcomes of a gradual and long-term process that spans the entire curriculum and which only really takes off in secondary school, after a somewhat less spectacular but necessary, formative start in primary school.

Thirdly, the results further demonstrate the often extensive range of variation in the rate and outcomes of L2 learning in the European Schools. Depending on such factors as L1 background and the status of the L1 and the L2 in the school and wider context, different ES pupils may experience the learning of a given second language in quite different ways.

6. Some wider implications.

Implications of the above findings can be summed up in five points.

6.1 Time and timing of L2-education

Starting age of L2 education. Although there are no conclusive research findings on the subject, there may be important cognitive, social, psychological, and psycho-linguistic arguments and some advantages for introducing an L2 at an early age (Stern, 1983; Clyne et al., 1995; Peltzer-Karpf, 1997), as is done in the European School system. Among the advantages mentioned in the literature, the following seem particular relevant:

a) Young children will usually be superior in terms of ultimate attainment ('younger is better', at least in the long run). Early L2-starters have a diminishing initial superiority in both speaking and listening proficiency but maintain a later superiority in speaking proficiency;

b) Young children respond more readily and intuitively to language 'acquisition' in social and communicative situations and are more likely to develop interpersonal communicative skills.

Length of L2 education. Given the gradual and lengthy nature of the development of L2-proficiency, L2-education should be allowed to span both primary and secondary education (and preferably beyond). This has the additional advantage of providing an important element of continuity in the curriculum.

Amount of L2 education. The amount of time devoted in the curriculum to the L2 depends on a variety of factors, including the sociolinguistic status of the L1 and L2 involved and the availability of additional, extra-curricular input and output opportunities inside and/or outside the school. Unless the L1 is dominant in the out-of-school environment, it is probably preferable to devote no more than 50% of the time-table to the L2 (including L2-subject and L2-content lessons) in the early years of schooling to avoid impairment of L1 development.

6.2 The L2 as a medium for teaching content matter

The European School experience also underscores the importance of using the L2 as a medium for teaching general content matter. This practice provides extra input and output reinforcement for the L2-learning process and also generates the pertinence which Baetens Beardsmore & Kohls (1988) identified as an important factor in the success of L2-programmes. Content-based use of the L2 is also different from subject-based use of the L2 and thus extends the range of input types to which pupils are exposed. For these reasons, it is advisable that at least one general subject be taught through the medium of the L2. The optimal or maximum number of subjects that can be taught through the L2 will depend on a variety of factors (including practical considerations such as the availability of qualified teachers and L2-teaching materials).

In principle, any type of content can be taught in the L2 and can make a valuable contribution to the global L2-developmental process, albeit it in different ways and at different stages in the curriculum. Activity-based lessons, like physical education, music, art and even basic science subjects create opportunities for con-textualised and cognitively undemanding input and output. They provide opportunities for introducing basic vocabulary items (e.g., for elementary concepts like shape, size, and colour) and basic speech acts (e.g., requests for information and materials, expressions of emotions, and giving instructions). After a few years, when basic threshold levels of receptive and productive proficiency have been attained, these subjects probably lose much of their value for the L2-learning process. At this stage, subjects like human sciences and social studies provide a suitable context for introducing pupils to increasingly more decontextualised and cognitively demanding aspects of L2 use and L2 proficiency.

6.3 The need for self-generated sustained output

The exigencies of traditional classroom interaction (which is typically teacher-centred) often provide insufficient opportunity for individual pupils to produce independent sustained L2 output. Therefore, the use of the L2 as a medium for teaching academic content advocated in the previous section will mainly contribute to the development of receptive skills. It needs to be complemented by communicative-rich contexts that promote the production of spontaneous continuous output to enable the development of productive L2 proficiency. The European Schools show that such contexts can be created outside and inside the L2-medium classroom (e.g., through interactive teaching, the use of monitored group- or pair-work rather than individual work, and by inviting L2-speakers to give oral presentations or guide debates). At the same time, the European Schools also show that this process is greatly facilitated if the pupil population is linguistically heterogeneous, which creates a natural context for the use of the L2. Therefore, one way in which an L2-programme modelled after that of the European Schools could offer more interactional input and output is through the extensive use of L2-resources available within and outside the school.

6.4 The need for (formal) L2-subject teaching

The European School experience in L2 learning demonstrates that there is a clear need at all stages for 'structured exposure' to the L2 in the form of L2-subject teaching to supplement the 'language in use' component of L2-medium instruction. In some cases it may even be beneficial to delay L2-medium instruction and start with L2-subject teaching, as is done in the European Schools.

Our research also corroborates the need in many multilingual education contexts for L2-subject teaching to be analytic and form-focused at some stage of schooling to help pupils acquire the less accessible aspects of the target language and to promote the development of metalinguistic awareness, linguistic accuracy, precision and appropriacy. Withholding this component heightens the risk of arrested grammatical development (fossilisation), particularly in situations where critical levels of comprehensible input, output and motivation cannot be guaranteed.

6.5 Functional specialisation of the L1 and L2

As Clyne et al. (1995) pointed out, the principle of functional specialisation is an extension of the 'one person – one language' principle in bilingual L1 acquisition. In bilingual education programmes this principle is reinforced by assigning different curricular subjects to the L1 and L2. In a programme where this principle is followed consistently, the L2-teacher speaks only L2 to the children inside and outside the classroom, and is completely identified with that language.

Observance of this principle has implications for the use of the L1, L2 and code-switching in both L2-subject and L2-medium lessons. Although we acknowledge the occurrence, naturalness and functionality of code-switching in bilingual communication, we would, on the basis of our findings in the ES in Varese (cf. section 3.4.3.), advise against its regular use in 'L2-poor' teaching contexts in the light of ensuring sufficient provision of comprehensible L2 input. Regular use of the L1 as a medium of instruction in L2-subject or L2-medium classrooms in such contexts may not only deprive pupils of vital comprehensible input for L2 learning but it may also lead them to 'switch off' whenever the L2 is used and render the L2 learning task less pertinent to their immediate communicative needs.

7. Conclusion

At the moment we only have a fragmentary view of the processes of second language learning and teaching in the system of multilingual education of the European Schools. Given the complexity of this system the two studies presented in this paper can only go a short way towards providing the missing information. Much more research is needed to complete the picture, including research on different L1-L2 combinations, different contexts and different aspects of communicative competence than have been investigated so far. Such research is valuable not only in its own right but also adds to our general understanding of variables, processes and outcomes in bilingual and second-language education.

7 Bilingual Education Equals a Bilingual Population? The Case of Brunei Darussalam

Gary M. Jones
Universiti Brunei Darussalam

Introduction

This paper compares bilingual education in Brunei Darussalam (Brunei) today with the situation in 1991 when Brunei hosted its first international conference on bilingualism – *Bilingualism and National Development*, or BAND'91 as it is usually referred to. The paper will also apply a cost/benefit analysis to bilingual education in Brunei before concluding with thoughts about the future of such education in the country.

The history of bilingual education in Brunei has been examined in earlier publications (Jones, 1996a; Jones et al., 1993, for example) and does not need to be described in detail here. Suffice to say, Brunei has a bilingual education system that uses both English and Malay as mediums of instruction. Some subjects are taught in English, others in Malay, but the two languages are not used in the same lesson. Officially, therefore, code-switching in class does not occur. What is notable is that the system switches from being predominantly Malay medium in Lower Primary school (years I to III) to one that is mostly English medium in secondary school (from year VI onwards).

Early conferences

As previously mentioned, in 1991 Brunei hosted BAND'91. It was hoped that insight might be gained from overseas participants about bilingualism in their countries as well as discussing issues specific to Brunei.

John Edwards, in a paper entitled Dilemmas of a Bilingual Society, talked about 'legislative tension' (Edwards, 1991: 49) that might occur in Brunei given that an educational role for Malay is a constitutional requirement while in reality English plays the dominant role in the education system. Edwards went on to describe a number of research questions that he felt should really be addressed. These included:

- The need for a language survey across domains.
- Language/identity relationships.
- Perceived changes over time.
- The matter of an emerging variety of Brunei English.
- The need to study 'what actually transpires in the classroom... how much Standard Malay is actually used, how teachers' competences are employed, how goals are set' (ibid: 56).

Edwards' comments were noted and acted upon. Two lecturers at the university at that time, Graeme Cane and Peter Martin, wrote doctoral theses on the fourth and fifth points respectively (Cane, 1993; Martin, 1997), while the other points were included in my own doctoral thesis (Jones, 1995).

Edwards went on to warn against relying too heavily on the schools as the sole agent of change: 'The second generality involves the reliance, the over-reliance, upon school as an agent of change. This problem is especially clear when the school is asked to lead, to take society in a direction not wholly endorsed by that larger body' (Edwards, 1991: 60-61). This point is particularly pertinent in Brunei given that it is widely assumed that bilingualism will occur through the action of the schools alone without any further official support. Recently, however, the widespread use of satellite television and the Internet has provided a new impetus and wish to learn English.

A final extract from Edwards that is also most pertinent concerns domains and perceived elitism. Within Brunei it would be wrong to assume that English, given that it is a widely used international language, must enjoy more prestige than Malay. To begin with, Malay, or various forms of the language found in Malaysia, Indonesia, Singapore and Brunei, is itself a Language of Wider Communication (LWC), at least within the Malay archipelago. In addition, Brunei Malay, the local form of Malay, enjoys prestige as an identity marker among Bruneians. (Bruneians are proud of the their country, its history and its relative importance, given its small size. As a result they are proud to be associated with things Bruneian, including the language.) Nevertheless, English does enjoy prestige in many domains and being fluent in the language does bestow academic and even social kudos for the user. This may create a problem, as Edwards noted: 'The problem is that some domains may be seen as more important than others and may, in fact, come to be the preserve of a social elite. Could this be a feature in Brunei, particularly since (as we've seen) most of the 'modernised' and 'modernisable' subjects at school are associated with English? Everyone goes to school; everyone gets a thin wash of English; but not everyone has equal opportunity to deepen this fluency, or to practice it in rewarding ways' (ibid: 62-63).

Similarly, in his paper at the conference, Culture Planning in Language Planning: What Do We Know about Culture Loss, Survival and Gain in Relation to Language Loss, Survival and Gain? Björn Jernudd also touched on the same theme: 'A proportion of the school cohorts will learn English well but many will not' (Jernudd, 1991: 523). Unfortunately Professor Jernudd's prophecy has materialised and among the school failures are many who have failed to learn English to any real extent. This is a problem that has yet to be fully addressed.

Participants from Brunei presented a number of papers in the BAND'91 conference. It is important to note that this was the first such conference to be held in Brunei, so most of what was presented was new, often groundbreaking, and paved the way for subsequent work. The impact that the conference had on the local community cannot really be over estimated: it received front page news, including headline news on the first day, and was attended by both the Minister and Deputy Minister of Education and many senior ministry officials.

Conrad Ozog, while discussing the role of media, made the point that in Brunei 'programmes broadcast at peak times are generally in Malay' (Ozog, 1991: 153) and went on to add 'English shares a radio station with Mandarin'. The point he was making was that at that time very little English was heard or seen on radio and television. Today the local radio stations (note the plural) still broadcast mostly in Malay, but Brunei also receives two London-based radio stations 24 hours a day (via satellite), Capital Radio and Capital Gold. While satellite is responsible for the introduction of two overseas English-medium radio stations, it is also responsible for the introduction of very many (often 24 hour) television channels. The number depends on the type of satellite receiver used, with many households enjoying access to over thirty channels. However, not all these channels broadcast in English: those from Malaysia and Indonesia usually broadcast in Malay, while Chinese, Indian, Thai and Japanese channels are also available. Nevertheless, the majority of channels, and often the most popular, are in English. These include MTV, Disney Channel and Cartoon Network – channels that are obviously popular, and most probably influential, with youngsters.

In my own paper, *From Here to Eternity? Bilingual Education in Brunei Darussalam* (Jones, 1991: 134-147), I lamented the rigid school syllabus and the lack of public awareness about the country's education system. Unfortunately not much has changed. The school system is still rigid and there is still confusion, even among educators, about the role of bilingualism in schools. However, today's parents are increasingly the product of the same education system and are likely to be more questioning, more knowledgeable and have a better command of English than their parents. Such parents have a much clearer perspective about the role of education in their lives and in the wider community than their own parents had and are therefore likely to bring more pressure to bear on those schools that are not meeting their own perceived standards. (One consequence of this is that there are now a lot more private schools in Brunei than ten years ago, suggesting that many parents have decided to opt out of government education altogether.)

One of the more important aspects of BAND'91 was that it brought together academics involved in both English and Malay. Wherever two or more languages overlap in a community there will inevitably be some tension, and the same was (and to a lesser extent, still is) true in Brunei. A deliberate theme throughout the conference was to realise the need for languages to work in harmony rather than in opposition. Too often the attitude seemed to be one of 'them and us', resulting in diatribes about the pernicious role of English in the community on the one hand and the 'unnecessary' burden of Malay on the other. Whether a language divide is real or imaginary it is important for both 'sides' to work together for the common good of the community. BAND'91 helped to bridge the differences and subsequent conferences have continued to try and involve language practitioners from both mediums. Today there appears to be a much better understanding and appreciation of the role of both languages in the community. The sort of language rivalry prevalent in 1991 now seems to be a thing of the past.

Following the success of BAND'91 a second conference on bilingualism was held in 1995. This was entitled *Bilingualism Through the Classroom: Strategies & Practices*. This conference looked specifically at the bilingual classroom and how teaching could be improved. Again it was instigated and supported by the Ministry of Education. Only invited papers were presented at the conference, together with discussant comments. More than half the papers were specifically on Brunei. The papers were published as a special edition of *The Journal of Multilingual & Multicultural Development*, Clevedon: Multilingual Matters. Vol. 17: 2-4, 1996.

Although all the papers must be considered important, two examples suggest the direction which Bilingual research in Brunei was taking at that time. Code-Switching in the Primary Classroom: One Response to the Planned and the Unplanned Language Environment in Brunei by Peter Martin examined an area that is much misunderstood, that of code-switching. That code-switching exists in Brunei classrooms is clear to everyone; that it is frowned upon by school inspectors is also well known. This paper attempted to explain a role for code-switching and for a greater appreciation of the processes of becoming bilingual. This paper was important because it brought the topic out into the open – for too long the topic had been avoided, presumably because nobody wanted to admit that what was actually happening in the classroom was different from what was officially prescribed. (Peter Martin went on to complete his doctorate on the subject of classroom code-switching. Its contents have been discussed by senior officials at the Ministry of Education in Brunei, so a subject that was once confused and confusing is now much better understood by the very people who make the important educational decisions in the country.) A paper of my own, Bilingual Education and Syllabus Design: Towards a Workable Blueprint, attempted to take what was currently known about language acquisition and bilingualism and match this to the needs of the Bruneian school syllabus. The paper provides a model, but actual implementation would need a certain amount of teacher retraining, a lot of textbook writing and a great deal of new teaching materials preparation.

Identifying problem areas within an education system is not particularly difficult: the real problem lies in being able to address them. For instance, teacher education or reorientation assumes an adequate number of teacher trainers who can perform this task. Similarly, textbook writing assumes a pool of writers and publishers who are willing and able to produce the necessary textbooks. In a small country like Brunei (population 330,000) the required human resources do not always exist.

While the conferences attracted a lot of attention to the process of bilingual education in Brunei, both within the country and from overseas, other research had been taking place at UBD and at the Ministry of Education.

Hugo Baetens Beardsmore visited Brunei during July and August 1993. He subsequently produced a report entitled *Visits to Schools and Discussions with Ministry Officials.* This report analysed Brunei's education system and offered suggestions for its future orientation. Perhaps the most important issue raised, and one that has subsequently been the subject of much further research, is that of the apparent radical shift from mostly Malay-medium to mostly English-medium subjects at Primary IV. (Baetens Beardsmore visited Brunei again and produced a second report in 1998. This reiterates many of the earlier comments and also attempted to dispel some of the preconceptions and mis-conceptions about bilingualism.)

A Research Fellow at UBD, Dr Lewis Larking, wrote a number of reports while attached to the Department of Language Education. While not focusing on bilingual education per se, his work is of interest because, among other subjects, he examined in a paper Reading Comprehension Ability of Primary 5 & 6 Children in Malay and English in Brunei Darussalam (Larking, 1994). This is important because it ties in closely with observations made by Baetens Beardsmore and focuses attention on the pupils when they are at a critical stage in the acquisition of literacy. Becoming literate is an absolute prerequisite for any sort of success in one's education. Like Baetens Beardsmore, Larking also questioned the abrupt switch to many English medium subjects at Primary IV.

A comprehensive attitude survey was conducted in 1994 (Jones, 1995). 1,000 questionnaires were distributed among all sectors of the Brunei population and throughout all four districts. Of these, 714 were properly returned and analysed. The end result, assuming an indigenous population of 230,000 at that time (based on 1991 census figures), was a survey that was distributed to 1 in 230 of the Brunei population and answered by 1 in 322. The survey revealed most conclusively that the vast majority of the Brunei population was in favour of not a Malay-medium or English-medium education system, but a system that teaches **both** Malay and English. It also revealed that Bruneians did not fear for their culture or religion as a result of acquiring English.

In addition to the work described thus far, other research in Brunei over the last ten years has examined subjects such as attitude and motivation, acculturation, gender differences, accommodation theory and literacy.

The Present

The following is an analysis that attempts to examine the present state of bilingual education in Brunei, it does so with a cost-benefit analysis. The approach is simple: the benefits are weighed against the costs to determine if one outweighs the other. In trying to apply such analysis to education some factors are immediately apparent, but not all. The factors included here are the most obvious and the ones most often raised in any discussion about the system in the country itself.

Money. This factor is most important, particularly during a recession. It undoubtedly costs Brunei a lot of money to implement and maintain a bilingual education system. Perhaps the single greatest cost is that of employing expatriate native-speaking English teaching staff. As well as their salaries, expatriate staff also receive air fares, subsidised accommodation and various education, transport and living expenses. It is not easy to place an exact cost on this, but Brunei $12,000 per expatriate employee per month is a figure that would be close to the mark (based on discussion with various government officers). This amount is probably twice that needed to employ a local officer (even though both would receive the same basic salary at the end of the month). Of course, even if Brunei had a monolingual system of education many expatriate Malay-speaking teachers would have to be employed, but not as many as for the current system and probably at a lot less cost. The country is well aware of this particular cost and is energetically trying to localise (employ local Bruneian teachers rather than expatriates) as many teaching posts (including university posts) as quickly as possible. With the large number of trained teachers now graduating from UBD this localisation process could be complete before the end of this decade.

Culture. What is the cost to Brunei's culture? Of course attitudes, values and beliefs are changing in Brunei, just as they are everywhere else in the world. And just as elsewhere, many Bruneians are concerned about a perceived erosion of cultural and moral values. The tension is at times more apparent in Brunei when behaviour differs from Islamic teaching and the values that the country is trying to inculcate through its MIB (*Malay Islam Beraja* or Malay, Islam Monarchy) civics courses that are now part of the school curriculum. Inevitably, part, if not the root, of the problem is regarded by many to be the introduction of western cultural values through access to western media and the English language. Brunei's youngsters are regularly reminded to avoid drugs and other unhealthy practices and to remain pious. These warnings come amidst a growing drug problem, increasing criminal activity and rising unemployment.

Brunei is paying a cultural cost, but it could just as easily be argued that it is gaining more culturally than it is losing. Bruneians have access to the English-speaking world and I do not know of a single young bilingual Bruneian who would trade this with the monolingual culture of their parents. From discussion with students and colleagues it is clear that the majority of Bruneians feel they are gaining a second culture rather than losing their first. They are bicultural and most seem to move easily between the demands of a predominantly Islamic Malay community and that of the English-speaking world and all its attendant (and often definitely non-Islamic) attractions. Nevertheless, it would be wrong to assume that such harmony will continue. Should recession and unemployment worsen then religious and social tension will become more apparent, just as it has in so many other parts of the world.

Identity. In the language attitude survey reported earlier an attempt was made to elicit any concerns that Bruneians might have about erosion of their identity as a result of becoming part of the English-speaking world. They had none. As suggested in the discussion about cultural change, respondents accepted that changes were taking place, but they were sure that they would not lose their Bruneian identity. One respondent noted that she was an English-speaking Bruneian, but that did not make her any less of a Bruneian or, for that matter, any less of a Muslim. In fact, given the widespread knowledge of English in Brunei the language has become something of an identity marker. Younger Bruneians especially are keenly aware that their knowledge of English is often greater than that of their Malaysian cousins and that use of the language, or at least mixing the languages concerned, marks them out as Bruneians.

Nationalism and Nationism. Bamgbose (1991) distinguishes nationalism from nationism. He argues that nationalism calls for sociocultural integration and the adoption of an indigenous language while nationism is concerned with efficiency and calls for the use of the most useful language. In the Brunei context the respective contestants would be Malay and English. Of course, in a bilingual context, it may be possible to have one's cake and eat it. At the moment this certainly seems to be the case, the two languages are performing their respective roles with little contentious overlap. The domains that one might imagine are for the most part Malay-speaking (home, market, mosque) are just that, while technical or professional tasks involving non-Malay speakers are usually conducted in English. Of course this is a huge simplification of what is a complicated language mosaic involving a lot more languages than just Malay and English. However, the point is, for the moment at least, Malay and English enjoy a peaceful coexistence.

Employability. Perhaps the most important benefit of being bilingual, and one of increasing benefit in a shrinking job market, is employability. Everyone clearly understands that today ability in English can often be the decisive factor when applying for a post. It is the needs of industry that ultimately determine a country's education system, and the need these days is to be able to communicate, and communicate well, in English, at least at the professional level. Ideally, a prospective employee in Brunei should be able to offer fluent Malay and English (while additional fluency in Mandarin would also be very highly regarded). Failure to achieve fluency in these languages does not mean that an individual is unemployable, but it does mean that they are unlikely to get employment in posts involving overseas travel or in ones that deal with non-Malay speakers – their careers and opportunities would be severely limited. Work is available for monolinguals, and it is possible to live quite easily as a monolingual in the country, but only within the confines of one's own linguistic group.

Internationalism. As part of a wider survey, UBD students studying sociolinguistics (trainee TESL teachers who have a good command of English) were asked to analyse the apparent language differences between themselves and their parents. Not unexpectedly, most referred to generation differences and the fact that their parents were mostly monolingual (or, at least, had limited access to English) while their peers were all English-knowing bilinguals. They went on to report on other language-related differences. It is clear that the students believe they are better informed about what is happening around them and believe that this is due to being able to read more, understand foreign broadcasts and surf the Internet comfortably. They see themselves as having a much better understanding of the world than their parents, and for the most part are proud of this without being condescending – they appreciate the often difficult lives their parents had compared to the rather cosseted ones they have enjoyed. They see this as a direct benefit of having studied in a bilingual school system.

The survey also included a group of Malay and Arabic medium students of the same age as the group mentioned above. However, while the sociolinguistics students are studying to become English language teachers, those in the Arabic and Malay medium are studying subjects such as religion and religious law, in Arabic and Malay rather than English. Most of these students did not follow a Malay-English bilingual schooling, but rather a Malay-Arabic bilingual schooling in schools that were run by the Ministry of Religious Affairs. (The number of pupils attending these schools, which have only just come under the umbrella of the Ministry of Education, is very small compared with the wider school population.)

Despite having only limited English compared with their English-medium peers, these students also felt that they were more advantaged and had a greater understanding of the world than their parents. However, and curiously, they also felt that their parents were better people because they had a simpler and less materialistic outlook on life. Nevertheless, when asked whether they would like to change places with their parents, all replied 'no' – they obviously felt that they could live with the guilt!

These two groups of students are the same age, the same nationality and from the same towns and villages, but in many ways they are so different. For a start virtually all the prospective English language teachers are female, whereas the sexes are evenly matched in the Malay-Arabic group. The students in the first group often wear very fashionable clothes while those in the second always wear regulation Malay costume. The students in the first group are often loud, brash and confident, both inside and outside of class; those from the second are almost without exception quiet and retiring. The differences must be due to their school experiences and I am looking forward to undertaking further research with these students.

School failures. Around the world and from all sorts of school systems, girls seem to be outperforming boys educationally. This phenomenon is certainly most marked in Brunei and is especially apparent among undergraduates at UBD where females outnumber males and it is females who are most likely to get the best degrees (Jones, 1998). The question that has not yet been addressed is whether the bilingual education system is in any way exacerbating this apparent problem. And problem it is. While the girls are to be congratulated and some may even argue that what is happening now is simply redressing the balance, the reality is that growing numbers of young men are becoming disaffected and if their plight is left unaddressed then social problems are sure to follow. I believe that this is currently the most important educational issue facing Brunei.

Comparisons

Are the costs and benefits that Brunei is experiencing being replicated elsewhere? The recent special issues of the *Journal of Multilingual and Multicultural Development* (Vol.19: 5-6; Vol.20: 4-5), covering language planning in Malawi, Mozambique, the Philippines, Nepal, Taiwan and Sweden, suggest that they are. For instance, there is popular demand for English in all these countries and also concern that English is eroding the place of other languages in the various countries. It is pertinent to note that in 1983 Mozambique was so concerned about cultural and language erosion that it decided to establish a protective body (Lopes, quoted in Kaplan & Baldauf, 1998: 460). However, since that time, nothing concrete has materialised. It is not unusual to hear fears expressed about cultural and language erosion in most countries (we hear this regularly in Brunei), but for the most part governments (and we must assume they reflect the will of the people) remain apathetic. I think that governments are being pragmatic: the most important consideration is to provide work and feed a populace – cultural considerations come a distant second. As Lopes suggests, developing countries have given greater emphasis to efficiency and nationism rather than nationalism, and in terms of language this has resulted in a desire for English language proficiency.

The desire to learn English, even in countries where it is not officially sanctioned, would seem to be getting stronger (although David Graddol's 1997 publication *The Future of English*, suggests that the situation is rather complex). In all the countries described in the special issues it is clear that where there is a demand somebody will supply, even if the supply is of doubtful benefit (Eagle, 1999, refers to the demand for English medium 'boarding-schools' in Nepal). As Baldauf and Kaplan (1999: 270) note 'the behaviour of a population may to some greater or lesser extent be at odds with the intentions of governmental (and educational) language planning'. I think it is clear that people from all parts of the world will vote with their feet and opt for an education system that fulfils their needs. Failure to provide such a system will mean that government schools are avoided (as is apparently happening in Nepal) and a private sector will flourish. Given the continued demand for the language it is necessary for planners to include some meaningful role for English in the curriculum.

Brunei Today

So what has been achieved and what still needs to be done? In listing factors for the cost-benefit analysis it was immediately clear that the benefits of having a bilingual education system in Brunei today outweigh those of a monolingual system. However, an education system that is not overtly bilingual but which achieves high standards in the national language as well as in English, would also, I believe, be equally acceptable to most Bruneians. There is a need for English, but this does not necessarily equate with a need for a bilingual education system.

Brunei today is a multilingual state and most locals use a variety of languages in their business. However, many sections of the community need no language other than their first, be it Malay, Chinese or English. Thus while a bilingual education system may have a bilingual population as its ultimate objective not all sections of the community actually need to be bilingual. Of course, it would be highly divisive to try and determine at an early age who is likely to need English in later life, but it is equally apparent that at the moment not all pupils are learning English equally well. Pupils who are struggling with English might benefit from having more of their studies in Malay. Career opportunities would be limited for such pupils, but perhaps no less so than they are at present given that such pupils are failing at school anyway.

There are a disproportionate number of boys among the weaker students. Girls now make up the great majority of Brunei's undergraduate students and it is girls that are most likely to graduate with good degrees. If any sort of two-tier education system is introduced it is most likely that girls would outnumber boys in any top tier and vice versa in the lower tier. The implications for the society are obvious and may be unacceptable in a traditional Islamic society, a society that has always been male dominated.

At the moment we are working on assumptions and a much clearer picture needs to be determined. A clear definition of 'failure' needs to be established, as does any correlation between failure and English language proficiency. Brunei's bilingual education system may be satisfying the needs of industry and commerce at present, but there are some sections of the community who are failing at school and whose career opportunities are therefore minimal.

Should changes need to be made to the present education system there would be implications, among others, for teacher training, curriculum, textbooks and examinations. Such change would lead to a certain amount of disruption anywhere, but in a small country like Brunei, with only limited human resources, any transition would be particularly difficult.

Conclusion

Over the last fifteen years Brunei has witnessed the development of its bilingual education school system. As a measure of success, the country's sixth form centres and university have no shortage good pupils and students. Indeed, the country faces something of an embarrassment of riches with many competent, well educated bilinguals being unemployed as a result of recession and a shrinking economy. Further down the scale, however, while still fairly competent in both school languages, there are pupils who are handicapped by their inability to fully grasp English. Although they understand English, and are able to use the language in most situations, many would be unable to use it competently in all domains. The weakest pupils include those who are abject school failures. All countries have such pupils, no matter what type of education system is used, but a question facing Brunei is whether the extremely weak pupils are unfairly handicapped by the particular demands of the bilingual education system and whether an alternative system, with greater emphasis on the use of L1 in class, would improve the situation.

In sum, after fifteen years experience with the education system, the present status is one of guarded optimism. The bilingual education system is bridging the gap between the needs of a Malay-speaking Islamic monarchy and those of a young and potentially energetic developing Southeast Asian nation. Nevertheless, it should be possible to improve on the present system without losing the benefits that have already been accrued. This would involve a certain amount of restructuring and a flexible attitude from all concerned and, most importantly, an acceptance of the need for changes.

8 Productive Bilingualism: 1 + 1 > 2

Gao, Yihong
Peking University

---

1. Current Models of Bilingualism and Multiculturalism
1.1 Subtractive bilingualism and additive bilingualism

Ever since their first use by Lambert (1974) to distinguish between two socially defined types of bilingualism, the terms 'subtractive bilingualism' and 'additive bilingualism' have become a significant part of the typology of bilingualism. In the past thirty years, in many works on societal bilingualism, the terms have been extensively used either explicitly (e.g., Gardner, 1982; Cummins, 1976) or implicitly (e.g., Schumann, 1978). There might be some slight meaning variations, yet a general definition can be derived. (For definitions, see Ellis, 1986: 117; Gardner, 1985: 134-135; Richards, Platt & Weber, 1985: 4; Baetens Beardsmore, 1986: 22-23; Romaine, 1995: 117). With subtractive bilingualism, the second or foreign language (L2) is acquired at the expense of the native language (L1), and target culture (C2) assimilation threatens to replace values and life styles of the native culture (C1).[1] With additive bilingualism, the acquisition or learning of L2 and C2 is not at the expense of L1 and C1 identity; the native language and cultural identity are maintained. Since both subtractive and additive bilingualism assume the combination of language and culture, they can also be considered concepts of biculturalism.

1.2 Acculturation as subtractive and additive bilingualism

Schumann's (1978) 'acculturation model' highlights the effect of C2 acquisition on that of L2:

---

[1] Unless specified, the author makes no special distinctions in this paper between 'second language' and 'foreign language', or between 'acquisition' and 'learning'.

By acculturation I mean the social and psychological
integration of the learner with the target language (TL) group.
I also propose that any learner can be placed on a continuum
that ranges from social and psychological distance to social
and psychological proximity with speakers of the TL, and that
the learner will acquire the second language only to the degree
that he acculturates (Schumann, 1978: 29).

Schumann further proposes that learners' integration
strategies can be classified into three major categories on the
continuum of acculturation: *preservation*, in which the learner
sticks to C1 norms and rejects those of C2; *adaptation*, in which
the learner adopts C2 but maintains C1 for intragroup use;
assimilation, in which the learner replaces C1 life styles and
values with those of C2. With preservation L2 learning is
inhibited; with adaptation L2 learning is partial; only with
assimilation L2 learning is maximal (Schumann, 1978: 30).

Schumann's scale of acculturation actually demonstrates a
gradual development toward subtractive bilingualism. Preservation represents the lowest degree of C2 learning. Adaptation can
be taken as additive bilingualism, as L1 and C1 are maintained
while L2 and C2 acquired. Assimilation is subtractive
bilingualism of a pure kind, characterised by cultural identity
substitution. So as far as maximising the level of L2 proficiency
to be achieved is concerned, Schumann's evaluation of preservation, which tends to produce additive bilingualism, is negative,
and that of assimilation, which tends to produce subtractive
bilingualism, is positive. However, in view of the influence of
bilingualism on cognition, some others (e.g., Lambert, 1974;
Cummins, 1976) propose that additive bilingualism has positive
effects, resulting in more cognitive flexibility.

There are other bilingualism models that parallel
Schumann's acculturation model. Andersen's (1983) nativisation
model, for example, sees L2 learning as a gradual process of
'denativising' L1 and C1 features in the learner's L2, hence
subtractive bilingualism. Acton and De Felix (1986) also stress
the adoption of C2 identity, and view such a process as consisting
of four acculturation stages: C2 tourist, survivor, immigrant, and
citizen. Their 'acculturation' is defined in an additive sense,
however, as 'the gradual adaptation to the target culture without

necessarily forsaking one's native language identity' (Acton & De Felix, 1986: 20). Similarly, Guiora's L2 ego model (Guiora, 1972) allows L1 ego to stay after L2 ego is developed. Thus these two models can be considered additive. There are also studies that talk about 'healthy acculturation,' and view culture shock as leading to 'a high degree of self-awareness and personal growth' (Brown, 1986: 42 & 38). However, the nature of the relationship between L1 and L2 egos or between C1 and C2 identities, especially in a *healthy* kind of learning that facilitates personal growth, remains to be examined.

1.3 Multiculturalism

Parallel to research on bilingualism is the research on multiculturalism. The focus of such research is on the development of cultural awareness and sensitivity, which will enhance the effectiveness of intercultural communication. Multi-culturalism does not assume multilingualism or bilingualism; it is not dependent on language. As an example, Hanvey (1990) proposes four stages in the development of cross-cultural awareness. At the first level, the learner develops awareness of superficial cultural traits, and C2 is perceived as unbelievable. At the second level, there is awareness of significant and subtle C2 traits that contrast markedly with those of C1. Cultural conflict situations occur. At the third level, 'empathy,' the learner is able to conduct intellectual analysis of C2, which then becomes cognitively believable. At the fourth level, 'transspection,' which is achieved through cultural immersion, C2 becomes believable because of subjective familiarity. Hanvey's model is based on French people's contact with North American Indians, and American Peace Corps volunteers' experience in the Philippines. In both cases, the socioeconomic status of C1 is high and that of C2 is low. No value change is involved, and replacement of cultural identities is out of the question. Such a model might be called 'additive.' Nevertheless, instead of being considered the simple addition of a new cultural identity, it might be seen as a general expansion of cognitive and behavioural repertoire, and softening of rigid emotional reaction patterns. In Hanvey's own words (1990: 240-242), the change from a 'traditional man' to a 'modern man' and then to a 'postmodern man' is the expansion of one's perspective from 'local' to 'national' to 'global,' i.e., from monoculturalism or ethnocentrism to multiculturalism.

From a pedagogical perspective, Wurzel (1988) proposes a seven-stage model of cross-cultural awareness development. These stages are: monoculturalism, cross-cultural contact, cultural conflict, educational interventions, disequilibrium, awareness, and multiculturalism. The following is Wurzel's definition of 'multicultural man':

> A multicultural man is the person who is intellectually and emotionally committed to the fundamental unity of all human beings while at the same time he recognises, legitimises, accepts, and appreciates the fundamental differences that lie between people from different cultures. This new kind of man cannot be defined by the languages he speaks, the countries he has visited, or the number of international contacts he has made. Nor is he defined by his profession, his place of residence, or his cognitive sophistication. Instead, multi-cultural man is recognised by the configuration of his outlooks and world views, by the way he remains open to the imminence of experience. (Wurzel, 1988: 13)

1.4 Comments on models of bilingualism and multiculturalism

Models of bilingualism tend to mostly focus on the acquisition of linguistic skills of a particular target language and take that as the final objective, for which acculturation is a necessary condition. Personality growth in general is not an essential concern; in some models it is quite irrelevant. Models of multilingualism take general personality growth as the end rather than the means, aiming at the expansion of self, the adoption of a 'world identity' or 'universal identity.' It does not pay much attention to the role of learning a particular L2 in the construction of such an identity. In related fields of research, 'bilingualism' as a keyword is more frequently used than 'multilingualism,' whereas 'multiculturalism' as a keyword is more frequently used than 'biculturalism.' This difference in preferred prefixes is symbolically revealing – bilingualism research is too much confined to two; multiculturalism research needs to scrutinise the source of its multiplex.

In both bilingualism and multiculturalism models, a question remains as to the interaction between C1 and C2 identities. In subtractive bilingualism, C1 identity is a hindrance to learning, hence it is discarded. In additive bilingualism, it is 'maintained,' 'not the expense,' or even 'enriching,' but the nature of its interaction (if at all) with C2 identities is still misty. In practice, education that takes additive bilingualism as the goal may well lapse into reduction of both L1 and L2 (Poon, 2001; Man, 2001). In multiculturalism models, C1 identity tends to melt into a 'world identity,' without detailed accounts of such a transformation.

Methodologically, most bilingualism studies that focus on 'affect', 'attitudes' and 'motivation' paradoxically adopt a *cognitive* approach, trying to single out in an 'objective,' 'scientific' manner the affective bits among a number of factors influencing language proficiency. Empirical basis is stressed, and quantitative research techniques are favoured. Some acculturation studies also adopt qualitative methods such as diary studies and autobiography studies (e.g., Schumann, 1998), to describe cases of acculturation. On the other hand, multiculturalism studies are often speculative and non-empirical, trying to categorise stages of multicultural awareness development (e.g., Hanvey, 1990; Wurzel, 1988). While bilingualism studies are mostly descriptive, multiculturalism studies are mostly normative.

There is no reason why the approaches to bilingualism and multiculturalism studies cannot be integrated, however. We may take a qualitative, descriptive look at the attitudinal aspect of actual learners, and conceptualise a general pattern of C1-C2 interaction from there.

2. An Empirical Investigation
2.1 Research question
An empirical study (Gao, 1994 & 2001) was carried out on some recognised 'best foreign language learners' in the People's Republic of China. The purpose of the research was to discover attitudes toward L1, L2 and C1, C2 respectively, and the pattern of interaction between L1/C1 and L2/C2.

2.2 Method

The informants of the study were 52 Chinese foreign language scholars working in the fields of teaching, research, and cultural exchange. Of these 52 informants, 26 were selected 'best foreign language learners' according to the result of a questionnaire. The questionnaire was conduced on 70 participants at two national conferences on foreign language teaching, asking them to select those people whom they considered 'best foreign language learners in China.' From the resulting name list, 26 (mostly in their seventies, sixties or late fifties) were within the researcher's reach and became informants for the study. The other 26 informants included in this study were mostly younger scholars recommended by the selected 'best foreign language learners,' and in a few cases, the researcher's acquaintances or colleagues. All the informants learnt their L2 as a foreign rather than second language. Among them, 42 had either lived in or visited countries where their L2 was spoken as a native tongue. Yet most of the informants had lived in their home country most of the time.

Individual interviews were carried out between the researcher and each informant. The informants were requested to describe their L2 learning process, with emphasis on attitudes and motivation. Some follow-up interviews were conducted for further clarification and exemplification. All the interview data were coded and analysed, and common features and patterns were identified.

As supplementary data, relevant works of and about the informants – academic articles, biographies and autobiographies, and photos were also examined.

2.3 Findings

The informants demonstrated some shared attitudes and tendencies toward L1/C1 and L2/C2, which may be characterised as openness, criticalness, and incorporation. While acquiring a 'world identity', their original Chinese identities were not reduced, but enhanced and enriched.

2.3.1 Openness

An open attitude toward the target culture was found to be common. Informant 28, who taught English movies in a college, reported her experience with *On the Golden Pond*:

I did not really appreciate the movie *On the Golden Pond* until I lived with a retired American professor during my one-year stay in the United States. This lonely old lady was constantly haunted by the fear that her dog would die. We soon became friends, and both of us felt sad when I had to leave. Now when I teach the film *On the Golden Pond,* I often recall the moments when the old lady and I watched videos together, and the dog lay by, as if watching with us. The appreciation of a movie has many dimensions – the concepts and morals, the artistic techniques, and also, the feelings and emotions. I believe love between human beings as expressed in *On the Golden Pond* is a universal theme. (#28)

Openness might be found at the emotional level and presented as empathy, as in the above case. It was also found at cognitive, behavioural and aesthetical levels. Moreover, openness was directed toward not only C2, but also C1. Interestingly, opening to one culture did not mean rejecting the other; very often, the more open one was to one culture, the more open he or she was to the other.[2]

I used to know very little about Peking opera and seldom went to see it. When I did go I found the music loud, the costume gaudy, the make-up exaggerated, the acting stylised, the singing affected and the pace unbearably slow. The first time I ever felt that there was something worth looking at in Peking opera was when I accompanied a Canadian friend of mine and her little son to see *The Romance of the Iron Bow.* Throughout the two hours I was amazed to find that both mother and child were absolutely charmed. When I looked back, I realised that the explaining process, during which I tried my best to look at the play from my friends' viewpoint and was anxious that they should enjoy it, had made me look at Peking opera with fresh eyes and helped me discover what's enjoyable in it. That was my first lesson in the appreciation of Peking opera. Some years after that, an American scholar-friend of mine showed me an article he had written about Peking opera, in which he discusses the relationship between artistic creativity and formal conventions. He argues that the creativity of Peking opera is realised in the actors and actresses creating beauty

---

[2]   It should be noted that international relations and historical situations had an impact on attitudes toward L2 and C2. Older informants reported hatred for foreign languages during the Japanese invasion (WWII).

within the conventions of the stylised motions and singing. The article represents a Western view of Peking opera, but it brings out the universal truth that any art form is a way of creating beauty under the constraint of particular conventions. One may say that beauty is created in spite of the conventions, but it will be nearer the truth to say that beauty is created owing to the conventions. Though I failed to appreciate Peking opera in the past, Western ballet has always had a fascination for me. Now I realise that ballet, as well as Peking opera, is a form of art with very rigid and apparently very artificial conventions. Ballet owes its creative beauty precisely to these conventions. Then why shouldn't I be able to see the beauty of Peking opera, which is likewise created precisely out of its own particular set of rigid conventions? (#26)

The appreciation of C2 offered Informant 26 a new aesthetical and cognitive perspective of C1. Such C1 revisits were also reported by other informants:

I obtained a deeper understanding of and greater respect for Confucianism in the United States. I did not realise the value of Confucianism until I was in the United States and adopted a Western view of my native culture. The humanism and the sense of social responsibility proposed by Confucius are necessary for the whole world. What strikes me after my return to China is that many of these things are lost. That's a shame. (#38)

It was in the United States that I first became interested in *The Book of Changes*. I read the English version first at a friend's home and then came back to find the Chinese original. In the past I thought it was no more than fortune telling. Now I realised that it contained much scientific thought in it. (#32)

2.3.2 Criticalness

Openness was coupled with a seemingly contradicting attitude, and criticalness. Informant 48 was daring in criticising Chinese culture, her C1, in the midst of a political campaign 'against bourgeois liberalisation,' during which individualism was considered one aspect of 'bourgeois liberalisation'.

In our culture sometimes the individual is considered unimportant; he or she should be subordinate to the group. However, it is impossible to dispense with the individual or the self. What makes things different is the quality of the self. A person who has a high-quality self will not be selfish. One who is only interested in protecting self-interest does not have a self. What he or she has is an empty shell. Such people are not very different from animals; they are not individual human beings. Those who have true selves, those individuals of high qualities are not selfish.

A society of high quality is a society that respects individuals. What makes a group is not a herd of cattle, a flock of sheep, a drove of horse, or a pack of pigs. Without excellent individual human beings, there is no excellent group. (#48)

Similarly, another informant critically reflected on the status of humour in Chinese culture:

I wouldn't say sweepingly that we Chinese have no sense of humour. ... But a sense of humour has never been seriously thought of as a trait that will win us admiration or success. At least I've never heard of Chinese parents in teaching their children the precept of life mention a sense of humour as a virtue to be cultivated, nor have I ever met a Chinese young man or woman who, while looking for a prospective mate, seriously stipulates a sense of humour as a requisite quali-fication. On the other hand in the Western world a sense of humour is universally looked upon as an admirable trait or a sign of good upbringing. And in British journals it is very common to come across 'mate wanted' advertisements in which a sense of humour is explicitly mentioned as a requirement. ... The common lack of a sense of humour in the Chinese perhaps has to do with China's feudal social structure which reduces all human relationships, such as between monarch and subject, father and son, husband and wife, elder and younger, master and servant, teacher and student, to a superior-subordinate relationship, in which everybody is either a superior or a subordinate, and in either position humour is frowned upon as improper. This is just as true with contemporary China as with ancient China. Take for instance a teacher teaching in a classroom. He is expected to keep up a 'dignified' image all the time. Some teachers manage this without obvious effort, while others, unfortunately, seem to be labouring all the time. One of the most painful sights left in my memory from my student days was the piteous look of the red-faced teacher who felt that he had been humiliated in front of his students. After I myself became a teacher and got to know a number of Western colleagues, I often asked myself why shouldn't we Chinese teachers have that sense of humour so many Western teachers have, which liberates them from slavery to their own outward dignity? This, of course, applies not only to teachers, but to other people as well. I am not saying that we should emulate Western witticisms and learn to crack clever jokes as we see Westerners often do. In fact with some Westerners the witticisms and jokes are no more than a manifestation of intellectual snobbishness. Anyway the superficial manifestation is not what we should imitate. What we should make an effort to acquire is the true sense of humour which enables a person to see himself as just one of the billions of funny little animals called human beings on this earth. I often feel a great admiration for the Westerner who, when he is fired by his boss or deserted by his wife, or even sentenced to death for something he has not done, can laugh and tell himself that it must be God having a joke with him. (#26)

Criticalness manifested in the views of Informant 26 quoted above was directed not only toward C1, but also toward C2.

Informant 31 was a well-known linguist and historian who studied in Europe and had a good command of many Western and Far Eastern languages. He made the following remark on the 'Western analytical mode of thinking' in an article:

Why is it so that toward the end of the 20th century, when the Western culture is like the blazing sun at noontime, some insightful Westerners have established the study of chaos, which is against the general trend of Western culture? There is only one answer. That is, these insightful people have deeply realised that infinite division will come to its end. In order that human civilisation should retain its vitality and advance itself, we must change our perspectives. ... Western thinking sees only the tree but not the forest. It does atomistic analysis of specific details, but often overlooks the interrelation among these details and fails to generalise from a macro perspective. Such a view portrays various things and phenomena as if they were all as clear as water. But that is not true. ... I think the Chinese and Eastern way of thinking is closer to truth, as it looks at the whole and the interrelation between objects and phenomena. In this respect, traditional Chinese medical science has its advantage over Western medical science. The Western doctor treats the head if there is headache, and the foot if there is toe sore. In contrast, the Chinese doctor examines the whole body in various respects and may work on the foot for the headache. The ingredients of one serving of Chinese medicine have primary and secondary contents, and therapy is directed to the core of the disease rather than the superficial symptom. This method of treatment is more scientific than the Western method. To extend a little bit, I believe the same principle of holistic thinking is embodied in fuzzy mathematics which now attracts the attention of modern scientists. (#31)

Critical attitudes towards C1 and C2 were not related to each other in a 'subtractive' or 'additive' manner. Like openness, criticalness seemed to be a general asset developed or enhanced during the process of L2 and C2 learning:

I believe I'm more Chinese than many Chinese, and more Western than many Westerners. This is because I have different perspectives; I can see the special features of a culture better (than monolinguals), and I'm freer and better equipped in critiquing either one (culture). (#11)

You can't really understand and appreciate your own language and culture unless you well understand and appreciate a foreign language and culture. You can't really understand and appreciate a foreign language and culture unless you well understand and appreciate your own. (#29)

2.3.3 Incorporation

Through constant conscious comparison of C1 and C2, the informants reached incorporation of the two cultures, each person in his or her unique way. They also engaged themselves in cultural exchange activities, as if they assumed a certain mission. For some, this was introducing Western cultures to China, for others, it was introducing Chinese culture to the world.

Informant 7 was a well-known translator in his seventies. He published some 40 books, mostly English and French translations of classical Chinese poetry. He proposed that good poetry translation should preserve three kinds of beauty in the source language – 'beauty in sense, sound, and form.' In his English and French translation of classical Chinese poetry, he made special efforts to render its original formal beauty:

Parallelism is important in Chinese regulated poetry, for at least in the two middle couplets of the eight-line verse, the paired lines are syntactically parallel, and each word contrasts in sense with its counterpart in the other line. For example, we may read the following couplet in Du Fu's *On the Height*:

The boundless forest sheds its leaves shower by shower;
The endless river rolls its waves hour after hour.[3]

It is said that in English strict parallelism without the repetition of a word is nearly impossible, while parallelism involving repetition will quickly seem rigid and monotonous. But in the above version we may find only unimportant particles repeated without entailing rigidity or monotony. It is true that in the second line of Du Fu's original couplet the word 'roll' is repeated (gun^3gun^3), while in this version it is not. Isn't it a loss? So it is, but the loss is compensated for by the repetition of 'hour,' which cannot be found in the original. Then this maybe called a loss at sunrise with a gain at sunset. (#7)

Such effort of rendering the formal beauty is quite different from some English-speaking translators of classical Chinese poetry, who try mainly to capture the meaning. Based on his translation practice, this Chinese translator proposed an 'eight-*yi*' theory, each *yi* as a translation principle. These eight points touch upon the relationship between the translator and various elements in translation: the original author, the cultural context, the linguistic codes, the reader, the nature and the effect of the activity. They embody the teleology, epistemology and methodology of poetry translation. Each of the points is rendered by a homonym *yi* in Chinese; thus his translation theory, like his practice, also has a formal beauty.

Informant 7's pursuit for congruence, harmony and incorporation in translation was consistent with his general views on cultures:

The West values truth; the East treasures goodness; as a poetry
translator I pursue beauty. Truth, goodness and beauty are
congruent with one another. (#7)

Informant 43 was a young lady in her earlier thirties, who married an American. The couple ran a Sino-American cultural exchange programme and a magazine introducing Chinese culture to the Americans. They travelled between the two countries every year, spending summer and autumn in China, and winter and spring in the US. The young lady was a college classmate of mine, and in her college days she remained in the memories of many as a 'Westernised' 'giggling girl'. When we

---

[3] wu^2bian^1 luo^4mu^4 $xiao^1xiao^1$ xia^4, bu^2jin^4 $chang^2jiang^1$ gun^3gun^3 lai^2.

met again several years after her marriage, she appeared to be a mature, capable and quite philosophical person. As a friend she chatted with me from time to time on cultural issues, lent me books on *Zen* and taught me how to meditate in a *Zen* style.

> I feel I am very Chinese now. In the past my Chinese identity was natural and taken for granted; I was unaware of it. Now I know *why* I am Chinese.
>
> This has something to do with my marriage. Before I met my husband H., I was only interested in enjoying myself, trying to go abroad, all the stuff that Chinese college students are commonly interested in. Yet H is a very cultured person and his interests in classical culture – Chinese, Greek, and many others – have influenced me a great deal. I did not enjoy reading as a college undergraduate, but now I enjoy it and can sit there reading for hours. H is a Buddhist, and it is from him that I learnt to practice *Zen* and *Qigong*. Now I can appreciate a lot of the Chinese things. I enjoy communicating with nature, that kind of man-nature harmony. When I practice *Qigong* or *Zen*, I communicate with myself. When I interview people for our magazine, I communicate with human beings. When I go out to the wild, I communicate with nature. All these communications help me to know myself and the world around. It's interesting that marriages bring out different things in different couples. In our marriage, our best things are brought out and combined. (#43)

Informant 43's view of cultural incorporation was restated by her husband (though not an informant in this study) from an American perspective:

> America is a young, up-surging country with a lot of *Yang Qi*; whereas China is a culture whose dominant *Qi* is *Yin*, a culture of tranquillity and calmness. The American culture charged with *Yang Qi* needs to incorporate some *Yin Qi* from the Chinese culture. The Americans have a lot to learn from the Chinese, those things in the traditions and inherited by the contemporaries. ... I am here in China to dig gold. Of course there are gold and rocks in a culture. What I want is the gold; I don't mind the rocks.

2.3.4 Cultural identities

Most informants, when asked about their cultural identities, made a clear and strong claim of Chinese identity, but this was an identity that got broadened and enriched in the process of L2 learning.

I never went through the process of travelling from cultural identity A to cultural identity B. I am always 100% Chinese. I never look down upon my own culture, but I've learnt to understand it and appraise it. What I have gained from learning English and English literature is an increased ability of social perception and cognition, an increased ability of analysis and evaluation, and an increased ability of appreciation. What I have gone through is a process from A_1 to A_2 to A_3 to A_n, for I am constantly enriched and empowered. I have gained an expanded and deepened insight of Chinese culture and of Western culture. (#48)

Some avoided answering the identity question directly, yet their responses implied a 'world identity'. Informant 45, a renowned scholar and translator in his seventies, cited comments from one of his international friends on his apparent cultural origin:

It's hard to tell which culture you are from. If I'm told you are from Beijing, I would believe it. Yet if I'm told you are from Washington D.C., I will not have any doubt. Again, if I'm told you are from Paris, I'll still be convinced. (#45)

Informant 20 was a young scholar and translator. He translated, among a good many works, *The Book of Lao Tze* into English, and Shakespeare's sonnets into Chinese. In an article written in classical Chinese yet accessible to modern Chinese readers, he proposed his view 'thousands of theories and schools, all share the same origin and complement one another'. For him, different cultures were ultimately congruent with one another. In the interview, he identified himself as a multicultural person:

I have long had the tendency of being multicultural. Foreign language learning helps to develop a thinking mode, a way of viewing the universe from multiple angles. It is only in this way that our cognition can be enhanced; it is only for its diversity that the world is significant and interesting. The more language one learns, the more broadened his or her perspectives should be. (#20)

2.4 General discussion

What is the nature of the interaction between L1/C1 and L2/C2 as found with the informants? Subtractiveness does not offer an accurate description. The majority of the informants had a clear and strong C1 identity, which was neither replaced nor reduced in the course of L2 and C2 learning. On the contrary, this C1 identity was strengthened. On the other hand, Schumann's 'preservation' does not seem to apply either. For one thing, the informants did demonstrate, apart from other things, an open attitude toward C2 and critical attitude toward C1. For another, instead of having their L2 fossilised at an earlier stage, they had high L2 accomplishments (e.g., in translation and writing), hence regarded as 'best language learners'.

Additiveness seems to be closer to the picture, but not very exact either. True, it might be said to apply when it means 'maintaining', 'without replacing' or 'not at the expense of' C1 identity. Yet the informants' C1 values and identities were not simply *maintained*, but *enhanced* or *enriched*; some qualitative *changes* or *differences* were brought about. C2 values and beliefs were not mechanically added to those of C1 for functional convenience. Nor were C2 and C1 averaged to result in a happy medium. Instead, they interacted, transformed each other, and were incorporated into a new self.

Another line of thinking is that the informants had an 'instrumental' rather than 'integrative' orientation (Gardner & Lambert, 1972); they used L2 for practical purposes, and cultural integration was irrelevant. It is true that many informants reported an instrumental motivation or absence of clear motivation at the beginning stage of L2 learning (e.g., Informant 7, the well-known translator). Yet in later periods, their L2 activities tended to derive from some inherent interest, and perception of meaning or significance was embedded in the creative language-use activities. Such interest, perception of meaning, and in some cases a sense of mission went far beyond instrumental purposes.

On the other hand, the L1-L2 and C1-C2 interaction presented above was a development of cross-cultural awareness or tendency of multiculturalism, as described in previous literature. Although the development of multicultural awareness does not have to depend on L2 proficiency, the mastery of a foreign language played a central role in the informants' in-depth understanding of different cultures. Therefore, it seems a new concept is needed to capture the bilingual and multicultural phenomenon as found in the data.

3. Theoretical Conceptualisation
3.1 Productive orientation

Erich Fromm's concept of 'productive orientation' seems to shed light on the nature of C2-C1 interaction described above. As a humanistic psychologist, Fromm (1948) proposes two large types of personality orientation – *'non-productive' vs 'productive.'*

> The 'productive orientation' of personality refers to a fundamental attitude, a mode of relatedness in all realms of human experience. It covers mental, emotional, and sensory responses to others, to oneself, and to things. Productiveness is man's ability to use his powers and to realise the potentialities inherent in him. (Fromm, 1948: 84)

> It is the paradox of human existence that man must simultaneously seek for closeness and for independence; for oneness with others and at the same time for the preservation of his uniqueness and particularity. As we have shown, the answer to this paradox – and to the moral problem of man – is productiveness. (ibid.: 96-97)

In such a relation, the two parties in the interaction will be mutually enhanced. For example, in 'productive love' which involves care, responsibility, respect and knowledge, one will try to do things for the other party to enhance his or her growth (motherly love is typical of this kind). In 'productive thinking,' the thinking subject is intensely interested in the object, and the more intimate this relation is, the more fruitful the thinking. At the same time, the subject is competent to understand the object as it is, not as he or she would like to see it. Productive thinking is marked by unity of the subject and object. In contrast, with non-productive orientations – 'receptive,' 'exploitative,' 'hoarding' and 'marketing,' one will tend to totally accept, exploit, possess, or trade with the other party in an interaction. In his later work (1989), the nonproductive-productive distinction is accommodated in a broader framework 'to have' *vs* 'to be.'

3.2 Productive bilingualism

Table 1 **Types of bilingualism**

Bilingualism Type	Productive Bilingualism	Additive Bilingualism	Subtractive Bilingualism
Symbolization	1 + 1 > 2	1 + 1 = 1	1 − 1 = 1
Feature	L1/C1 & L2/C2 benefit and enhance each other	L1/C1 & L2/C2 divide up communicative functions	L1/C1 replaced by L2/C2

'Productive orientation' well captures the nature of interaction between C1 and C2 as demonstrated in the informants. We may call this phenomenon 'productive bilingualism [4].' For a productive bilingual, the command of the target language and that of the native language positively reinforce each other; deeper understanding and appreciation of the target culture goes hand in hand with deeper understanding and appreciation of the native culture. In the process of learning another language and related culture, the learner's personality becomes more open and integrated at the same time. Such mutual enhancement can be symbolically represented as '1+1>2.'

In contrast, additive bilingualism can be formulated as '1+1=1,' or more exactly, '1+1=½ + ½'. For an additive bilingual, the two linguistic and cultural identities divide up the total communicative functions. In the situation of Schumann's 'adaptation', for instance, L2 and C2 are used in intergroup context, whereas L1 and C1 are used in intragroup context. Such bilinguals will readily adapt him- or herself to the communicative situation so as to achieve communicative effectiveness at a functional level. A typical case of additive bilingualism might be an immigrant child who adopts L2 and C2 identity in school, and L1 and C1 identity at home. Each language and cultural identity has its own role to play in the individual's communicative activities. They are like two handy masks put in two different drawers, and each one is taken out for use in a different type of situation. In a context where the functional division is not that clear, additive bilingualism often presents itself as mixture of reduced codes and identities.

---

[4]   The concept here is distinguished from 'productive bilingualism' as contrasted with 'receptive bilingualism,' difined by the type of L2 skills (Cf. Baetens Beardsmore, 1986: 18-19).

Additive bilingualism of a functional kind might be related to a 'marketing orientation.' According to Fromm, those with such a personality are concerned about external success, and sell their various personalities for success. They do not feel 'I am what I do,' but 'I am as you desire me.' That is, they take a practical, instrumental attitude and feel the self is composed of different social or situational roles.

> 'The very changeability of attitudes is the only permanent
> quality of such orientation. In this orientation, those qualities
> are developed which can best be sold'. (Fromm, 1948: 77)

Subtractive bilingualism can be represented by '1-1=1,' as one linguistic/cultural identity is replaced by another. In a typical case, such as 'assimilation' in Schumann's model, L1 together with C1 identity is replaced by L2 and C2 identity. Thus C2 minus C1 equals C2.

Subtractive bilingualism or acculturation of the assimilation kind is probably related to Fromm's 'receptive orientation.' Such learners will see the external world as the only source of what they want to get. Their central concern is being loved, and they depend highly on people's acceptance, acknowledgement, and help. Ironically, this kind of 'bilingualism' or 'biculturalism,' portrayed as an ideal by some bilingualism researchers such as Schumann, is in fact *monolingualism* and *monoculturalism*, a mere shift from L1/C1 to L2/C2.

Productive, additive and subtractive bilingualism are theoretical categories. Individuals may well combine different types of bilingualism or change from one type to another. For example, those who are primarily 'additive bilinguals' might have productive experiences, and as their productiveness increases, become 'productive bilinguals'.

4. Conclusion

The findings of my empirical research reported above have a number of limitations. The informants were exclusively from the People's Republic of China, and were a small group of successful intellectuals. They learnt their L2 as a foreign language in their native culture, although short term C2 experiences were obtained later in most cases. Also, as interview was the major data collection method and the interviewer herself was working in the same field as many informants, the depths, details and objectivity of data obtained might be affected to some extent. Therefore, caution should be taken when generalising the findings to other contexts. Productive bilingualism as a new concept calls for further supporting data, especially in other contexts and with other groups of learners. Another line for further research is the process of productiveness development, and the relationship between 'personality orientation' and L2 learning. It remains to be examined whether one leads to the other, or the two are involved in mutual construction.[5]

In spite of important research limitations, the present study has its own theoretical significance and practical implications. Integrating approaches to bilingualism and multiculturalism, the present study highlights the relationship between language learning and growth of the learner as a whole person. Theoretically, it suggests a new typology of bilingualism. The enriching nature of L2 learning, part of which already noted in previous studies (e.g., Lambert, 1974; Cummins, 1976), is examined in affective, aesthetic as well as cognitive dimensions. Such an orientation is captured under the new concept 'productive bilingualism,' distinguished from the passive state of 'being maintained' in 'additive bilingualism.' Both 'subtractive bilingualism' as an ideal model for individuals and 'additive bilingualism' as a pedagogical objective are put under a critical light, requiring reconsideration and reevaluation.

With a combined development of intercultural communication and foreign language education, bilingualism is achieved increasingly with C2 components yet in C1 contexts. The productive model may have practical implications especially for those who learn and teach L2 and C2 in C1 contexts, including English learners and teachers from developing countries and regions. For these people, how to deal with the relation between C1 and C2 values, beliefs and life styles has been an important issue. There is a need for bilinguals to go

---

[5]   Some preliminary results were found in a resent study on Chinese college English majors, with productive orientation and its constructive process evident in one of the three cases (Gao, Li & Li, 2001).

beyond the 'instrumental' level of language learning, to expand horizons while affirming one's own cultural heritage and constructing an integrated self-identity. For that purpose, the perception of '1 + 1 > 2' is expected to be beneficial.

9 Some Considerations for Additive Bilingualism: A Tale of Two Cities (Singapore and Hong Kong)

Benjamin K. Tsou
City University of Hong Kong

Introduction

Singapore became a part of the British Empire in 1819 and Hong Kong in 1850. Both have been known as typical examples of modern city states which are vibrant and thriving plurilingual urban hubs. Yet there have been parallel concerns in both cities regarding language problems which have come about as a result of the transition from triglossia[1] to diglossia. More specifically, while there have been massive language shifts as a result of the primarily proactive language policies in Singapore and primarily reactive languages policies in Hong Kong, the linguistic competence of each population is considered by some to be weakening according to local societal requirements.

In the case of Singapore, the future of the Chinese dialects and the Chinese language is seen to be in jeopardy. On the other hand in Hong Kong, English is seen to be in jeopardy among young people, in spite of long years of English education and their additional inadequacy in Modern Standard Chinese (MSC) confounds educationists and policy makers as the latter frantically search for solutions.

This paper proposes to examine the major language shifts within a relatively short time-span in the two communities, and the impact these might have on their emerging sociolinguistic profiles. Associated issues of bilingualism and semilingualism, or possibly double semilingualism will also be addressed.

Singapore

Singapore as a city state may trace its beginning to after the Second World War when Britain was preparing to set its Straits

---

[1]   Tsou, 1983.

Settlement of Malaya and Singapore on the course of independence, just as it conceded independence to India, Pakistan and Sri Lanka. Long an immigrant society with an unusually rich mixture of diverse races from the Indonesian Archipelago and traders from different regions in Southern China, Singapore was transformed from a way station on the sea route between the Suez Canal and the Far East into a thriving port city. Its population swelled quickly with additional immigrants from China because of turmoil arising from civil war there in the mid-20th century. Although records of the varieties of people residing in Singapore exist, extensive information on the language background of the residents is relatively scarce, especially in the early years. Early useful data on language use is available for 1957. After independence in 1964 much more extensive official data became available, and useful secondary data also became available from the 1970's. While they are not all compatible, it is nonetheless possible to draw some interesting and useful comparisons.

Table 1 shows some Census data on language and ethnicity for Singapore in 1957, when its population had already reached 1,442,929.

In 1957 three of the four largest groups in the Singapore population were Chinese: Hokkien (30.62%), Teochew (16.96%), Cantonese (14.23%) and Malay (9.38%).

The cultural diversity among the Chinese can be seen by the existence of six other additional dialect groups, though only two groups were represented by more than 5% of the population: Hainanese and Hakka. According to Kuo (1981), the top four groups also had higher than 96% mother tongue retention. Moreover, the top three Chinese groups also represented more than 60% of the entire population.

There is reasonable mutual intelligibility between the two largest groups: Hokkien and Teochew, such that 'translingualism'[2] is common, where two speakers of different dialects speak with each other in their own dialect in a productive social encounter, especially when bilingualism does not exist between the interlocutors. Given the numerical superiority of Hokkien Chinese under these circumstances, it is easy to see why the situation rapidly developed into one of stratified sociolinguistic dominance,

---

[2]   A term proposed by Prime Minister Lee Kuan Yew in 1977.

Table 1 **Population Ratio and Mother Tongue Retention, By Ethnic/Language Community, Singapore, 1957 (adapted from Kuo, 1981)**

Ethnic/language community[a]	Percentage of total population (N = 1,445,929)	Mother tongue retention rate
I. Chinese		
Hokkien	30.62	96.0
Teochew	16.96	98.2
Cantonese	14.23	99.1
Hainanese	5.40	95.2
Hakka	5.05	90.1
Foochow	1.16	83.7
Other Chinese dialects	0.64	78.8
II. Malay[b]		
Malay	9.38	99.8
Javanese	2.49	40.0
Boyanese	1.53	63.9
Bugis	0.07	29.5
III. Indian[c]		
Tamil	5.41	91.7
Malayali	1.51	90.9
Punjabi	0.54	87.3
Ceylonese Tamil	0.24	86.0
Sikh	0.24	86.4
Sinhalese	0.10	61.8
IV. Other		
Eurasian[d]	0.79	96.0
European[d]	0.75	84.8
Arab	0.24	12.0

Notes: [a]   Including all communities with population size of over 1,000. The categorisation follows that officially and commonly adopted in Singapore, which need not be valid in linguistic and anthropological senses.

[b]   Including those of Indonesian origin

[c]   Including Pakistani and Ceylonese

[d]   The 'mother tongue' of the Eurasians and Europeans is assumed to be English in the calculation of retention rate.

Sources: Computed from S.C. Chua, Report on the Census of Population, 1957: 155-61. Taken from Kuo, 1981 where the Hokkienese were less prone to speak the other dialects than speakers of other dialects to speak Hokkienese, and why Hokkienese developed into the *lingua franca* among the Chinese in Singapore[3], as can be seen in Table 2.

It is therefore no surprise that by 1978 (Table 2), 97% of the Chinese could '*understand*' Hokkien, as compared to only 82.1% who could '*understand*' Mandarin (Kuo, 1981). To better appreciate the ascendancy of Hokkienese, it will be useful to examine some longitudinal changes.

Table 1 provides two kinds of data: (1) Census data on percentage of population who could *speak* a particular language variety (not just as a *Home language*), in 1957, and (2) data on percentage of population who could *understand* the same varieties of language in 1972 and 1978. The assumption is that active 'ability to speak' assumes greater competence than passive 'ability to understand'. Thus from Table 1 it can be seen that the smaller dialect groups in 1957 were experiencing initial language loss and language shift more so than the larger groups, with those represented by less than 5% of the total population undergoing as much as 34.6% language loss (i.e., Shanghainese). At the same time, whilst there is no information on bilingual ability involving more than one dialect, it is interesting to note from Table 2 that 26.7% of the Chinese population spoke Mandarin in 1957 even though no significant group had it as the mother tongue as would otherwise have been registered in Table 1. This implies that about 26.7% of the Chinese population were bilingual in Mandarin and a Chinese dialect and would most likely be those who had learnt Mandarin in Chinese medium schools. This also implies 19.9% of the total population were bilingual in Mandarin and Chinese in 1957 (Table 2). The percentage of the population who could speak both English and some other Chinese dialect, Malay or an Indian language was most likely smaller than the 22.2% reported to speak English in Table 2 because there were monolingual English speakers among this group. In actual fact, bilinguals in Mandarin

---

[3]   This kind of stratified sociolinguistic dominance can be seen in other Chinese communities: Hokkien in Penang, Muar, Seremban, and Jakarta; Teochew in the Riau Archepelago; Cantonese in Kualar Lumpur and Ipoh, and in Hong Kong; Hakka in Tahiti, Calcutta, Reunion, and Mauritius (Tsou, 1991).

Table 2 **Percentage of Population Aged 15 and Over Competent in Various Languages in Singapore by Ethnicity, 1957 and 1978 (adapted from Kuo, 1985a)**

Ethnicity	Major Languages				
	Malay	English	Mandarin	Tamil	Hokkien
Malays					
1957, % speak	99.4	23.5	b	b	b
1972, % can understand	100.0	60	1.7	1.7	6.2
1978, % can understand	100.0	84.2	3.0	1.3	15.8
Chinese					
1957, % speak	32.5	18.0	26.7	b	b
1972, % can understand	45.8	41.2	69.5	0.1	91.1
1978, % can understand	58.1	56.1	82.1	0.2	97.0
Indians					
1957, % speak[c]	88.3	35.5	b	76.7	b
1972, % can understand	95.9	66.3	<0.1	86.7	5.1
1978, % can understand	97.4	67.0	1.7	79.1	8.7
Total[a]					
1957, % speak	48.0	22.2	19.9	8.2	b
1972, % can understand	57.1	46.6	54.4	6.7	72.7
1978, % can understand	67.3	61.7	63.9	6.0	77.9

Notes: a   Including 'other ethnicities'.
         b   Data not available.
         c   Not including Ceylonese, most of whom were Tamil speakers.
Source: 1957 data based on Chua, Report on the Census of Population, 1957, pp. 162-65, Tables 44-47.
         1972 data based on Survey Research Singapore, *SRM Media Index*, 1972, vols. 1 and 2.
         1978 data based on Survey Research Singapore, *SRM Media Index*, 1978, vols. 1 and 2.   Taken from Kuo, 1985(a)

and a Chinese dialect should be less than 19.9%. By contrast, almost half the Chinese population spoke a Min dialect such as Hokkien, Teochew and Hainanese (Table 1). On the other hand, if we compare Tables 1 and 2, we see that there were more Malay speakers among the Chinese than Chinese speakers of any dialect group, which truly reflects the linguistic diversity and complexity of Singapore in 1957.

Table 2 shows that by 1978, the percentage of Chinese population who could *understand* Hokkien (i.e., at least receptive bilinguals) had reached 97%, as compared to 82% for Mandarin.

This probably represented the zenith of dialect prevalence in Singapore, even though Hokkien had little or no official status in the media, education, or for formal occasions.[4]

Following independence in 1965, the Government of Singapore saw a need to foster greater national unity and social-cultural integration. It recognised four national languages: English, Chinese, Malay and Tamil, with English as the working official language. Chinese referred to spoken Mandarin (know as *Hanyu* in Singapore) and written Chinese has come to be based on Modern Standard Chinese (MSC), which also draws its norm from spoken Mandarin. The Government began to implement language planning in nation building. The efforts included educational reforms, whereby the previous system of separate English medium or Chinese medium schools was reformed in favour of bilingual schools emphasising skills in the First Language, which was to be English, and a second language which was to be a mother tongue selected from one of the other three national Languages. They also included a new language policy regarding the media, such that imported dialect TV programmes or films were to be dubbed into Mandarin before release. The Government also vigorously mounted a 'Speak Mandarin (less dialects)' Movement. The campaign was controversial in respect of its reception and successful outcome in the early stages. Many surveys were conducted and Table 3 contains interesting results from a sizable evaluation exercise published in 1985.

The results reported in Table 3 indicate that there was an overall growing trend among respondents to agreeing that the campaign was a success, where approval went up from 31.5% in 1981 to 46.2% in 1983 (Question 9). Also more than 90% of the

---

[4]   It seems that the only official status Hokkien had was in unusual or temporary contexts: When National Service was introduced via the Singapore Armed Forces, Hokkien platoons were formed for those who were not fluent in any of the four official Languages: English, Mandarin, Malay and Tamil. Also in the 1977 National Cultural Show and Rally Prime Minister Lee Kuan Yew gave his speech in Hokkien after Malay and English (Straits Time, 18 Apr 1977).

population thought the campaign should continue (Question 10), and community centres should offer more free Mandarin lessons (Question 7). By comparison, the negative responses were limited to less than 40%. Question (3): The Campaign has had little effect over the past two years (35.6%); Question (4): The civil groups are largely indifferent to the Campaign (37.3%); Question (6): Mandarin is of little use in daily life (40.0%).

Table 3 **Assessment of the Speak Mandarin Campaign (adapted from Kuo, 1985b)**

Statements	1981	1983
1. The Campaign has received wide support from the public.	74.9	84.2
2. The government has made a great effort in promoting the Campaign.	87.6	90.0
3. The Campaign has had little effect over the past two years.	35.7	35.6
4. The civil groups are largely indifferent to the Campaign.	33.4	37.3
5. The press has shown its great influence in promoting the Campaign.	82.9	80.1
6. Mandarin is of little use in daily life.	35.0	40.0
7. Community Centres should offer more free Mandarin lessons.	86.6	90.6
8. Mandarin has become more commonly used among Chinese in the past two years.	76.8	79.5
9. The Speak Mandarin Campaign has succeeded.	31.5	46.2
10. The Campaign should be continued.	93.1	91.6
11. Mandarin programmes on TV have made a great contribution to the Campaign.	---	81.4

If there was scepticism in the 1980's, a review of the sociolinguistic situation some 20 years later would lay to rest earlier reservations and queries. Some relevant findings from the 2000 Singapore Census are presented in Tables 4, 5 & 6.

From Table 4, it can be seen that in contrast to 1957 (Table 1), where over 90% of the population spoke Chinese dialects, the percentage of those speaking Chinese dialects as the *Home Language* had dropped to 50.3% in 1990 and to 30.7% in 2000. At the same time, use of Mandarin as the *Home Language* had gone up from 30.1% in 1990 to 45.1% in 2000.

Table 4 **Resident Population Aged 5 Years and Over by Languages Most Frequently Spoken at Home (adapted from Singapore Census, 2000)**

Ethnic Group/Language	1990	2000
Chinese	100.00	100.0
English	19.3	23.9
Mandarin	30.1	45.1
Chinese Dialects	50.3	30.74
Others	0.3	
Malays	100.0	100.0
English	6.1	7.9
Malay	93.7	91.6
Others	0.1	0.5
Indians	100.0	100.0
English	32.3	35.6
Malay	14.5	11.6
Tamil	43.2	42.9
Others	10.0	9.9

Table 5 **Literate Resident Population Aged 15 Years and Over by Languages Literate in (adapted from Singapore Census, 2000)**

Ethnic Group/Language Literate In	1990	2000
Chinese	100.00	100.0
English Only	19.8	16.4
Chinese Only	40.6	32.0
English & Chinese Only	37.8	48.3
Others	11.9	3.3
Malays	100.0	100.0
English Only	3.2	2.0
Malay Only	27.3	19.8
English & Malay Only	68.1	76.7
Others	1.4	1.5
Indians	100.0	100.0
English Only	22.1	21.5
Tamil Only	14.5	8.9
English & Tamil Only	31.5	37.5
English & Malay Only	19.1	17.4
Others	12.8	14.6

Table 6a **Resident Population by Languages Most Frequently Spoken at Home and Age Group (adapted from Singapore Census, 2000)**

Ethnic Group/ Language	5-14 1990	15-24 1990	25-39 1990	40-54 1990	55 & Over 1990
Chinese	100.00	100.00	100.00	100.00	100.00
English	23.3	19.9	24.6	16.1	5.3
Mandarin	57.6	28.5	30.4	24.8	6.1
Chinese Dialects	18.9	51.5	44.8	58.8	87.7
Others	0.2	0.2	0.3	0.4	0.9
Malays	100.00	100.00	100.00	100.00	100.00
English	8.3	7.0	7.3	3.4	0.7
Malay	91.6	92.9	92.6	96.4	99.1
Others	0.1	0.1	0.1	0.1	0.2
Indians	100.00	100.00	100.00	100.00	100.00
English	39.6	37.0	36.3	25.7	13.4
Malay	18.4	15.1	14.5	13.7	9.4
Tamil	35.6	41.0	41.3	47.5	56.2
Others	6.3	6.9	8.0	13.0	21.1

Table 6b **Resident Population by Languages Most Frequently Spoken at Home and Age Group (adapted from Singapore Census, 2000)**

Ethnic Group/ Language	5-14 2000	15-24 2000	25-39 2000	40-54 2000	55 & Over 2000
Chinese	100.00	100.00	100.00	100.00	100.00
English	35.8	21.5	25.2	25.1	9.9
Mandarin	59.6	59.8	46.5	43.9	17.8
Chinese Dialects	4.3	18.4	28.0	30.7	71.8
Others	0.4	0.3	0.3	0.3	0.5
Malays	100.00	100.00	100.00	100.00	100.00
English	9.4	8.2	10.5	6.1	1.7
Malay	90.1	91.3	89.0	93.4	97.6
Others	0.5	0.5	0.5	0.5	0.6
Indians	100.00	100.00	100.00	100.00	100.00
English	43.6	37.9	35.5	35.5	20.5
Malay	12.9	14.7	9.6	12.5	9.2
Tamil	36.3	40.6	43.0	43.6	54.6
Others	7.2	6.7	11.9	8.4	15.7

What is significant in the Singaporean situation is that it seems to have undergone two critical stages in language shift, and sociolinguistic realignment, within 50 years:

Stage I: from the 1950's to 1970's, there were critical changes in Language Loyalty among the Chinese population. They either underwent language shift towards Hokkien, or acquired ability in Hokkien as receptive or productive bilinguals, resulting in about 97% who could *understand* it in 1978 (This shift is clear because only about 46% of the Chinese population had clearly related linguistic background and only 30.6% were Hokkienese).

Stage II: beginning in the1970's, a second major language shift from the dialects to Mandarin and, surprisingly, English, took place as a result of conscious Government language planning policies to promote Mandarin and English. Thus, Mandarin which was the *Home Language* of a tiny percentage of the Chinese population in 1957 (though *understood* by 26.7%) had gone up to 30.1% as the *Home Language* in the 1990s and 45.1% in 2000. On the other hand, those who spoke a Chinese dialect as *Home Language* (i.e., maintaining *language loyalty*) drastically went down from 96%[5] in 1957 to 50.3% by 1990 and thereafter further went down to 30.7% in 2000.[6] Also the number of people who use English as the *Home Language* has increased by 20% with overall increase to 23.9 of the entire population while the figure has gone up from 23.3% to 35.8% for

---

[5]   By comparison, the overall language loyalty of the "Malay" group is 84.3% (though the language loyalty among the Malays was already at 99.8%). This indicates that the non-Malays within the "Malaysian" group, such as Javanese and Bugis were undergoing language shift toward Bahasa Malay. By comparison, the Indian group's dominant members (Tamil and Malayali) showed high levels of language loyalty while the much smaller sub-groups were showing signs of language shift. The overall Language Loyalty for the "Indian" group is 90.6%. In the case of the smallest communities of "others", the overall Language Loyalty is 80%, with Eurasians retaining English and Europeans yielding ground to mostly English. It is interesting to note that the very small group of Arabs underwent most language shift, probably to Malay.

[6]   The incipient decline of Hokkien in the late 1970's can be seen from the significantly lower rate of increase (from 91.1% to 97%) in the number of Chinese who could understand it, when compared to at least 20% increase in ability to understand Malay, English or Mandarin.

the youngest (5-14) age group. By comparison the percentage of the population which used English as the *Home Language* was very likely between 6.36% and 1.5% in 1957.[7]

It would seem from these reports that the Chinese in Singapore had, within less than half a century, gone through two major language shifts: (1) from dialects to Hokkien, and (2) then from Hokkien to Mandarin or English. The official Census in 2000 also shows that by 2000, 48.3% (Table 5) of the population claimed biliteracy in English and Chinese. These phenomenal language shifts were further supported by the 40-54 age group who reported that their use of dialects as the *Home Language* had dropped from 58.8% in 1990 to 30.7% in 2000 (Tables 6a & 6b), while their use of Mandarin as the *Home Language* had gone up from 24.8% in 1990 to 43.9% in 2000. Such phenomenal language shifts are unprecedented if they could be more fully substantiated, and would testify to the exemplary and successful implementation of language planning policy.

From the critical sociolinguistic realignments indicated above, it is not surprising that there are many other concomitant changes. The Government in Singapore has also been vigorously promoting English in their official bilingual education policy. As noted before, its success had led the Chinese population to increase the use of English as the *Home Language* from 19.3% in 1990 to 23.9% in 2000 (Table 4), and much more significantly, for the youngest age group (5-14) the percentage having English as *Home Language* has gone up from 23.3% (1990) to 35.8% (2000), while the use of Chinese dialects for this group went down from 18.9% in 1990 to 4.3% in 2000. These unusual figures draw a picture of massive language shifts and phenomenal sociolinguistic realignments.

---

[7]   The overall rate for Language Loyalty is 79.92% on the basis of data obtained from Table 1. The only groups which might have used English as the *Home Language* for certainty would be the Eurasians and the majority of the Europeans. Assuming they provided the lower-limit, then not more than 1.5% of the population in 1957 used English as the *Home Language*. If we further assume that all those who underwent Language Shift in 1957 took an English as their *Home Language*, then the upper limit on using English as the *Home Language* would be (100 − 93.64)%, i.e., 6.36%.

What then may be some consequences of such colossal change? Language after all is intimately linked to culture and cognition. One simple conclusion to be drawn is that Chinese dialects could become extinct within one generation. What is interesting, however, is that not just the continuation of Chinese dialects is threatened but that the continuation of the Chinese language itself also appears to be losing ground. This is however quite surprising and not readily supported by the census data. But a persistent public perception on such decline has been frequently expressed, as can be seen from the following newspaper cuttings from the Chinese media.

(1) Fossilisation Fate Of Chinese Language
According to archaeologists, dinosaurs became extinct mainly because room for their existence was threatened. The room for existence for our Chinese language should not be threatened, yet there are worries that the Chinese language may be losing ground (in Singapore). What actually is the problem?
(*Lianhe Zaobao*, 13 Aug 2000 'Public Forum' – Cai S.)

(2) Will Chinese Language Perish?
The low competence level of Chinese is a regular topic of concern. Cai Shenhong recently revisited the matter (*Lianhe Zaobao*, 8 Aug 2000) because of the (problematic) language competence of a certain local singer.
In the past, our Chinese curriculum was revised again and again to resolve problems of Chinese competence. We thought there were rays of hope. But, have the results shown any improvement?   Regrettably, the situation has not changed for the better because of these tumultuous debates and reformation.
(*Lianhe Zaobao*, 18 Aug 2000 'Public Forum' – Li Huimin)

(3) The Future Of Chinese Language Worrisome
Recently, while casually chatting with friends, the topic of students studying Chinese in our country came up, and she suddenly took on a sad intonation to say: 'I believe in 20 years the Chinese language will disappear from Singapore.'
(*Lianhe Zaobao*, 4 Sept 2000 'Public Forum' – Yen Lizhen)

(4) Scholars From China: If Trend To Replace Chinese By English Not Turned Around, Mother Tongue Will Be Foreign Language to Singaporeans
Even though the Speak Mandarin Movement has obtained definite results in the last 20 years, the Chinese language now

faces the danger of being replaced by English. If this trend is not reversed in time, the Chinese language will be a foreign language to Singaporeans in 30 to 50 years.

Two specialists on the Chinese language voiced concerns at the 'The Incomplete Half' of 'Speak Mandarin Movement' Forum, in response to comments by the Senior Minister Lee Kuan Yew that 'Speak Mandarin Movement' has only done a half-job.'   (*Lianhe Zaobao*, 24 Sept 2000)

The reports of concern on Chinese dialects losing ground are supported by the Census data (Table 6), which show incredible gains by Mandarin at the expense of dialects. In fact, such gains by Mandarin are much more spectacular than the gains by English in absolute terms (except perhaps with the 5-14 Age Group) and the reported trends support this. Thus, it is surprising that the popular media singled out the likely replacement of the Chinese Language by English, which does not appear to be readily supported by facts. To appreciate and unravel this puzzle requires more extensive explorations, even though it is a commonly accepted worry in Singapore that Chinese dialects are losing ground rapidly while Mandarin (MSC) and especially English are gaining ground.

One major explanation for this inconsistency may be due to quantitative versus qualitative differences, and the relationship between the two. When respondents in a survey report not speaking or not understanding a certain language, there is little equivocation possible. However, when a respondent claims that he/she speaks or can understand a certain language variety, there can be considerable granularity in the intended meaning of the respondent and much of the validity of the findings depends on the existence of commonly accepted thresholds. It would seem that if the popular perception is correct, responses given in the survey to possible knowledge or ability (to use Chinese) might have been over-rated and thus a gap could very well exist between reality and self-perception on linguistic competence in Chinese. In other words, the population's competence in Mandarin or (MSC), and possibly English, both of which have no deep cultural roots in Singapore, might have been lower than reported or expected. This could mean the existence of *semilinguals*[8] who would show signs of language fatigue and alienation. That this is the case may be seen in the following newspaper item on the English performance of the Tale of the White Snake'.

(5) **English Performance of 'Tale of White Snake' – Enjoyment of Vernacular Opera for Non-dialect Speakers**
Using English to perform Vernacular opera – perhaps not known to many people. This Saturday evening (2 Nov), if you go to Bedok, you can listen to this newly arranged Westernised Cantonese opera, and it will be a new experience. The Natural Arts Council sponsored Wow Wayang ('Appreciative of Operatic Arts') Activities will begin with Dung-huang Drama workshop's 'Tale of White Snake ' performance in English – this Saturday 7:30 p.m. at the vacant lot next to the Bedok MRT Station.

(Lianhe Zaobao, 29 Nov 2000)

The 'Tale of the White Snake' is a popular Chinese folktale, and is a favourite not only in Chinese vernacular operas, but in Mandarin as well. That this opera was not performed in a Chinese dialect is understandable in view of the language policy in Singapore, but that not even a performance in Mandarin was offered was quite surprising.[9] It could indicate that Chinese culture, and not just the Chinese dialects or Chinese languages, is losing ground, and it also appears to justify some of the lamentations cited in the newspapers. This kind of cultural dislocation is a manifestation of alienation and anomie, and not uncommon among semilinguals.[10]

---

[8]   Skutnabb-Kangas, 1981 ; Tsou, 1986.

[9]   In contrast to this, it is interesting to note that in Hong Kong attempts were made in the 1980's to perform Shakespearean plays in Cantonese, which would appear to be solidification of Cantonese culture, and possibly weakening of English status when no comparable performances were available in English.

[10] An early and extreme case of semilingualism was provided by Bloomfield's 1927 description of a Menomini Indian in North America: "White Thunder, a Man around 40, speaks less English than Menomini, and that is a strong indictment, for his Menomini is atrocious. His vocabulary is small, his inflections are of ten barbarous, he constructs sentences of a few threadbare models. He may be said to speak no language tolerably." It was Skutnabb-Kangas and Toukumaa (1976) who began to really draw attention to this phenomenon. However, there

A possible manifestation of such cultural dislocation or even alienation may be manifested by the recent and growing fad among young people in Singapore and other Asian cities such as Hong Kong and Tokyo to lighten their hair colour like Europeans. Other manifestation may be just as revealing, though controversial.

(6) Professor defends race survey results

A professor whose survey revealed that many young Chinese Singaporeans would rather be Caucasian or Japanese yesterday defended his study of values in the city-state and criticised the controversy triggered by the findings.

The survey by Chang Han Yin, a senior lecturer in sociology at the University of Singapore, showed that 23 per cent of the Chinese surveyed said they wished to be either Japanese or Caucasian and 18 per cent of Indians said they would opt to be Caucasian if given the choice. In contrast, nine out of 10 Malays said they would still choose to be Malay.

Several young people said they would prefer to have been born into another race, perceiving that would enhance their opportunities.

The survey's results prompted a deluge of letters to newspapers and calls to talk shows confirming or attacking the results, with some questioning the validity of the ethnic identity research.

In response to the outcry over the results from elder Singaporeans, Parliamentary Secretary Chan Soo Sen said there was no need to be alarmed by the desire of young Chinese Singaporeans to be foreigners.

---

are some major differences between Bloomfield's initial description and the focus of the work Skutnabb-Kangas. Whilst both were concerned with minority groups within a larger dominant society, the latter was concerned with children, as has been the cases in most studies (Cummins, 1979; Skutnabb-Kangas, 1981). As pointed out by Baetens Beardsmore, 1986; Romaine, 1989; Edwards, 1994, the notion of semilingualism has been extensively politicised because of the conflict of interests between minority rights and educational policy when immigrant minority children are concerned. At the same time, there have been also less politicised and hence less noted cases concerned with adults who constituted minority groups (Dorian, 1982; Tsou, 1981).

There is a fundamental difference between the past studies and the ones here, which are concerned with the dominant society's majority population, who might have, according to some exonomic criteria, less than native like ability in the language concerned, with detrimental cognitive and cultural consequences.

'These young people are still searching for their own identities,' Mr. Chan said. Chinese should treat the response as a very frank reply from 'a group of people who may be a little naive, but do not mean any harm'.

'Let the young people say their dreams out loud,' said Mr. Chan, recalling his own experience as a student abroad with friends who felt the environment overseas was more liberal and less stressful.

In a letter to the Straits Times, Professor Chang said it was too early to judge his work since the survey was part of a larger project.

Political and ethical values, achievement, life-orientation, philosophy and identity were among the factors under study, as well as national, ethnic, work, family and personal inclinations.

Professor Chang, initially from China but now a Singapore citizen, said he planned to compare the outcome against values in countries such as China and the United States with the aim of identifying those, both Western and Asian, which were most effective.

While the answers to the ethnic identity question could not capture all the different dimensions posed by the survey, Professor Chang said they would be used as an indicator to measure a person's appreciation of and confidence and pride in his or her ethnic group.

The survey of 800 secondary and tertiary-level students found young Chinese Singaporeans who have weak ethnic identify tend to be more educated and to speak English at home.

(Deutche Presse-Agentur in Singapore)

Whilst these findings were controversial, it is interesting that weak ethnicity is correlated with the better educated, English-dominant Chinese. This supports the common view that when the language divide is crossed, cultural lines may not be sacrosanct. This is not surprising for Singapore. When the younger generation gives up the native dialects of their fore-bearers for whatever reason, they also lose contact with, if not become alienated from, the older generations, who often provide and reinforce a traditional culture base via their native dialects. Such a sociolinguistic gap tallies well with the generation gap often mentioned in Singapore. If the popular sentiments are correct, as borne out to some extent by the shifts towards English noted in the Census data, Singapore could ultimately move towards a predominantly monolingual

English society. This is because when the linguistic roots of the home environment have been sufficiently weakened, the choice between Mandarin or English, as *home language* replacement, is no longer that crucial because the determining factors tend to be extrinsic to the family.

However, the move towards English may not be acceptable in the long run for two major considerations: (1) ethnically Singapore is not Caucasian, but it is predominantly Chinese and Asian, and it is situated in Asia. Moreover and more importantly, (2) its economic future well being must involve mediation between China and Southeast Asia, if not the world at large, where its Chinese roots and cultural advantage could be fully exploited, as was the case in a bygone era. Thus a rapid shift towards a pre-dominantly English based society could be undesirable to Singapore, and remedies should be taken, even as there are discussions on the possibility of retaining or cultivating Asian/Chinese values and culture via English.

It would seem from the Singapore case that rapid and frequent language shifts do not lead readily to additive bilingualism deemed desirable by society and the likely outcomes of such cases must be carefully assessed before vigorous attempts at social engineering.

Hong Kong

Like Singapore, Hong Kong began to emerge as a major city after the Second World War, especially in conjunction with the founding of the People's Republic of China in 1949 which was followed by the Korean War, as well as several subsequent colossal campaigns in China culminating in the Cultural Revolution. The population increased more than eight times within half a century, from 0.44 million in 1911 to 3.65 million in 1966, with the greatest growth in the two decades since the end of World War II. The British administration brought significant numbers of Europeans and South Asians, but the majority were drawn from the southern regions of China, covering seven dialect groups. Like Singapore, early useful data on language use is rare; some interesting data are provided in the Census report of 1911, when there were also numerous refugees from Qing Dynasty China which gave way to the founding of the first Republic. Thereafter, other census surveys have provided relevant data, notably 1961 to 1971. Table 7 below provides data on the distribution of the speakers of different dialects.

The situation on the use of Cantonese shows moderate growth from 79% speaking Cantonese as the usual *home language* in 1961 to 88.7% in 1996, the year prior to the reversion of sovereignty over Hong Kong from Britain to China. This situation allows for useful comparison with the rare but useful data provided in the 1911 Census, which reported 81% of the population speaking Cantonese (and 15.1% Hakka). However it is quite likely that in the subsequent years leading to the population explosion in the 50's and 60's, the influx of non-Cantonese speakers outnumbered local residents and that in the 1950's the percentage of Cantonese speakers was probably much lower than 79%.[11]

To better understand the dynamics of language shift in Hong Kong, it will be necessary to examine details from quite extensive data available for 1966 and 1971.

Table 7 **Percentage Distribution of Population by 'Usual Language Spoken' in Hong Kong (adapted from So, 1998 and Tsou, 1997)**

Language	1961	1966	1971	1991	1996
Cantonese	79.0	81.4	88.1	88.7	88.7
Fukien	6.3	6.5	@[12]	1.9	1.9
Hakka	4.9	3.3	2.7	1.6	1.2
Szeyap	4.4	3.1	1.2	0.4	0.3
Chiu Chow	---	---	@[11]	1.4	1.1
Putonghua	1.0	---	@[11]	1.1	1.1
Shanghainese	2.6	---	@[11]	0.7	0.5
English	1.2	0.8	1.0	2.2	3.1
Others	0.6	3.1	@[11]	2.0	0.1
Total (%)	100.00	100.00	---	100.00	100.00

---

[11]   see Tsou (to appear).

[12]   There is considerable overlap between Fukien, Hoklo, and Chiuchow because at various times they were seen to belong to a single linguistic group in census surveys. Until there are clearer figures on these groups some of the other projections will be affected and so should be held in abeyance.

Table 8 **Percentage Distribution of Sub-Speech Communities in Hong Kong Population, by Home Language and Ethnicity, 1966. (Tsou, 1993: Language Shift and Consolidation of Ethnicity 1966)**

	English	Cantonese	Hakka	Hoklo	Szeyap	AOCD	AOL
Hong Kong	0.98	81.65	14.80	2.17	0.04	0.6	0.12
Canton, Macau and vicinity	0.01	94.42	3.79	1.44	0.17	0.11	---
Szeyap	0.01	83.78	0.04	0.08	15.48	0.09	0.06
Chiu Chow	---	43.38	1.97	54.57	0.03	0.03	0.03
Hakka	---	[55][13]	[43][12]	---	---	---	---
Elsewhere in K & K	0.05	94.28	4.35	0.46	0.14	0.46	0.23
Elsewhere in China	0.25	48.92	0.11	16.22	---	34.32	---
All Other Places	56.39	15.86	1.98	1.76	---	2.86	21.15
Unknown	8.80	91.20	---	---	---	---	---
Total	0.80	81.43	3.33	8.19	3.08	2.79	0.31

*AOCD: Any other Chinese dialect   AOL: Any other language

Table 9 **Percentage Distribution of Sub-Speech Communities in Hong Kong Population, by Home Language and Ethnicity, 1971. (Tsou, 1993): Language Shift and Consolidation of Ethnicity 1971**

	English	Cantonese	Hakka	Hoklo	Szeyap	AOCD	AOL
Hong Kong	0.2	85.5	12.8	@[11]	0.1	0.3	---
Canton, Macau and vicinity	0.1	95.7	3.0	@[11]	0.1	0.4	---
Szeyap	---	92.3	0.3	@[11]	6.2	0.6	---
Hakka	---	---	38[12]	---	---	---	---
Chiu Chow	0.2	67.1	1.3	48[12]	0.3	3.5	---
Elsewhere in China	58.9	78.4	2.0	10[12]	0.2	11.7	0.1
All Other Places	1.0	15.8	0.5	---	0.1	0.9	23.2
Total	---	88.1	2.7	---	1.2	2.3	---

*AOCD: Any other Chinese dialect   AOL: Any other language

---

[13]   see Tsou, 1997; Tsou & You, 2001.

From Tables 8 and 9, several groups could be seen to undergo varying degrees of language shift to Cantonese: Szeyup, Chiuchow (as with Teochew in Singapore), Hakka, Mandarin and Wu dialect speakers. It is interesting to note that whereas the Chinese in Singapore quite readily became bilingual or multilingual by expanding their linguistic repertoire through the adoption of another dialect or language, the Chinese in Hong Kong underwent wholesale language shift and language loss in favour of Cantonese.

There is reason to believe that the 9.1% increase between 1961 and 1996 has obscured the much more significant sociolinguistic developments than what it appears to represent.[14]

During the initial period from 1961 to 1981, the population of Hong Kong dramatically grew from 3.13 million to 4.99 million, a 59.3% increase represented by 1.86 million people. The period of greatest growth can be further narrowed down to 1961-1971 when the population grew by 55.96%, or 835,430 individuals yielding a very robust average of 2% more per year. This was the period when the Cultural Revolution and all its excesses were in full swing in China and numerous refugees, especially those located in the neighbouring Pearl River Delta, were added to the Hong Kong population when informal immigration control was quite free. This was the period when the Cultural Revolution spilled into Hong Kong with communal riots in 1967 and when China placed a 'Bamboo Curtain' between herself and the rest of the world. Hong Kong had to secure her own economic future and reassess her identity. Given Britain's 'laissez faire' policy or policy of 'no policy', it is not surprising that the status of spoken Cantonese was consolidated. In contrast

---

[14]   In 1966, Language loyalty among the four major sub-groups in the population mentioned above varied from 15.48% for Szeyap to 54.57% for Chiu Chow. These percentages were further decreased for all groups in 1971. It would be reasonable to extrapolate and suggest that there was higher Language Loyalty among these groups prior to 1966, and progressively also in 1961. Thus, the proportion of the population speaking Cantonese as the *home language* should have been lower than the 79% for the 1950's. It would not be surprising that the figures could have been much lower, perhaps between 70% to 75%, and that hence the massive and decisive language shift to Cantonese might have been easily 20% to 30%.

to elsewhere, where Mandarin was replacing dialects in increasing official domains such as *education, courts, government agencies* and *mass media* (e.g., Taiwan and Mainland China), Cantonese continued to develop in all official domains (Zou & You, 2001). Thus there was massive language shift towards Cantonese by the residents within the population who were not of basic Cantonese stock, as Cantonese became symbolic of a life and society which was distinct from those then prevalent in Mainland China *and* as the new arrivals were quick to cast off their emotional and cultural baggage. This could account for the ascendancy of spoken Cantonese for the majority of non-Cantonese speakers and for their descendants in Hong Kong, who at their peak represented more than half the population. Thus while only 88.1% of the population since the 1970's have reported their *home language* as Cantonese, 95% or more of the population could understand or use Cantonese, a figure comparable to Hokkien at its peak in Singapore.

Two developments in the 1980's served catalytic functions for new directions in sociolinguistic development: (1) China became more open after the conclusion of the Cultural Revolution and vast economic opportunities have increasingly opened up there since the late 1970's. (2) Hong Kong's return to China was not raised openly and discussed in earnest until the early 1980's, and 1997 was the date of the return set by the Sino-British Joint Declaration of 1984. In both cases a reassessment of Hong Kong's economic and cultural priorities was called for, and the role and function of Putonghua (Mandarin) would be important in such a review. The adoption of the 'One Country Two Systems' approach provided a counterbalance between the urgency of the reassessment and the likely reality to emerge with respect to the language scene after 1997. In the run-up to 1997 there were already relevant discussions as sentiments began to surface between the majority who preferred the initial *status quo*, and those inclined towards integration sentiments. But it was only after the departure of the British Administration that some of the critical issues came out in the open. What is clear is that the consolidation of Cantonese had peaked by the 1980's, thus ending the first stage of critical sociolinguistic realignment in Hong Kong. The second stage has begun but the outcome is far less conclusive than in Singapore, though indicative trends are discernable.

To understand this, let us look at some of the most recent practical issues which have focused on the English competence of the workforce and its perceived decline, as well as the inability of the population to effectively use written Chinese based on Modern Standard Chinese (MSC).[15] All these have given rise to heated debates and reflect new sociolinguistic realignment in the offing. These issues came to a head in the world of finance and service industries. However, the concerns were usually distinctly compartmentalised: the concerns about English are often taken to be distinct from concerns about Chinese, and the two concerns are seldom discussed in the same common forum. There have been rarely any holistic considerations. As will be seen later, such a situation in itself constitutes a major cause of the language problem in Hong Kong, and the severity of the situation is rarely recognised, as may be expected under the circumstances.

The following newspaper cuttings will serve to illustrate some of the basic concerns:

(7) British   Chamber   of   Commerce: To   Maintain Advantage – Must emphasise English
The new Chairman of the British Chamber of Commerce, Mr Mervyn Davis, considers that Hong Kong, being an important international city, must work hard to retain English as a major

---

[15]   Whilst on the one hand there has been little defense offered on the decline of ability to use written Chinese, on the other hand there has been often a consistent effort at defense on behalf of English mounted by some stake holders and in some quarters that the case of declining English standard was understandable. Thus when interviewed by the popular Chinese weekly *Asiaweek* on whether the English standard of Hong Kong students might have declined, the Secretary for Education, Fanny Law, pointed out: "It is hard to compare the past and present Hong Kong students, because in the past only 1% to 5% of the appropriate age cohort attended university, whereas it is now 18%".
"Hong Kong has been transformed from an industrial society. Its need for students good in English has greatly increased and the education system has not been able to cope. I feel that the English standard of the new university students is not inferior to that of the "old elites". SCOLAR (The Standing Committee on Language and Research) will review this question and make suggestions" (*Asiaweek*, 6 Feb 2002)

language. It must also set very high standards for English. Short term political or economic differences are not of utmost concern to the Chamber.   (*Ming Pao*, 8 Aug 2000)

(8) Hong Kong English Weak – Competitiveness Reduced

The Hong Kong Branch of the Australian Association of Accountants released yesterday their 2001 Survey on Hong Kong Economy. It pointed out that most companies in Hong Kong did not plan to expand in the next 5 years. At the same time, they face certain issues: The most important is the quality of the employees, especially the lower than expected level of English, higher cost of transportation and competition from Mainland companies.

Those interviewed indicated that if Hong Kong could not improve its English and Putonghua standards, reduce transportation costs, as well as re-adjust its orientation as China enters WTO, its status as an international city would be weakened.

(*Ming Pao*, 21 Nov 2000)

(9) Canada Says: Hong Kong Police Speaks Little English

The new edition of the Hong Kong Tourism Report published by the Foreign Affairs Department of the Canadian Federal Government pointed out 'the Hong Kong police in general speak very little English or no English'.

(*Ming Pao*, 25 Jul 2000)

It is interesting to note how sometimes concern regarding inadequate English standards in Hong Kong might be muted but no less eloquently expressed by the very absence of expressed concerns:

(10) Participants dazzle with English-speaking skills – Shanghai student grabs first prize

Chen Heng, a student at the Shanghai International Studies University, took first place at the fifth annual 21st Century Cup National English Speaking Competition, which was held on Friday in Guangzhou.

He will represent China in an international speaking competition to be held in London in June.

'Ke Fai, a student at Sichuan University, came in second followed by Bao Ling here representing Macau,' Betty Lam Mong-chi an English major at the University of Macau, told *Campus Post*.

'The contestants were terrific English speakers. They were very enthusiastic in the competition,' Ms Lam said.

Participants had five minutes in which to define success. They were then given three minutes to discuss a topic such as whether students studying abroad should return home after finishing their studies or if Chinese characters should be replaced by pinyin. This was followed by *Post* after competition had ended.

'The students did very, very well,' Kim Lee, one of the judges, concurred.

A former English teacher, Ms Lee, who works in Guangzhou for Stone Cliz International, said she was impressed with the ability of the students to perform so well under pressure – especially in a foreign language. 'I've judged at competitions in the United States and anyone on that stage could compete on an international level with no difficulty' Ms Lee said, 'They all put convincingly to an international audience,' she added. The competition's first winner, Liu Xin of Nanjing University, went on to become an anchorwoman at China Central TV. She was also one of the masters of ceremony at last week's event.

Other winners are still in university. Li Shu, who won in 1997, is now doing postgraduate studies at Northwestern University in the United States. Liang Limin, 1998's winner, is doing postgraduate studies at Beijing Foreign Studies University.

(*South China Morning Post*, Michael Taylor in Guangzhou)

The above reports show a wide range of concerns, particularly relating to the business sector and tourism sector, both major employers in Hong Kong. But the seriousness of declining English standards can be further gauged by reports on threats relating to the miscarriage of justice and the need to consider lowering the entrance requirements for Law school, in a system which is largely based on the Common Law system operating in Hong Kong through the medium of English for one and a half centuries before 1997:

(11) HKU Law Head: Relax Admission, Lower Standard

The English Standard of Hong Kong lawyers has drawn criticism recently. Last year there was a case of industrial compensation. Because of the inadequate English standard of the lawyers, multiple versions of events appeared, causing the validity of evidence to be questioned, thereby almost causing the injured party to receive no compensation.[16]

---

[16]   The relevant judgment from the High Court of Hong Kong on June 3, 1999 provides an example of the seriousness of the problem at hand:

The Head of the Department of Law at Hong Kong University, Johannes Chan, indicated that in the late 1990's, the June 4th event and emigration waves out of 1997 had influenced the Government, which became concerned with the brain drain and the need to train replacements. One consequence was to lower entrance requirements, thus giving rise to the declining standard of English among lawyers today.

(*Ming Pao*, 8 Sept 2000)

There are many other non-social but plausible reasons for this declining standard of English (and Chinese) and some hints on the causes may be drawn from the mix code of Chinese in English commonly used in Hong Kong:

(12) Ability Below Standard – Chinese-English Mix Code

Hong Kong people's English have been criticised, as has been their Chinese, but Hong Kong people likes to mix Chinese and English in their 'Chinglish' (English with Chinese grammar). This is even true of the Chief Executive, Mr. Tung Chi Hua – Legislative Councillor Emily Lau finds this most regrettable. She feels that Hong Kong people mix Chinese and English mainly because of their weak language skills. 'Because their ability in Chinese is weak, they cannot produce a sentence which is purely Chinese. Of course neither is their English ability good, their English grammar is not correct'. Moreover, she feels Hong Kong people are lazy because they simply mix

---

"The facts stated in the Particulars of Claim in the Employees' Compensation claim before the District Court and the witness statement for this action are the work of the Plaintiff's solicitors. They appear to be inaccurate partly, as I have explained, due to language problems. There is an additional language problem in that the solicitors cannot even write a complete grammatical sentence in the Particulars of Claim. Notice too the use of the word plank instead of board...

Thus I have every reason to believe that solicitors [*10] for the Plaintiff are unable to translate the Plaintiff's account of the accident accurately into English... I have mentioned during the trial I do not like to criticise solicitors or indeed any lawyer. I do not think solicitors for the Plaintiff tried to mislead the court [*11] or to dishonestly inflate the claim; but, I regret to say, solicitors for the Plaintiff put in shoddy work. If the Plaintiff loses this common law claim for doubts on his credibility generated by solicitors who do not take care to represent his case accurately, he might well have a claim against his solicitors. It is very important to ascertain and put down one's client's case fully and correctly."

the two languages up when they communicate without any determination to correct the bad habits.

(*Ming Pao*, 28 Oct 2000)

Aside from language planning policy, or the lack of it, two major common causes on the declining standard of English have been identified: (1) Problematic Medium of Instruction (MoI) and (2) inability of teachers to teach in English.[17] When Hong Kong first became a British Crown Colony, there was the gradual introduction of English medium schools primarily to produce a work force to serve in the Civil Service where English was the only official language for much of its colonial period. In time, they began to compete with the Chinese Medium schools which taught English in most cases as a subject. By the 1950's, one hundred years after the founding of the Colony, the number of English medium Anglo-Chinese Schools was almost on par with Chinese medium schools. However, by the late 1980's, Anglo-Chinese schools out-numbered Chinese medium schools by six times, and the combined Anglo-Chinese school population outnumbered the Chinese medium school population by more than 10 times. It became clear that Chinese medium schools were moribund. This critical trend of development in Hong Kong education can be seen in Table 10.

Table 10 **Hong Kong Enrolments in Anglo-Chinese Schools and Chinese Medium School**

Year	ACSS		CMS		Total School	Total Student	% (CMS)
	School	Student	School	Student			
1958	74	25,863	89	21,210	163	47,073	45
1963	147	81,163	106	41,079	253	122,242	34
1968	223	149,921	123	50,596	346	200,517	25
1973	239	223,254	96	57,321	335	280,575	20
1978	330	375,470	104	58,548	434	434,018	14
1983	351	380,203	68	38,671	419	418,874	9
1988	343	365,330	57	32,973	400	398,303	8

ACSS = Anglo-Chinese Schools   CMS = Chinese Medium Schools
Source: Hong Kong Government, Hong Kong Annual Review, Chapters on Education, various issues (adapted from So, 1998).

---

[17]   There is a full range of literature on the historical background. See, for example, Asker, 1998; Lord & Cheng, 1987; Luke, 1994; So, 1998.

In actual fact many of the Anglo-Chinese schools were not fully English Medium schools. Many only nominally used English as MoI. The classroom situation would in the majority of cases involve English textbooks, but the teaching would be conducted in a combination of English and Cantonese, or mostly Cantonese, and only a small minority of prestigious schools would be able to maintain an intensive or exclusive usage of English.

The mixed code approach to a large extent mirrors the elite Cantonese society in Hong Kong (Tsou, 1986), but has been increasingly seen to be a major contributing factor to the students' inability to adequately manipulate either English or Chinese. This approach was not sanctioned but developed gradually and naturally in ways not dissimilar from comparable situations in Singapore, Malaysia or the Philippines. In part, the population explosion since the 1960's and the natural growth in importance of the English language led to a phenomenal growth in the education sector. This meant a concomitant increase in demand for teachers to provide instruction in English.

One solution was simply to make do with existing teachers, who might not be fully qualified to provide instruction in English (but perhaps qualified in other subjects, such as mathematics or science) to teach other subjects in English as well as to teach English when needed. The rationale was that, after all, the teachers, who were graduates from local universities, should be able to teach *in English* as well as *English*, because they came from the elite English medium universities.[18] Thus a vicious cycle began with teachers weak in English producing students with weaker competence in English, so that English competence progressively dropped for each subsequent generation. It is understandable that the Government had to engineer changes even in the run-up to 1997.

The Government in the 1990's changed its previous policy on 'Bilingual education' to one of mother tongue education for the majority of the students. This was a concerted effort to stamp out the use of mixed code in teaching, and to develop wholesome ability in both Chinese and English. There were three major factors which contributed to this decision. (1) an overwhelming

---

[18]   See Lord & Tsou, 1986; Lord & Cheng, 1987, also footnote 16.

majority of research findings supporting the use of mother tongue as MoI, (2) there is much consensus in Hong Kong that it needs people who are proficient in English, and so the most effective way must be found and (3) research findings showing mixed code being ineffective for teaching.

Following assessment, the implementation of this policy resulted in only 100 schools (with slight revisions subsequently) which could use English as the MoI, in a continuation of previous policy, but the remaining 300 and more secondary schools had to use Cantonese as the MoI, as has been the case for primary school. Moreover, teachers must meet benchmark requirements before they could be considered qualified English teachers, or they have to undergo Benchmark Tests. The new and inevitable negative (re-) labelling for many schools and teachers was de-moralising and drew considerable sympathetic concern as well as claims and counter claims.

(13) Civil Servants First Time Support Anti-Benchmark Test March – 2,500 Teachers On Streets Again
2,500 people marched in the rain yesterday to ask the Government to scrap the Language Bench Mark Test and to openly debate with the Chief Executive, Tung Chi Hua on the Test. Many Civil Service organisations also sent representatives for the first time. The Secretary for Education, Fanny Law, criticises the teachers for politicising educational matters, and finds it regrettable.   (*Ming Pao*, 22 Oct 2000)

The concerns and actions were intensified when the Education Department took certain actions and a whole series of claims and counter claims followed as events unfolded:

(14) Education Department Should Clarify
'Chinese-English Mix Code Teaching' Soonest Possible
The Education Department quietly selected 10 Chinese middle schools to pilot-test the mixed use of Chinese and English in classes. This has raised another wave of concern in educational circles with many opposing it. Some organisations even pointed to the Government reversing it position on mother tongue education. We have consistently supported mother tongue education, but we have an open mind on the Education Department experiment with mixing Chinese-English as a medium of education. However, we feel it inappropriate for the Education Department to take such a 'clandestine' approach to this kind of experimentation and in terms of the double

standards for Chinese Medium Schools and English Medium Schools. This raises doubts on whether the Government will insist on mother tongue education. Hence we believe the Education Department should as soon as possible come clean on this to the teachers, parents and society.

(*Ming Pao*, 23 Nov 2000 *Editorial*)

(15) Teacher Alliance Salvo on Chinese English Mix Code Introduction as Regression

The Hong Kong Alliance of Educational workers criticises the Government for going back on its language education policy in the case of allowing 10 Chinese medium middle schools to choose either Chinese-English mix code or all English as media of instruction. They say it is an admission of the failure of the mother tongue education policy in disguise. They also question the Education Department in the selection of the experimental schools. The Alliance is worried that there would be three classes of middle schools, the top class could be English medium schools. Chinese-English mixed medium school would be second class, and purely Chinese medium schools would be third class.

The vice president of the Alliance, K. Y. Wong, says: when the Education Department publicises the benefits of mother tongue education on the one hand, but allows Chinese medium middle schools to learn through English junior middle school on the other, it is whittling away mother tongue education and self-contradictory.

(*Ming Pao*, 23 Nov 2000)

(16) Education Department Denies Policy Change On Mother Tongue Education

The Education Department has been criticised for involving more than 10 middle schools to participate in bilingual education experiment as reversing its policy on mother tongue Education. The Education Department yesterday for the first time publicly offered an explanation and defended its policy on mother tongue education. Assistant Director, K. S. Lee, re-emphasised that there was no intention to change the policy of mother tongue Education. He said: 'A single research effort is not enough to provide enough data to change the policy (of Mother Tongue Education)… or shake confidence in Mother Tongue Education. But, this should not mean that we don't do research'.

(*Ming Pao*, 25 Nov 2000)

(17) English and Mother Tongue Education – The Struggle Continues

From a Middle School Teacher:

The Government invited about 10 Chinese middle schools to be 'English Teaching Medium Experimental Schools'. Under this scheme, junior middle school classes would use English as medium of instruction or both Chinese and English as mixed medium of instruction for either some classes or some subjects, in an effort to investigate the impact of bilingual education. In turning back to pursue such research, the Education Department has not operated in a logical manner, because it has already conducted many similar research in the past. The results from these researches have in fact provided an important basis for the Education Department setting down the current policy on mother tongue education.

(Lau Sau Yin, *Ming Pao*, 12 Dec 2000 Forum)

From the foregoing, it should be clear that the importance of English remains paramount for Hong Kong in economic terms, even though its relevance to power and elite has waned. Any discussion on the extent of the adequacy of the current English standard in Hong Kong often introduces emotionally charged debates. But English standards have clearly fallen in the perception of the majority consumers of language or at least do not meet their expectations. This is lamentable because of the enormous efforts and resources which have been earmarked to deal with these problems in recent decades.

The situation with MSC competence is comparable. There are two aspects to it. They relate to: (1) the growing importance of written Chinese based on MSC or Putonghua in an increasing range of domains, and (2) the increasing economic and professional opportunities associated with it in Mainland China. These two concerns have had wide ramifications in Hong Kong, just as national leaders from China who have replaced those from Britain in media coverage use exclusively Putonghua on public occasions and as Putonghua broadcasts have increased. Hong Kong leaders are also expected to be fluent Putonghua speakers, as increasingly exemplified by the new leadership in Hong Kong.[19]

---

[19] At the inauguration ceremony for the Hong Kong Special Administrative Region on 1 Jul 1997, all principal officials of the Government swore an oath of office. Unless they were ethnically non-Chinese, their oath of

These new sociolinguistic requirements have substantial impact in wide ranging areas, especially in education. There are two extremes in opinion on what mother tongue means for Hong Kong education. While the majority of local educationists and other concerned individuals recognise Cantonese as a mother tongue, there are others who see Putonghua as the mother tongue and Cantonese only as the Mother Dialect. The fallacious argument has also been advanced, as has been the case for English before, that early exposure to Putonghua, by for example, using it as MoI would help to foster ability in it. The significance of the problem has attracted considerable attention across the community. Let us look at some of the views expressed in the media.

(18) Michael Tien Advocates Putonghua as Medium of Instruction:

Whilst the *Standing Committee on Language and Research* remains divided on the matter, its Chairman, Michael Tien, broke new grounds by suggesting in his personal capacity that Putonghua should replace Cantonese and be used along with English as the Medium of Instruction for Secondary Schools in the long run. This was to raise the bilingual ability of students and to be in line with economic developments worldwide: 'We shall not speak of English Medium School or Chinese Medium Secondary School in future, but rather English Media (Secondary) School or Putonghua Media (Secondary) School'.

(Ming Pao, 18 Nov 2001)

This new line of thinking is very contentious, and there is no shortage of opinions, including some who query whether such a suggestion is against the spirit of mother tongue education. In the same newspaper report, the Secretary for Education, Fanny Law, when interviewed, indicated this to be an 'extremely long term view', and that 'before implementation, it must await a certain threshold standard to be reached by teachers and students alike, and even by the society as a whole'. But she emphasised that in the short term the Government will continue to support mother

---

office had to be in Putonghua, even though the individuals might not have been competent or comfortable with it. Thus, a significant number of them, including the Chief Justice, Andrew Li, valiantly took the oath in Putonghua, and have taken to being tutored in Putonghua.

tongue (i.e., Cantonese) education to reduce language obstacles in the learning process, and to improve teaching strategies for raising the language standard of students. This was echoed by others, including the Deputy Director of Education, Mr. K. T. Tong, who was reported on the same occasion to have reservations on the suggestion, because 'it could lead to a situation of neither good Chinese nor good English, and would (adversely) affect the students' acquisition of knowledge'.

Tien's controversial view drew considerable public interest and reactions, ranging from editorials (suggesting varying degrees of caution) to opposing professional stands. That such a personal view as Tien's was released in public, given his special position, is seen as a test balloon on public opinion. But the suggestion is not surprising and its timing quite interesting, given views such as the following expressed quite a few month earlier:

> **(19) Specialist Teacher from Mainland on Inspection Tour: Hong Kong Student Language standard Lower than Mainland**
>
> Two specialist and senior teachers, after spending half a year observing classes... (one) points out that the local media overflows with dialect, thereby directly influencing the communication model of the young people.
>
> He believes Hong Kong is well equipped to promote teaching through Putonghua in order to raise the students' ability with respect to pronunciation, vocabulary and grammar. 'Canton has also gone through a long period of the transition in going from teaching through Cantonese to teaching through Putonghua... (I) believe Hong Kong could do it in 10 years.'
>
> (*Ming Pao*, 20 Apr 2001)

This appeal to exocentric references and models is common, for there are also others who think it expedient and readily justified to use Putonghua as MoI. For example, the Director of the Putonghua education Research and Development Centre at the Chinese University of Hong Kong, Wai-kit Ho, wrote to a newspaper forum to allay concerns in the Legislation Council of Hong Kong that a shift towards using Putonghua as the MoI would have deleterious effects:

(20) Mother Tongue Rights – A Beautiful Misunderstanding
California implemented bilingual education through legislation in 1968 to allow new immigrant children to learn via English and their mother tongue. The results showed that not only resources were wasted but also the children involved drifted away from the mainstream English medium education. They found it difficult to be integrated into the (mainstream) society and to improve their economic well being. This led to the recension of the legislation. When we look at the developed countries, we see them using the national common language as MoI. We could today grant our students greater rights to learn through Cantonese, so that they would temporarily find relief. But in future they will have to spend even more efforts to solve their language problems. Can we afford the time and resources?   Must we be responsible for finding extra room for our next generation to develop?

(Ming Pao, 24 Jan 2002)

There are many controversial issues, and, unless considerable rigour is exercised, piecemeal supporting evidence can be usually found. California has gone through cyclical alternation between support for main stream education and bilingual education, and Hong Kong has only recently recognised that the early introduction of a non-mother tongue target language, such as English, as MoI, does not guarantee success but could in fact lead to learning difficulties. Given the Government's plan to review mother tongue education in 2003, it is clear that the debates will continue and there are hints on how the agenda may be shaping up.

It can be seen also that the outcome of the second stage sociolinguistic realignment in Hong Kong is still less clear than Singapore. However, some indicative trends are apparent: (a) the drive to uplift ability in Putonghua and MSC may be fairly encouraging, but perhaps not fast enough for some segments of society; (b) status and function of Cantonese are being reduced; and (c) the drive to uplift English has not been successful.

Hong Kong seems to be developing sociolinguistically away from an international and cosmopolitan urban centre, and there is pressure for it to quickly develop into another urban centre in China. There are wide ranging and serious consequences. The primary cause for this state of affairs is the absence of holistic concerns and consistency in policy, as indicated by one view expressed by an academic from the Department of Public Administration and Government of a local university in Hong Kong.

(21) Education Change Lacks Global Vision
Even though the Education reforms of the Education commission embody many long-term ideals, they unfortunately raise many questions when it comes to substantive content. One major issue which has not been noticed much is that the reforms do not contain a global vision for the 21st Century. Under these conditions, if the reforms are forcefully carried out, Hong Kong's long range competitive edge will be severely hampered.

                                        (*Ming Pao*, 21 Jul 2000 Forum)

Concluding Remarks

The comparison of the situations in Singapore and Hong Kong has brought forward some key issues in sociolinguistic change, and also has provided an object lesson in language planning. Both communities have been involved with two drastic language shifts:

Stage (1): Within a short period of basically two to three decades towards the mid-20th century, a dominant local LOW language managed to gain ascendancy. In the case of Singapore, it is HOKKIEN, and in the case of Hong Kong, it is CANTONESE. This phase of Language shift was completed in both communities by the 1980's.

Stage (2): Further sociolinguistic realignment has been in the offing because for a variety of reasons neither situation has been found to be acceptable for a variety of reasons. In the case of Singapore, active Government policy has promoted English and Mandarin as effectively the High and low languages respectively at the expenses of dialects in rigorous attempts at sociolinguistic engineering. One clear result from such efforts is a further shift from Hokkien to the exonormic Mandarin, but in actual fact the ultimate end result could well be a shift to English. In the case of Hong Kong, the importance of Mandarin or Putonghua-based Modern Standard Chinese (MSC) has been increasingly recognised and Putonghua is rapidly gaining ground. In spite of the continuing economic importance of English, and the enormous resources and efforts committed by the Government, the *lassez faire* policy of Hong Kong has, by comparison with Singapore, meant English ability could well be on the way down, as Hong Kong appears to move towards becoming just another city in China. For this reason, the debate is still raging as to whether Putonghua, which has already replaced English in some significant domains, would displace Cantonese in increasing *High Language* domains to the point where Cantonese would gradually move to function as one of the local dialects in a typical coastal city of China.

Neither outcome in Singapore or Hong Kong is seen to be desirable by different groups and stake holders. The power elite in Singapore is relatively satisfied with the spread and, possible uplifting of English ability there, but is concerned with the possible emergence of semilinguals and cultural eunuchs as their Chinese linguistic and cultural roots become increasingly and significantly weakened. They are not certain how the tide may be reversed. However, given her geographical location, historical background, and economic priorities, Singapore must target herself to be a wholesome bilingual community.

On the other hand, the power elite in Hong Kong is concerned with increasing inadequacy in both English and Chinese standards to meet on-going and new societal requirements respectively, and appears to be still frantically groping for direction. There is general agreement that Hong Kong cannot afford, at least economically, to be just another coastal Chinese city, against which the 'One Country Two Systems' approach and the publicly advocated 'Hong Kong remaining unchanged (i.e., not-integrated into China) for 50 years' policy are meant to guarantee. Many efforts have been put into preventing the economic contingency, but, by comparison, there is relatively little concern about the linguistic and cultural correlates of a policy to prevent the economic contingency. Given that English standard has been seriously compromised by most practical accounts, what if the school leavers someday also cannot compete with their Mainland cousins in their ability to use Chinese? What really could and must be the role and function of Cantonese, the mother tongue, in the larger schemes is apparently lost.

There is now no dearth of concerned individuals who may be enthusiastic but much less informed, who are focused on English and Chinese as targets but who care little about how to help Hong Kong students, whose home language and the language of socialisation is Cantonese, to make the transition Cantonese to either target language.

Singapore's *proactive* and *holistic* approach to language planning has been effective under a forceful and visionary leadership. It has produced both positive and negative results. Hong Kong's primarily *reactive* and *piecemeal* approach to language planning has introduced much more negative results than positive ones. While no ideal combination of outcomes can be recognised, an objective comparison between Singapore and Hong Kong has been useful. The outcome thus far appears to favour Singapore, whose population may be better rooted at least in one language, even though it may be non-indigenous and exocentric.

A cosmopolitan and urbane community typically strives for additive bilingualism in its search for new identity in the post colonial setting, but resurgent and substitutive exocentricism becoming a key issue is not common in such a setting, as typified by Singapore and Hong Kong. However, in both unusual cases, the sociolinguists and policy makers alike could note that there are prerequisite and global factors which one could ill afford to overlook, lest there be contrary results of subtractive bilingualism.

10 Whither Bilingual Education in Hong Kong: Stakeholders' Views (1974-1999) and Their Implications on the Way Forward

Daniel W. C. So
The Hong Kong Polytechnic University

Introduction

Neither the present government of the Hong Kong Special Administrative Region (HKSAR) nor the past British regime of Hong Kong attached the label 'bilingual' to the system of education in Hong Kong. However, in many studies about this system (e.g., Lord & Tsou, 1979; Ripple et al., 1984; Bickley, 1988), the label 'bilingual education' has often been used to characterise it as such where one finds (1) the presence of two categories of schools at the secondary level formally differentiated on the basis of their medium of instruction (MoI) (Chinese *vs* English), and (2) the manifest objective of the government both before and after 1997 to develop among school graduates proficiency of various levels in both Chinese and English (e.g., Education & Manpower Branch, 1993: 16; Education Commission, 1999: §3.4).

However, at the turn of the millennium, the future of this bilingual system of education so defined has become uncertain. First and foremost, the use of the English language as a MoI in schools has been deemed undesirable by the government, or to be more specific, by the Department of Education. In September 1997 the Department issued the policy document *Medium of Instruction Guidance for Secondary Schools* wherein it stipulates that (1) Mother tongue teaching has positive effects on students' learning; (2) Most students prefer learning in the mother tongue; (3) Students learning in the mother tongue generally perform better than their counterparts using English as MoI; and (4) students of traditional Chinese-medium (CM) schools consistently achieve a higher pass percentage than the territory-wide average in both Chinese Language and English Language in the Hong Kong Certificate of Education Examination. Accordingly secondary schools are encouraged to use Chinese as MoI. On the other hand, the use of mixed code, i.e., a mixture of Chinese and English in teaching and learning, is discouraged. Henceforth, subsidised and government secondary schools which wish to practise English-medium (EM) instruction have to demonstrate to a vetting committee chaired by a non-official member on the Board of Education that they satisfy the requirements necessary for the effective use of English as a MoI. An appeals committee chaired by another non-official member designated by the Secretary for Education and Manpower was also set up in 1998 to consider any appeals against the decisions of the vetting committee. As of September 1998, 114 schools were in the EM category (the number was 100 as of 1 December 1997 and revised up to 114 on 13 March 1998), about 300 were in the CM category.

The new policy is initially applicable only to the secondary-one intakes of 1998/99 as the implementation of this policy is to be done in a phased manner. But if the policy is to be pursued to its logical end, in a few years' time, the system will be radically different from what it is today. For example, the present numeric dominance of the EM schools traditionally known as Anglo-Chinese Secondary Schools (ACSSs) will be replaced by that of the CM schools. Furthermore in the secondary sector there will be a government-sanctioned compartmentalisation of the schools into CM and EM streams. While it is not the focus of this paper to examine the validity the four claims made by the Department that form the rationale behind its MoI policy, it is necessary to note that its fourth claim concerning the higher pass rate in English Language achieved by CM school students in the Hong Kong Certificate of Education Examination is disingenuous. The better performance of these students *vis-à-vis* their counterparts in the EM sector should be understood in the context that the CM sector has a less than 10 per cent share of the school population and its students have a relatively small in-group variance in academic and language standards. Whereas the EM sector has a more than 90 per cent share of the school population and the in-group variance concerned is much larger. If such variance is controlled in the comparison, the statistics about the ACSS students' performance in English Language in the Examination will be much more favourable. Given the significance of the language agenda to the future of Hong Kong, it is very dangerous to give people the impression by a twist of statistics that the CM sector is better able than the EM sector to spread English proficiency among Hong Kong students when it is not quite the case. Moreover if ACSSs are considered to be a flawed instrument for achieving horizontal spread (in terms of the number of English speakers) and/or vertical spread (in terms of level of proficiency) of the English language in Hong Kong, then other than the CM model, by what other ways and means will the proficiency standards of English be maintained and promoted? Also, should the mother tongue of the Hong Kong students be the only oral MoI in most classrooms, then how is Putonghua to be effectively promoted among a school population the majority of which are now taking merely 35-70 minutes of Putonghua instruction per week? The *status quo* apparently will do little to turn Hong Kong students into fluent speakers of Putonghua at the end of secondary-five when a sizable fraction of them leave school to work.

Given these and other considerations, it does not come as a surprise that the new policy has triggered an uproar. Particularly its streaming approach has pleased neither mother tongue education advocates nor conservatives who favour maintaining the *status quo*.[1] Accordingly the government announced on 13 March

---

[1]   David Chi-Kong Cheung's letter to the *South China Morning Post* published on 1 November 1997 under the caption 'New Education Policy Socially Divisive' reflects the disappointment of most mother tongue education advocates, who, like him, are worried that the policy "will further divide society"; and question respectively   "whether to allow a pseudo-English-medium education to continue will enhance the standard of English of the Hong Kong population ..." and "Is it not ludicrous that the Government, having described convincingly the educational benefits of mother-tongue teaching, still does not wish to impose it during the years of compulsory education?"   Whereas J. Garner's letter to the same newspaper published on 8 May 1997 under the caption 'Proposals Repeating Mistakes of the Past' reflects the anguish of those who are appreciative of "the tremendous efforts made by voluntary and religious groups which have sponsored schools using English as a medium of

1998 that a Joint Working Group on MoI would be established and 'the Board of Education and the Standing Committee on Language Education & Research would be invited to carry out jointly a study on promoting and implementing the Government's MoI objectives and to make recommendations in a year's time.' (Press Statement from the Secretary for Education & Manpower's office). In early September 2000, the Education & Manpower Bureau announced that, based on the recommendations of the Group, the streaming policy will be maintained for the time being until the 2003/2004 school year when a more thorough evaluation will have been completed. These subsequent actions of the government indicate that the new MoI policy as it stands now is unlikely to remain the final blueprint shaping the form and the practice of the bilingual system of education in Hong Kong in the early decades of the new millennium.[2]

At this juncture of continuity and change, it should be helpful to derive a clearer picture about the relevant views of the stakeholders, other than that of the policy-makers, involved in the issues of MoI and the language agenda of biliteracy and trilingualism by re-examining the data of a number of surveys, five of which were conducted wholly or partly by this author between 1983 and 1999. The reasons for this attempt are as follows: (1) The Department of Education has adopted a top-down approach in the form of an administrative decree to implement the new policy; a strong dosage of bottom-up views should therefore benefit its evaluation. (2) Given the amount of effort spent by the government to educate the stakeholders, especially the parents, about the merits of the new policy with a supposition that they have misguided views about the issues involved, it is only fair that the views of the stakeholders be made known in a more systematic fashion in order to see what these views are so that

---

instruction..." and question the wisdom of "going back to the days of the Chinese Middle School system which parents overwhelmingly rejected?"

2   The plasticity of the situation can be seen from a public speech made by the chairman of the Standing Committee on Language Education and Research that is involved in the review of the new MoI policy, in which, according to the *South China Morning Post* of 18 November 2001, he made known his hope that all secondary students could eventually learn in English and Putonghua starting from Form (Secondary) One.

one may then judge whether or not they are indeed misguided. (3) An exercise of this nature has never been done before and it is hoped that by presenting the views of the stakeholders of various backgrounds within a single rubric it would facilitate, albeit in a small way perhaps, the formulation of the right step forward into the new millennium for the bilingual education system in Hong Kong. In the next section, however, we will first establish the context for the interpretation of the stakeholders' views by briefly tracing the steps of the development of the MoI-based bifurcation of the secondary sector of education in Hong Kong.

MoI-based Bifurcation of the Secondary Sector

The development of a MoI-based bifurcation in the secondary system is a result largely of the following historical circumstances: (1) the cultural backwardness and foreign encroachment of Modern China (dated from the end of the Opium War with the signing of the Treaty of Nanking [Nanjing] in 1842); (2) China's loss of sovereignty over Hong Kong to Britain between 1842 and 1997, and the needs of the British regime to cultivate a class of bilingual brokers to mediate between itself and the governed; as well as (3) the Chinese Nationalist Party's political platforms on modern education and on the Overseas Chinese including those in Hong Kong.

As a result of the first two sets of circumstances, the development of modern education in Hong Kong was mostly the work of personnel and organisations with European and/or American backgrounds. Their efforts were in turn facilitated by the British regime which found in its collaboration with these bodies a convenient way for it to cultivate the talents it needed. From 1902 until the eve of the Second World War, a substantial amount of the resources allocated to education were funnelled, via the Grant-in-aid Scheme, to EM schools with the manifest purpose of cultivating a Westernised and English-speaking elite among the local population. The consequence of this policy can be seen from a remark in the *Annual Colonial Report-Hong Kong 1946*: 'The grant-aided schools mainly use English although one school is entirely taught in Chinese... secondary education in English is to a great extent in the hands of Government and grant-aid schools ...' (p.44).

Accordingly, modern education through the EM enjoyed a head start in Hong Kong, especially at the secondary level. It was not until 1926 with the founding of the Vernacular Middle School (renamed Clementi Middle School in 1951) that Hong Kong had its first government Chinese Middle School (CMS). Together with Munsang College, which was probably the subsidised CMS mentioned in the foregoing *Annual Colonial Report*, the two formed the core of the CM sector that would undergo rapid expansion in the years between 1926 and 1941. This expansion had little to do with the Hong Kong government but had much to do with the third set of historical circumstances mentioned above. Since its founding by Dr Sun and his associates, the Chinese Nationalist Party regarded itself as the leader of all Chinese nationalist movements both at home and abroad. It also treated all Overseas Chinese citizens of the Republic regardless of whether or not they were citizens of their respective host countries. Accordingly, the Nationalist Party found it politically opportune to promote nationalist education for its overseas citizens, and in fact, as early as 1921, when the Nationalist Party consolidated its power in Canton (Guangzhou), agents were sent to Southeast Asia and beyond to assist local Chinese communities in the development of nationalistic modern education for their children (Akashi, 1970: 1-14). 1928 saw a semblance of national unity achieved with the founding of the Nationalist Government in Nanjing. The temporary political unity facilitated the implementation of a national curriculum – which was largely based on the American model and had been adopted earlier in 1922 – as well as the popularisation of a national language – better known as *Guo Yu* or Mandarin rather than Putonghua at the time – in the nation's schools. After 1932 when the problem of establishing the standard pronunciation of *Guo Yu* was sorted out, it was vigorously promoted as a MoI in schools. By the early 1930s, a Chinese model of modern education and a linguistic medium of its transmission were finally taking shape, and were ready for large-scale export.

However, the climax of the expansion of CM secondary education in Hong Kong did not come until the out-break of the Second Sino-Japanese War. After the outbreak of this War, many CMSs in China simply moved across the border and re-established themselves in Hong Kong which, for four years, became a haven for escapees from the War in China. While it took more than eighty years after the founding of the Colony for CM secondary education to get started, a mere fifteen years after 1926, upon the eve of the Second World War, at least forty-nine institutions offering a CM education up to either junior or senior secondary level can be identified (Wong, 1982: 270-353). On the other hand, this period saw the British regime largely pursuing a policy of providing respectively an EM education up to university level for children from well-to-do families, and a vernacular primary education for children from less well-to-do families (Irving, 1914).

Therefore, by the early 1930's, the MoI-based bifurcation of the secondary sector was complete. While the EM sector enjoyed better endowments and resources, as well as a larger proportion of students with well-to-do family backgrounds, both sectors had their share of strengths and weaknesses. The choice between having one's secondary education in a CMS or an ACSS often depended on one's cultural orientation and career plans. But this balance of drawing power between the two sectors was upset soon after the Second World War.

The competitive edge of the CM sector was soon undercut by two developments after the Second World War. First, China's victory in the Second World War failed to accelerate the decolonialisation process in Hong Kong, which would benefit the CMSs. On the other hand, the collapse of the Nanjing regime in 1949 also deprived the CMSs of their centre of reference, and source of logistic support. As early as 1950, the Hong Kong government already indicated its concern for the problems faced by CMS graduates as a result of this deprivation (Colonial Office, 1950: 61). Nevertheless, as shown in Table 1, the sector experienced a steady decline in its share of the enrolment of secondary school students between the late 1950s and early 1990s despite a number of public policy changes which were apparently in its favour, among these were the rapid expansion of CM subsidised primary education in the 1950s and 1960s,[3] the founding of the

---

[3]   For example, in October 1954 the government launched the seven-year primary school expansion programme and when it was completed in 1961, primary school places were increased from 171,536 to 484,536. In

Chinese University of Hong Kong in 1963[4] and the passage in 1974 of the Official Languages Ordinance, which accords official status to the Chinese language. On the other hand, during the same period and especially after 1978 the EM sector expanded steadily in its number of intakes. At its height it had more than a 90 per cent share of the enrolment.

The MoI-based bifurcation of the secondary sector in Hong Kong in the last century and the decline of the CMSs in its latter half were a very complex process. A proper examination of this process will require much more space than what is available here.[5] However it may suffice to conclude this section with three observations: First, the bifurcation is rooted in a particular set of historical circumstances which cannot be ignored albeit gradually they are becoming irrelevant to Hong Kong in the new millennium. Second, while government policy definitely plays a role in the ebb and flow of the fortunes of the CM and EM sectors, forces that are exogenous, ideological and economic in nature have also driven the dynamics of school selection in Hong Kong. Third, the dynamics of school selection remain relatively favourable to ACSSs in spite of the heavy cost of EM instruction. The views of the stakeholders will not be fully understood if these factors are not taken into account.

---

other words, 313,000 new places were created, which amounts to an expansion of more than 82 per cent. (Colonial Office, 1962: 112-113).

[4]   In the Preamble of founding Ordinance of the Chinese University, it is clearly written, "the principal language of instruction [in the University] shall be Chinese." Moreover, the four-year norm of its curriculum structure also reflects the intention of the authorities at the time to have the Chinese Middle Schools as the major supplier of students to the University.

[5]   For an examination of this process, see So, 1984: 51-166.

Table 1 **Hong Kong School Enrolment at the Secondary Level (By Medium of Instruction), 1958-1988***

	ACSS		CMS		Total School	Total Student	% CMS
Year	School	Student	School	Student			
1958	74	25,863	89	21,210	163	47,073	45
1968	223	149,921	123	50,596	346	200,517	25
1978	330	375,470	104	58,548	434	434,018	14
1988	343	365,330	57	32,973	400	398,303	8

Source: Hong Kong Government, Hong Kong Annual Review, Chapters on Education, various issues.
*The figures in this table refer to enrolment at day grammar schools only. 1958 and 1988 are the year when such enrolment figures were reported in the Annual Reviews for respectively the first, and the last time.

Over-selection of the EM Sector

Its colonial past notwithstanding, the sociolinguistic conditions in Hong Kong have never been favourable to providing its ACSSs with a good supply of teachers highly proficient in English and students with a sufficient command of English for EM instruction.[6] Therefore inevitably the relentless growth of the EM sector in the past several decades has led to an over-selection of ACSSs, which in turn has given rise to a wide range of consequences many of which have been considered undesirable by educators. Here it may suffice to identify just three of them: First, the over-selection turns the processes of teaching in many ACSSs into a dreary chore of translating textbook texts to students many of whom, in turn, have to resort to crude coping measures such as rote-memorisation of key words and phrases to survive (Johnson, 1997). Second, the down-side of EM instruction has given rise to a widely held belief that such instruction may have serious damaging effects on students' cognitive and linguistic developments (Siu et al., 1979). Third, in order to compensate for the lack of English skills on the part of students and/or teachers, much of the classroom talk in many schools is conducted in mostly Cantonese and/or a mix of

---

[6] See So, 1998 for a discussion of these sociolinguistic conditions.

English and Cantonese. Many investigators believe such practices are not conducive to developing proficiency in English, which, as noted earlier, has been the *raison d'être* of EM instruction in the schools (Johnson, 1983). The first two concerns provide a rationale for change, albeit whether or not the changes initiated by the Department of Education are appropriate is another question. The third concern is particularly relevant to this paper because it reflects the pronounced mismatch between expectations and realities of the standards of English and the quality of its use in ACSSs.

The English Language Standards of Students

Given the sociolinguistic circumstances, ACSSs are at best a blunt instrument for spreading EM instruction and English proficiency among their students. It should be a big surprise if they were otherwise. However, probably because of their strong belief in the significance of English standards, many people fail to connect the two dots – circumstances and standards – and entertain unrealistic expectations of English standards in ACSSs. Indeed the steady growth of ACSSs since the founding in 1862 of their prototype the Central School has been punctuated by alarms about students' English language standards as shown in the founding of the Language Campaign discussed in the next section. These alarms can be dated back to 1878 when, in his dispatch to the Secretary of State for the Colonies, Sir John Pope Hennessy indicated his disappointment of not being able to identify a single English-speaking student out of a class of 150 at Central School, the government's flagship school of the day (quoted in Sweeting, 1990: 232). In 1916 Legislator Lau Chu Pak expressed his concern about the English standards of Chinese students in a speech at the Legislative Council (see Cheng, 1949: 83; Sweeting, 1990: 346). In more recent years, Lord (1974: 4) was quite alarmed by the fact that out of a total of 228 students in the Faculty of Arts of Hong Kong University who took a diagnostic test of their English skills, between 24 and 71 per cent of them required remedial assistance in one form or another to enhance their proficiency in English in order to function in the EM environment of the university. In 1989 Roy

Harris gave his inaugural lecture from the Chair of English Language the provocative title 'The Worst English in the World' which referred not only to the English abilities of the Hong Kong people in general, but also to his students at the Hong Kong University. The ringing of the language alarm bell has been getting more and more frequent especially since the implementation of nine-year free and compulsory education in 1979, which has eventually led to a sustained debate in the local media and among educators about whether students' English language standards are declining. While academic investigators of the issue tend to dismiss the warnings of falling language standards as alarmist and are in favour of alternate views (e.g., see King, 1982; Joseph, 1996; So, 2001), the debate has become impertinent to the community at large because stakeholders with real clout, e.g., employers in the business sector, have switched the tenor of the debate from whether or not standards are falling to whether or not their language demands are met by the schools.

Views of the Stakeholders: the Business Sector

The use of the term stakeholders in policy documents in the area of education appears to be a new phenomenon.[7] However, it has been a long standing practice that when major decisions in education are to be made, educators are not the only group that the government will consult. Efforts to solicit views of employers, parents, education personnel and students on major proposals in education have been common. Whether or not the views will then be adopted is of course another matter.

---

[7] It is the impression of this writer that the term gained currency only after the mid 1990s when it was used to refer to "the public concerned" in government documents about education such as *ECR7* (1997): § 6.17 (As the quality of our teachers is a key element in the entire education system, we recommend that the General Teaching Council (GTC) should have a substantial representation of other "stake holders"...); *The Outstanding School Awards* (1998) (Detailed Award Criteria: 1. Management and Organisation...and such plans are adequately communicated to stake-holders); *UGC Report* on the 1995-98 Triennium (1 Mar 2000) ... In 1994, the Heads of the UGC-funded institutions decided that... and exchange of views within the UGC-funded sector and between it and its various stake-holders. (Chapter 8)

In the following, the survey data will demonstrate that, contrary to the policies of the past and present governments on the bilingual system of education in Hong Kong, which have become increasingly inconsistent in recent years, the stake-holders have been quite consistent in terms of their expectations during the period of our examination. And they have also communicated these expectations of theirs in a consistent manner in surveys such as the ones conducted by this author. The data of the business sector will be first examined.

Ever since the late 1970s, the business sector has voiced its concern about language standards in the media regularly. In 1989, in an unprecedented manner, it served notice about its concern of language standards by founding The Hong Kong Language Campaign which was a consortium of leading corporations in Hong Kong[8] that opted to work together as a registered charity to help maintain and improve language standards in Hong Kong, particularly the standard of English. The aims of the Campaign were to heighten public awareness of the need for English and to encourage the community to take appropriate action.

Since the early 1990s, the debate about whether or not students' standards of English are declining has evolved and been replaced by the concern about whether or not our society is producing sufficient bilingual talents to meet the demands of the market. There are findings indicating that this is a genuine concern. For example, in connection with the validation of an academic programme, this author conducted a content analysis of job advertisements placed in four newspapers in 1994, namely *Recruit*[9] of 8 July (Friday), *Ming Pao* of 10 July (Sunday), the *Sing Dao Yit Pao* of 11 July (Monday) and the *South China Morning Post* of 9 July (Saturday). After making adjustments to obvious duplications, a total of 11,335 pieces of advertisement advertising job[10] vacancies were found in the sampled papers

---

[8]   Members of the consortium included The HK & Shanghai Banking Corp., Hutchinson Whampoa, Shell Hong Kong, the Swire Group (HK), Hong Kong Telecom, the China International Trust & Investment Corp HK (Holdings), The South China Morning Post.

[9]   *Recruit* is not a traditional newspaper; it is primarily a paper of job advertisements.

[10]   The unit of counting is jobs, not posts the number of which is

out. Of these advertisements, 27.1 per cent (N=3,076) of the jobs advertised make explicit stipulations concerning language requirements. Among these requirements 47.1 per cent (N=1,448) require a certain level of proficiency in *more than* one language. Accordingly when the counting was done on the basis of proficiency requirement *per* language, the total frequency of language requirements found in the advertisements rises to 4,783. The frequency distribution of these language requirements is shown in Table 2. The demand for bilingual skills, especially that of English skills, is further corroborated in the 1994 Education Commission survey,[11] as shown in Table 3.

The findings of these two studies provide evidence indicating there is much demand for bilingual talent in the Hong Kong economy. Given the executive-led style of the HKSAR government and its close connection with the business sector, it is therefore not surprising that well before the transfer of sovereignty, Mr. Antony Leung, a banker and a then member-designate of the Executive Council of the Hong Kong SAR government, in a speech[12] given to a seminar on 9 May 1997, included the development among local students of biliteracy and trilingualism as one of the demands and challenges of education for Hong Kong in its new era. This objective was subsequently endorsed by the Education Commission (1999: §3.4). At the transfer of sovereignty over Hong Kong, the stake of the business sector in the issue of whether or not in the post-1997 era the local education system will continue to be able to supply it with employees skilled in more than one language has been made loud and clear. Interestingly enough, based on an understanding of such concerns and on the assumption of the decisive role played by the business sector in policy decision making in Hong Kong,[13] one would hardly have anticipated the

---

understandably much larger than 11,335.

[11] Department of Chinese, Translation & Interpretation 1994. For a profile of the survey, see Endnote 5.

[12] The title of the speech was "The Demands on and the Challenges of Education for Hong Kong in a New Era".

[13] The clout that the sector used to have and may still have can be seen from this observation made by Hughes (1968: 23) "Power in Hong Kong, it has been said, resides in the Jockey Club, Jardine & Matheson, the Hong Kong and Shanghai Bank, and the Governor – in that order. There

bold moves made by the Department of Education in the question of MoI in the latter half of 1997.

Table 2 **Frequency Distribution (By Language) of the Number of Explicit Language Requirements in Advertisements Found in Four Newspapers 1994**

Newspapers	*A	B	C	D	E	F	G	**Row Total**
Recruit	110	745	238	13	1	1	1	1,109
Ming Pao	48	134	42	0	0	0	2	226
Sing Dao	62	289	117	10	2	0	0	480
SCMP	602	1,629	651	64	5	3	14	2,968
Column Total	822	2,797	1,048	87	8	4	17	4,783

Number of Sampled Advertisements=3,076
*A= Chinese (17.2%);   B= English (58.5%);   C= Putonghua (21.9%);
  D= Japanese (1.8%);   E= French (0.16%);   F= German (0.08%);
  G = Others (0.36%)

Table 3 **Graduate & Employer Respondents' Evaluation of The Importance of Different Language Skills At Work 1994**

Language skill important at work (% agree)							
S5* Graduates N=245		Employer/S5* graduates N=138		Tertiary graduates N=213		Employers/Tertiary graduates N=183	
Spoken English	86.4	Spoken English	80.2	Spoken English	89	Spoken English	87.4
Written English	45.7	Written English	73	Written English	82	Written English	83.1
Written Chinese	18.6	Written Chinese	64.6	Written Chinese	67.5	Written Chinese	51.4
Putonghua	15.4	Putonghua	51.9	Putonghua	48.3	Putonghua	43.7
Cantonese	13.3	Cantonese	42.7	Cantonese	32.5	Cantonese	35.7

*S5 = Secondary Five.

Views of the Stakeholders: Parents

The bold move in 1997 of the Department of Education to introduce a policy on the thorny issue of MoI was in fact not its first, albeit this move is unprecedented in terms of its vigour and determination. For example, as early as 1973, the Department put forth its first MoI policy statement in its Green Paper for Education wherein it proposed the option that 'Chinese become the usual language of instruction in the lower forms of the

is more than a grain of truth in the observation."

secondary schools' (Board of Education 1973: §16 & §17).[14] In this connection, a study of the stakeholders' views was conducted (Home Affairs Department, 1974). A major part of the study was a questionnaire survey of parents of three city districts, namely Kwun Tong, Wong Tai Sin and Kowloon City. 4,231 questionnaires were distributed and 4,012 (94.8%) were returned. More than 67% of the parents' agreed with the proposed option (Table 4 refers).

Table 4 **Parents' Views on Chinese Become the Major MoI in Lower Forms 1974**

Strongly agree	1,073 (26.8%)[15]
Agree	1,650 (41.1)
Uncertain	870 (21.7)
Disagree	313 (7.8)
Strongly Disagree	93 (2.3)
Non-response	13 (0.3)
Total Number of Responses	4,012

N=4,012

In three surveys conducted by this author in 1983, 1996 and 1999, a similar question was put to the parents.[16] Similar to the 1974 survey, for the surveys of 1983 and 1996, the option of having Chinese as the major MoI in lower forms with the EM to be phased in gradually received a positive response from a majority of the respondents (Tables 5A & 5B refer). The exception is the 1999 survey where the option was rephrased according to the government's new MoI initiative. Here there is no majority view and the plurality chose to withhold their judgement by returning a 'no opinion'. Otherwise the views of the parents would have been quite consistent.

---

[14]   For the full text concerned, see Endnote 1.

[15]   Unless stated otherwise, the percentages reported in this paper are based on total number of 'valid' responses.

[16]   For a profile of the parent respondents of these surveys, see Endnote 2.

Table 5A **Parents' Views on Introducing EM Instruction in a Gradual & Phased Manner 1983**

Agree	275 (70.2%)
Disagree	30 (7.7)
No Opinion	87 (22.2)
Total Number of Responses	392

N=404

Table 5B **Parents' Views on Introducing EM Instruction in a Gradual & Phased Manner 1996**

Agree	102 (56.4%)
Disagree	31 (17.1)
No Opinion	48 (26.5)
Total Number of Responses	179

N=186

Table 5C **Parents' Views on 70% of Subsidised secondary Schools to Adopt CM Instruction 1999**

Agree	41 (22.9%)
Disagree	65 (36.3)
No Opinion	73 (40.8)
Total Number of Responses	179

N=180

Another item included in the surveys of 1983, 1986, 1996 and 1999 that received consistent responses from parents is the one asking them to rate a set of criteria that define an ideal school. As shown in Tables 6A and 6B, it appears that the parents know what counts in quality education and that while no satisfactory explanation could be offered to account for the drop in ratings of the criteria Whether English is used for Instruction in the 1999 survey, it seems that the primary concerns of the parents for their children are a quality education and good language standards. It is probable that the issue of MoI is important to them only in the context of these primary concerns. As shown in Table 7, if parents are forced to choose between CMSs and ACSSs, the majority of them tend to opt for the latter, but if they are offered third alternatives like the aforementioned option of introducing the EM gradually (e.g., by level) or the much discussed option in recent years of introducing the EM by subject, it appears the majority of them are also quite prepared to accept the compromise (Table 7 refers).

Table 6A **H.K. Parents' Rating of Criteria for an Ideal School Ranked by Mean Rating 1983-1999**[17]

Ranked according to Parents' rating Criteria	1983	1986	1996	1999
Quality of the Teaching Staff	1	1	1	1
Students' English Language Standards	2	2	2	2
Endowment & Equipment of the School	3	2	6	6
Students' Chinese Language Standards	4	7	8	4
Prestige of the School	5	---	3	3
Performance in Public Exams	6	6	7	5
Whether English Textbooks are used	7	4	4	7
Whether English is used for Instruction	---	5	5	8
Whether Chinese Textbooks are used	8	9	9	9
Whether Cantonese is used for Instruction	---	8	10	10

Table 6B **H.K. Parents' Rating of Criteria for an Ideal School Their Top Four Choices 1983-1999**

Ranked according to Parents' rating Criteria	1983 June	1986 August & September	1996 November & December	1999 April
Quality of the Teaching Staff	1	1	1	1
Students' English Language Standards	2	2	2	2
Endowment & Equipment of the School	3	2	---	---
Prestige of the School	---	---	3	3
Students' Chinese Language Standards	4	---	---	4
Whether English Textbooks are used	---	4	4	---

Table 7 **Percentage of Parents Agree with the MoI Option 1983, 1986, 1996, & 1999**

MoI Option	1983 N=404	1986 N=227	1996 N=186	1999 N=180
English as Major MoI from S1 – S5	58	52	50.3	47.2
Chinese as Major MoI from S1 – S5	37	31	11.5	13.9
Combined Use of CM & EM from S1 – S5	---	91	---	---
CM & EM By Subject	55	---	61.0	66.5

---

[17]   For the tabulation of mean ratings by each survey, see Endnote 4.

Views of the Stakeholders: Teachers & Students

Unlike employers and parents, students and teachers are not only stakeholders; they are also part of the issue. Three of the surveys (1983, 1986 & 1994) conducted by this author cover student subjects.[18] Among these three, the two conducted in 1986 and 1994 also cover teacher subjects.[19] It is also in the returns of these three surveys that one finds a convergence of the historical and sociolinguistic factors that shape people's MoI choices in Hong Kong. Firstly, the 1994 survey indicates that the great majority of sampled students, educators, parents, graduates and employers do not have a favourable view of the level of English and Putonghua proficiency attained within the schools (the views of student and educator respondents are summarised in Table 8). And the situation of Putonghua appears to be even more serious than English. Therefore, whether or not language standards are falling, there is apparently much room for improvement in students' standards of English and Putonghua, which underscores the fact that biliteracy and trilingualism is a goal that would require much effort to achieve.

Secondly, these returns bring out a paradox that lies in the heart of the bilingual system of education in Hong Kong: On the one hand both students and teachers appear to perceive that the English proficiency of the majority of the students is not up to par. On the other hand when students are asked to indicate their preferred types (by MoI) of secondary schools for their secondary education, ACSSs remain the choice of a clear majority (Table 9 refers). The gist of the paradox is that people opt for EM secondary education not so much because their English is good. Rather the contrary, it is exactly because their self-perceived inadequacy in English and the perceived connection between English proficiency and ACSSs that have driven the forces that select ACSSs, especially in the past fifty years.

---

[18]   For a profile of the student respondents, please refer to Endnote 3A.
[19]   For a profile of the teacher respondents, please refer to Endnote 3B.

Table 8 **Percentages of Respondents Agreeing with Items about Students'**
English and Putonghua Proficiency 1994

Respondents	*A	B	C	D
**PS English Teacher N=275	20.5	---	---	---
PS Putonghua Teacher N=30	---	---	0	---
PS Heads N=60	29.9	---	4.3	---
SS English/Putonghua Teacher N=302/20	23.6	---	0	---
SS English Panel Heads N=61	23.5	---	---	---
SS Heads N=60	24.2	---	0	---
Primary Five Students N=1,375	---	33.1	---	16.7
Secondary One Students N=1,460	---	18.6	---	6.8
Secondary Six Students N=949	---	14.2	---	7.3

*A: Generally speaking, my students' English language ability is good.
B: Generally speaking, my English language ability is good.
C. Generally speaking, my students speak fluent Putonghua.
D. Generally speaking, I speak fluent Putonghua.
**PS=Primary School; SS=Secondary School

Table 9 **Students' Most Preferred Choice of School Type**
For Their Secondary Education 1983, 1986

School Type (By MoI) 1983		School Type (By MoI) 1986	
Government ACSS	51.1%	ACSS	62.3%
Subsidised ACSS	29.9	ACSS*	26.8
Government CMS	15.2	CMS	5.2
Subsidised CMS	3.5	ACSS**	3
Private ACSS	0.38	Others	2.6
N (Total)	519	N (Total)	231

*With some subjects taught in the CM
**With some students learn in the CM

Similarly, in the 1986 survey, when the teacher respondents were asked 'Whether it is reasonable to reserve access to EM instruction to the more capable students', 55.7% (N=93) returned a negative response; whereas only 23.4% (N=39) returned a positive response. In the same survey, when the teacher respondents were asked 'Whether the problems associated with EM instruction is surmountable', 53.1% (N=86) returned a positive response; whereas only 22.8% (N=37) returned a negative response.

Table 10 **Helping Factors for English Proficiency Deemed Important By School Personnel Arranged According to Rank 1994**

Factors	Three Helping Factors Present			Three Helping Factors wanted but Absent			Total (Rank)
	*A	B	C	A	B	C	A+B+C
Given Priority by The School	#74.9	36.9	48.5	0	18.9	9.9	189.1(1)
Good Teaching Staff	31.3	43.5	32.9	40.5	26.8	5.6	180.6(2)
Flexible Teaching Methods	23.1	26.5	18.4	27.3	26.7	21.2	143.2(3)
Reading Scheme	27.7	30.8	32.6	21.4	13.9	14.3	14.07(4)
Sufficient Supply of AV Equipment	24.1	16.6	16.9	25.9	32.9	23.5	139.9(5)
Supplementary Classes	38.7	36.2	35.9	1.0	7.2	6.3	125.3(6)
Syllabuses Relevant to Everyday Life	3.1	7.1	12.7	28.7	32.7	37.3	121.6(7)
EM Instruction for Other Subjects	13.2	10.4	12.9	17.2	35.7	32.1	121.5(8)
Sufficient Supply of Supplementary Teaching Material	13.8	33.0	27.8	15.6	9.8	17.1	117.1(9)
English Extra-curricular Activities	15.4	17.1	17.1	17.4	10.7	22.2	99.9(10)
Sufficient Supply of AV Teaching Material	6.8	7.6	4.6	23.2	20.4	25.5	88.1(11)
Native Speakers as English Teachers	8.7	0	5.9	32.7	12.1	27.0	86.40(12)
Good Textbooks	4.3	16.6	12.6	16.6	15.0	15.9	81(13)
Interesting Assignments	0	0	1.2	6.3	13.2	18.8	39.5(14)
Education TV	9.7	7.8	9.1	2.0	1.4	3.9	33.9(15)

*A = Secondary School Head (N=60); B = Head of English Panel (N=61); C = Secondary School English Language Teacher (N=302)
#Percent of respondents choosing the option.

In the 1994 survey, MoI options were not included. But the views of the Secondary School Heads, Heads of English Panels and English Teachers of secondary schools on the role EM instruction could be adduced from their response to the item where they were asked to identify, out of a checklist of 15 factors, three factors that are respectively present and absent in their schools that are helpful to enhancing English standards of their students (i.e., they have to make six choices). As shown in Table 10, in one aspect their responses have a close match with that of the parents: be it an ideal school or an ideal situation for teaching English in Hong Kong, the most important factors are more related to whether or not the schools have got their priorities right, as well as the necessary programmes and equipment, and quality teaching staff. Similar to the parents, the importance of EM instruction to them appears to be of an importance secondary to these primary factors.

Conclusions & Observations

This analysis has many limitations especially in the case of the surveys of 1983, 1996 and 1999, which are self-funded and the sampling designs and processes have all the usual constraints of a one-man job. However, it is submitted that the consistency of the responses of the respondents, which is very much in evidence among the survey findings, should merit attention of the policy makers when they are re-charting the government's language policy in education. For example there is general agreement among the stakeholders that school graduates' language standards, especially that of Putonghua and English, are low while at the same time there is genuine demands for biliterate and trilingual skills at the workplace. Another view consistently returned by the survey respondents is that they are receptive to mother tongue instruction but prefer the ACSS model as the norm in secondary education. Indeed the people of Hong Kong are not stupid. They understand that mother tongue instruction is an easier option. But at the same time they understand a quality education in the geographical context of Hong Kong and in the temporal context of the new millennium encompass relatively high levels of biliteracy and trilingualism. If the language agenda of the post 1997 administration and the problems of bilingual education in Hong Kong are to be resolved in the future, the Department must first come to grips with the paradox that it is exactly because the Hong Kong students' English has been found wanting that they are being sent by their parents to ACSSs to further their secondary education. If their children could pick up English at home or in the streets, we would not have to grapple with this vexing issue of MoI today.[20]

---

[20]   In this regards, the parents of Hong Kong are no different from the

At least five pointers may be derived from the findings for the consideration of stakeholders involved in the bilingual education debate: (1) the stakeholders in general have a clear idea about what makes an ideal secondary education system, *viz.* schools with quality teaching staff, good equipment, and high language standards. (2) EM instruction appears to be important only in this context. (3) In connection with (2) there appears to be no popular demand for secondary education to be conducted exclusively in either the CM or the EM. However if parents and students are forced to choose between CMSs and ACSSs, the majority of them will opt for the latter. (4) There appears to be general acceptance of options that use both linguistic mediums in various combinations and at different levels of the secondary curriculum and finally (5) language standards are perceived to be low by the stakeholders.

In the following, with reference to these pointers, the major mistakes of the Department of Education's MoI policy are examined. The biggest problem at present is that the Department is in a state of denial which can be seen when it asserts in its policy document *Medium of Instruction Guidance for Secondary Schools* that 'Most students prefer learning in the mother tongue'. Students of Hong Kong may prefer learning in the mother tongue but for the majority of them the school type of preference remains ACSSs. And they and their parents need not be told about the benefits of mother tongue instruction because they do know it is indeed the best MoI with all things being equal. However, given the world as it is, things are seldom equal. Ever since my doctoral research, I have taken exception to a common practice of many mother tongue education advocates who caricaturise Hong Kong parents' preference for ACSSs as some sort of 'irrational exuberance' driven by the herd instinct.[21] Instead, based on the findings of my studies and my contact with parents, there are good reasons to believe that the majority of them have a clear idea and a

---

[21]   parents of students of French Immersion programmes in Quebec.
For example, Cheung (1990) characterises the parents' preference for ACSSs as follows: "As far as possible, Ah Mou, Ah Sau, Ah Chu--the Chinese expression for every Tom, Dick and Harry – all rush to English grammar schools, resulting in endless problems in learning motivation, attitude and school discipline."

reasonable expectation of what they want for their children's education. As posited in my doctoral dissertation (So, 1984), it just so happens that as a result of historical circumstances the profile of many ACSSs match their expectations. If the Department refuses to confront this reality head-on, a satisfactory resolution of the MoI issue may never be obtained.

Earlier it is pointed out that the success of ACSSs has led to their over-selection and it is indisputable that many ACSSs are not offering authentic EM instruction for their students, especially after 1978. While measures should be taken to ensure that EM instruction be done authentically and appropriately, it does not necessarily entail a blanket imposition of mother tongue instruction in the majority of the schools. In doing so, the Department puts itself in a ludicrous position wherein on the one hand it vows the merits of mother tongue instruction and then on the other hand it enforces by decree that the mother tongue cannot be used, for example in a mixed/switched-code fashion, in schools sanctioned to be EM schools.

Furthermore, as indicated in the survey findings, if parents are confronted with only two MoI options in secondary education, it is very likely that they will opt for ACSSs because in the years after 1949, these schools have delivered the kind of education that parents aspire for their children. As I argue elsewhere, the parents and students of Hong Kong are not against CM instruction; they simply prefer the ACSS model to the CMS model. (So, 1992) The current problems of the Department are to a great extent a result of its attempt to impose the CMS model on the majority of the stakeholders as a way to resolving the over-selection problem. One may predict with confidence that if the Department persists with its MoI blueprint of 1997 and makes the CMS model the norm of the system, the selection pressure for EM instruction will be heightened rather than moderated. And the second class status of a CM secondary education would be reinforced, rather than diminished. The reinforced compartmentalisation of the two sectors is also socially divisive over time.

In this connection, it should also be pointed out that the dichotomy of CM vs EM education revived by the Department is false and counter-productive in the context of Hong Kong. As shown clearly in the survey data, the majority of the people of

Hong Kong are not demanding CM or EM education in a dichotomous, 'either all or nothing' form. Probably most of them are looking for an amount of both that is appropriate for their children. What parents aspire to is that their children are able to acquire a good education and in the course of doing so, achieve a good measure of biliteracy and trilingualism at various levels. As for the schools, there are also good reasons to believe that among the 300 schools sanctioned to be CM schools, many of them have the desire and the ability to deliver part of the curriculum in a medium other than Cantonese. There are also good reasons to believe many of the 114 schools sanctioned to be EM do not have the desire and the ability to deliver the entire curriculum exclusively in the EM. The Hong Kong people are indeed falling between the CM and EM stools.

Another big mistake made by the Department is that instead of rising to meet the challenge of fulfilling the demand for EM education, it has chosen to cast EM education under a dubious light and ration it on the assumption of limited supply. There is no question that for the majority of the Hong Kong people, an EM secondary education, which is perceived to be closely associated with bilingual proficiency development, has long been regarded as a desideratum. While it is taken that demand for such instruction has far outstripped the local education system's capacity to provide it properly, a sensible way out is to spend greater efforts and more resources to increase the supply of its authentic and appropriate form rather than confining it to a few. To make matters worse, serious efforts are made by the Department to persuade the majority to believe that the few are actually having EM education at their peril, apparently without knowing that second-language education, as shown in many papers in this volume, is already a trend in many parts of the world (See Lüdi, Genesee, Coyle, Wolff, Gajo & Serra and Housen in this volume).

Hong Kong people's aspiration of achieving a good measure of biliteracy and trilingualism in the course of having a quality education is by no means peculiar and out of the ordinary. In fact it is becoming a common expectation in the European Union and many parts of the world like Canada. The way forward is to confront the challenge embodied in the language agenda and to seek and develop a technology of second-language education such as language immersion and/or Content and Language Integrated Learning and to make an appropriate form of bilingual education accessible to all those people of Hong Kong who aspire to have it. This author is confident that a few decades down the new millennium, as far as MoI-based school type is concerned, the norm in the public education sector of Hong Kong will be neither CM schools nor EM schools. Of course there will be a small number of such schools in Hong Kong, but the infrastructural forces will select plurilingual schools that are able to develop a good combined use of Cantonese, Putonghua and English to deliver a quality education. The challenge to bilingual education advocates is to facilitate their coming into being.

Endnote 1

§16. The medium of instruction bears significantly upon the quality of education offered at post-primary level. Pupils coming from primary schools where they have been taught in the medium of Cantonese have a grievous burden put on them when required to absorb new subjects through the medium of English. We recommend that Chinese become the usual language of instruction in the lower forms of secondary schools, and that English should be studied as the second language. We recommend that every effort be made to develop good textbooks for all subjects written in Chinese, to train teachers capable of instructing through the medium of Chinese, and to adopt improved techniques of language teaching for both Chinese and English. Whilst we are aware that our recommending Chinese as the language of instruction in lower secondary forms will affect the large number of children who will complete their education at Form Three level and for whom a high standard of English will not be essential to gain employment, we are nevertheless conscious of the need to maintain and improve standards in the teaching of English for those who will proceed beyond Form Three level in preparation for continuing their education at the tertiary level.

§17. With the introduction of Chinese as the medium of instruction at lower forms, greater emphasis will need to be placed on the teaching of English in the upper forms to ensure that students are given the opportunity to become genuinely bi-lingual, so obviating the need for tuition in the English language at tertiary level in their education. In this connection, we have noted that many countries in Southeast Asia have accepted the need for bi-bilingualism, and that in Hong Kong, 1974 will be the first year of the combined Certificate of Education in which candidates may select to be examined in either English or Chinese.

Endnote 2

A PROFILE OF THE PARENT RESPONDENTS OF THE SURVEYS OF 1983, 1986, 1996 & 1999

The 1983 survey on parents was part of my fieldwork conducted for my doctoral dissertation; it was conducted in June. The respondents were parents of grade five students from three primary schools located in residential areas of different socioeconomic backgrounds. The questionnaires were both distributed and collected via the school authorities. One school from an upper-middle class neighbourhood (School A) and another school from a middle class neighbourhood (School B) were each given 180 questionnaires. The one from a lower class neighbourhood (School C) was given 220 questionnaires. 143 persons from School A, 141 from School B and 120 from School C responded.

The 1986 survey on parents (re So, 1986) was conducted in August. Based on data provided by the participating schools, 285 samples were selected in a random manner and contacted. 254 successful contacts were made and 227 accepted our invitation to be interviewed. All of them were parents of students of various grades studying in the Tsuen Wan, Kwai Chung & Tsing Yi District.

The 1996 survey on parents was a self-funded effort and was conducted between November and December. Six secondary schools were approached and five agreed to distribute the questionnaire to parents of one class of Grade Seven (secondary one) students. The sampling design was that of judgment sampling and the guiding principle was to have a sample profile that had a reasonably good coverage of the spectrum of schools from Bands One to Five. This principle was fulfilled to a certain extent: Two of the five sampled schools had mostly Band One intakes, The other two had mostly Bands Two and Three intakes, and the fifth had mostly Bands Three & Four intakes. The participating schools were situated respectively in The Western District, Shatin, Shamshuipo, Tai Wai, and Un Long. A total of 225 questionnaires were sent to the schools and 186[22] were returned.

The 1999 survey on parents was also a self-funded effort and was conducted in April. Eight secondary schools were approached and five agreed to distribute the questionnaire to parents of one class of Grade Seven (secondary one) students. The sampling design was the same as the one conducted in 1996 which was that of judgment sampling, and

---

[22]   The numbers of returns from the five schools are 37, 37, 39, 36 and 37.

the guiding principle was to have a sample profile that had a reasonably good coverage of the spectrum of schools from Bands One to Five. This principle was not quite fulfilled: Four of the five participating schools had mostly Band One intakes and the fifth had mostly Bands Three & Four intakes. The participating schools were situated respectively in Yaumatei, Homantin, Kwun Tong, Tai Wai, and Tsing Yi. A total of 225 questionnaires were sent to the schools and 180[23] were returned.

Endnote 3A

The 1983 survey on students was conducted between February and June. The respondents were from the same classes (N=14) where this writer conducted classroom observation of classroom language. 550 questionnaires were sent out and 530 students responded. Half of the questionnaires were both distributed and filled in during class periods, and the rest were distributed and collected via the school authorities. In terms of entry level, 140 of the respondents were band-one students, 179 were band-two students, 174 were band three students, eleven were band-four students and one was a band-five student. The bands of twenty-five respondents were not known. In terms of sex, 374 of the respondents were female. (Two of the eight sampled schools were girls' schools, the rest were co-eds). 148 were male. The sex of eight respondents was not known. In terms of grade level, ninety respondents were from grade seven, 154 from grade eight, 197 from grade ten, and eighty-nine from grade eleven. Finally, 159 of the respondents were from two CMSs and the rest were from six ACSSs.

Endnote 3B

The 1986 survey on teachers was conducted in the second week of August in the form of a mailed questionnaire with a cover letter and a self-addressed and stamped returning envelope enclosed. A total of 300 questionnaires were sent. Four non-deliveries were recorded. 168 subjects responded. All of the respondents taught in schools in the districts of Tsuen Wan, Kwai Chung and Tsing Yi Island. Their mean age was 30.2. 78 of them were male and 81 were female. In terms of teaching experience, 43 had one to two years; 44 had three to five years; 48 had six to nine years and 33 had 10 or more years. In terms of qualifications, 73 held bachelor degrees as well as college of education diplomas; 42 had college of education diplomas, 30 had bachelor degrees, seven had teaching certificates and 16 had other qualifications.

As indicated in Endnote 5, the 1994 survey on teachers and school heads was part of a larger survey and the teacher respondents constituted only a small part of the study population (Table 11 refers).

---

[23]   The numbers of returns from the five schools are 35, 37, 39, 30 and 39.

The respondents were from a representative sample of 60 primary and 60 secondary schools. For a more detailed description of their profile, see Department of Chinese Translation and Interpretation, 1994. In the following, only basic information about the respondents cited in this paper is provided.

Because of various constraints, data on only two attributes of the school-head respondents were collected *viz.* gender and subject major. 33 of the primary school heads were male and 27 were female. 29 of them were major in Chinese language during their tertiary education and 16 were major in English language. 46 of the secondary school heads were male and 14 were female. Eight of them were major in Chinese language and six were major in English language.

As for the 61 respondents who were English panel heads of secondary schools, 22 of them were male, 39 were female. 52 of them were major in English language. In terms of their English-teaching experience, seven had one to five years; 13 had six to ten years and 42 had eleven or more.

In case of primary school teachers, out of a total of 271 who responded, 56 of the English-teacher respondents were male and 215 of them were female. 144 of them were major in the English language. In terms of teaching experience, 81 of them had one to five years, 51 had six to ten years and 140 had 11 or more years.

There were 30 Putonghua-teacher respondents from primary schools. Four of them were male and 26 were female. 18 of them had received training in teaching Putonghua. In terms of teaching experience, 20 had one to five years; seven had six to ten years and three had 11 or more years.

There were 301 English-teacher respondents from secondary schools. 97 of them were male and 204 were female. 148 of them were major in English language. In terms of teaching experience, 133 had one to five years; 77 had six to ten years and 92 had 11 or more years.

There were 20 Putonghua-teacher respondents from secondary schools. Three of them were male and 17 were female. 17 had received training in teaching Putonghua. In terms of teaching experience, 15 had one to five years; two had six to ten years and three had 11 or more years.

Endnote 4

Table A Mean Rating of H.K. Parents of Grade 5 Students on Criteria for An Ideal School 1983

Criteria	N	Mean Rating	S.D.
Quality of the Teaching Staff	404	2.72	0.57
Students' English Language Standards	404	2.49	0.59
Endowment & Equipment of the School	403	2.39	0.74
Students' Chinese Language Standards	403	2.23	0.66
Prestige of the School	403	2.11	0.88
Performance in Public Exams	404	2.06	0.84
Whether English Textbooks are used	396	1.38	1.07
Whether Chinese Textbooks are used	397	1.30	1.04

N=404 (Self Administered Questionnaire Survey)

Table B Mean Rating of H.K. Parents of Secondary School Students of Criteria for An Ideal School 1986

Criteria	N	Mean Rating	S.D.
Quality of the Teaching Staff	227	1.5	0.6
Students' English Language Standards	227	1.1	0.7
Endowment & Equipment of the School	227	1.1	0.7
Students' Chinese Language Standards	227	0.6	0.9
Prestige of the School	---	---	---
Performance in Public Exams	227	0.7	1.0
Whether English Textbooks are used	227	0.9	0.8
Whether Chinese Textbooks are used	227	0.4	0.9
Whether Chinese is used for Instruction	227	0.5	0.9
Whether English is used for Instruction	227	0.8	0.9

N=227 (Questionnaire-based Interviews)

Table C Mean Rating of H.K. Parents of Secondary One Students of Criteria for An Ideal School 1996

Criteria	N	Mean Rating	S.D.
Quality of the Teaching Staff	186	4.60	0.63
Students' English Language Standards	186	4.51	0.62
Prestige of the School	184	4.33	0.76
Whether English Textbooks are used	186	4.21	0.70
Whether English is used for Instruction	185	4.04	0.91
Endowment & Equipment of the School	183	3.98	0.76
Performance in Public Exams	185	3.78	0.83
Students' Chinese Language Standards	181	3.41	0.77
Whether Chinese Textbooks are used	182	3.30	0.86
Whether Cantonese is used for Instruction	184	2.89	1.10

N=186 (Self-Administered Questionnaire Survey). The figures are the nummber of response to the item.

Table D **Mean Rating of H.K. Parents of Secondary One Students of Criteria for An Ideal School 1999**

Criteria	N	Mean Rating	S.D.
Quality of the Teaching Staff	180	4.63	0.68
Students' English Language Standards	179	4.45	0.79
Prestige of the School	179	4.36	0.79
Students' Chinese Language Standards	178	4.29	0.81
Performance in Public Exams	179	4.22	0.86
Endowment & Equipment of the School	177	4.15	0.79
Whether English Textbooks are used	179	4.10	0.87
Whether English is used for Instruction	177	4.08	0.93
Whether Chinese Textbooks are used	178	3.67	0.95
Whether Cantonese is used for Instruction	179	3.49	1.01

N=180 (Self-Administered Questionnaire Survey). The figures are the number of response to the item.

Endnote 5

The Education and Manpower Branch commissioned in March 1994 a research team based in The Hong Kong Polytechnic University to carry out the captioned Survey in order to provide one form of input to the Education Commission Working Group on Language Proficiency for its deliberation on ways of enhancing the helping factors which promote language proficiency in schools and removing the hindering factors.

The survey was conducted between April and June 1994. It seeks the views on the current students' and recent graduates' levels of language proficiency of Chinese, English and Putonghua from five categories of people: (1) educators, (2) students and (3) their parents, in primary, secondary and tertiary sectors; (4) graduates from secondary and tertiary sectors, and (5) their employers.

In exploring and identifying the helping and hindering factors, attention is focused on the presence and/or absence of these factors in formal education, especially in the primary and secondary sectors.

The samples of students and educators are drawn from the study population in a statistically random manner. On the other hand, the samples of graduates and parents are drawn from the sampled schools and tertiary institutions, while the samples of employers are drawn from the sampled graduates.

Altogether 7,228 people from a sample comprising 60 primary schools, 60 secondary schools and all seven UPGC-funded tertiary institutions were surveyed (see Table 11). A report of the findings was submitted to the aforementioned Working Party in July 1994.

Table E **The Sample of the 1994 Survey**

Category	Primary	Secondary	Tertiary	Total
Principal	60	60	---	120
Chinese Panel Chairman	59	59	---	118
English Panel Chairman	58	61	---	119
Chinese Teacher	254	280	---	534
English Teacher	275	302	---	577
Putonghua Teacher	30	20	---	50
Lecturer	---	---	212* (Year 1: 131) (Other: 81)	212
Student	1,375(P5)	2,409** (S1: 1,460) (S6: 949)	213(Y1)	3,997
Parent	360(P1-P6)	365*** (S1, S3, S5)	---	725
Graduate	---	245(S5)	210	455
Employer	---	138(S5)	183	321
Total	2,471	3,939	818	7,228

*131 were students in the first year of their university education. The rest (81) were from other years.

**1,460 were S1 students, 949 were S6 students.

***The figure covers S1, S3 & S5 students.

11 Defining Taiwanese Mandarin

Shouhsin Teng
National Taiwan Normal University

Taiwan is a truly plurilinguistic community. Mandarin Chinese, Southern Min Chinese, Hakka Chinese speakers, as well as Austronesian languages are spoken on this mountainous island where cross-linguistic interactions are common.

This paper attempts to examine Taiwanese Mandarin (cf. Kubler, 1985), which has emerged recently as a *lingua franca* on the island. Specifically it will focus on the syntactic features of this spoken variety of Mandarin with an aim to clarify whether this variety is a pidgin or a creole, as defined in Hymes (1974). This paper will propose that Hymes' bipartite system to define languages in contact is not an adequate system, at least as far as Taiwanese Mandarin is concerned.

This paper attempts to demonstrate that mainland China. Taiwanese Mandarin is a continuum. At one end of the continuum there is the non-native variety which embodies the presence of many southern Min syntactic features and a highly unstable Mandarin vocabulary. At the other end of the continuum there is the variety spoken by native speakers, which show significant influence from southern Min and departure from the norms of Putonghua spoken on.

Sampling from both written and oral sources abused prominent public figures in Taiwan will be employed to document and substantiate the demonstration.

1. Taiwan as a Plurilinguistic Community

Taiwan is a truly plurilinguistic community. The native Taiwanese have their own Austronesian languages; the Fujian people brought to Taiwan their southern Min Chinese dialects; the Kejia people brought their Hakka dialects to the island; the Japanese ruled the island from 1895-1945 and brought their language to the island; and finally in 1945 when the Nationalist government moved to Taiwan, it brought not only the national official language, Mandarin, but also various other Chinese dialects to the island. It is truly an island of many tongues. The statistics below are taken from Huang (1993: 21), against a rough count of the then entire population of 20 million.

Southern Min origin	73.3%
Mainland origin[1]	13%
Hakka origin	12%
Formosan origin[2]	1.7%

A natural question to ask then is how people on such a small island with so many languages and dialects communicate with each other? Do they have at their disposal all the languages or dialects they need for their livelihood? Or do they have a *lingua franca*? If so, how did this language come about?

A simple explanation is that before the Japanese left the island in 1945, Japanese was the *lingua franca* (and had been for about 50 years), and after they left, and after the Nationalist government moved in after the war, the *lingua franca* became *de facto* Mandarin Chinese.

2. The Mandarin Movement

Thanks to the unprecedented success of the Mandarin movement in Taiwan since 1945, as promoted through the organisation of the Mandarin Promotion Commission, Mandarin as the official language has penetrated into every inch of land on Taiwan. Such success is not reported or observed on Mainland China in spite of the enormous amount of effort spent on the Putonghua movement there. As a result of the Mandarin movement in Taiwan, communication throughout the entire island plus offshore islands proved to be a simple and smooth task. The bonding effect via Mandarin has taken the nation to great agricultural and industrial strengths. The so-called economic miracle in Taiwan would not have been possible

---

[1]   This category refers mainly to those who came to reside in Taiwan at the time of the Nationalist government retreat to Taiwan in 1949.

[2]   This category refers to the native tribes who were resident in Taiwan/Formosa before the Chinese/Han immigration, consisting of nine tribes with different languages/dialects.

without the development of a high level of education which is delivered through the medium of Mandarin.

3. Erosion of Mother Tongues

But there was a price to pay for the tremendous success of the Mandarin movement. The success of Mandarin was built on the suppression of local dialects and languages. Only Mandarin was to be used at schools, in various media, and governmental organisations. The native Formosan languages and non-Mandarin Chinese dialects, the so-called mother tongues, eroded, especially in and around the capital of Taiwan, Taipei. The most severely affected are native Formosans who reside in the plains, who have more or less lost their native languages. Next came the Hakka people in urban areas. Thanks to the strongholds of Southern Min (usually referred to as Taiwanese) in southern Taiwan, the dialect has retained its vigour, but only in the south.

4. Emergence of Taiwanese Mandarin

What takes the place of mother tongues when they decline? Mandarin, but not the kind of Mandarin spoken in Beijing. It is not the equivalent of the Putonghua in Mainland China. Thus the label Taiwanese Mandarin came to pass. Contributions towards the formation of Taiwanese Mandarin came mostly, if not entirely, from Southern Min, i.e., Taiwanese. Cheng (1985) attributes the shaping of Taiwanese Mandarin to (1) a drift towards common Chinese characteristics, (2) borrowings from local dialects or native languages, and (3) internal adjustments. Formosan and Hakka elements in Taiwanese Mandarin have not been explicitly documented in Cheng (1985). For the first time in the recent history of Taiwan, Taiwanese Mandarin is the mother tongue of many, especially in northern Taiwan where the capital city of Taipei, hence the central administration, is situated.

5. Is Taiwanese Mandarin a Pidgin or a Creole?

Taiwanese Mandarin can be defined as a mixture of the linguistic structures of Southern Min and Mandarin[3]. Following

---

[3]   This is in addition to the internally motivated structures such as the

the polar dichotomy of Pidgin and Creole as stipulated in the classic Hymes model (1974), Taiwanese Mandarin is bit of both and not entirely either. It is a Creole because it is the mother tongue of a sector of the population in Taiwan, and for them, it has its own well-defined phonological, lexical, and syntactic structures. At the same time, it is a pidgin because, for the other sectors of the Taiwanese population, it is created more or less spontaneously each time. In the latter category, the linguistic structures are not well defined and vary with each individual, giving rise to a wide range of the Taiwanese Mandarin features.

6. Taiwanese Mandarin as a continuum

The concept of continuum, as vigorously defended in Rickford (1987), captures the state of Taiwanese Mandarin in Taiwan rather well, albeit to be tightened further to do justice to Taiwanese Mandarin. At one end of the continuum, we have stable, well-defined Taiwanese Mandarin, which is the mother tongue to a sector of the population. This lect is at the same time different from Putonghua in Mainland China and from other varieties of Taiwanese Mandarin at the other end of the continuum, though it does contain linguistic structures from southern Min. At the other end of the continuum we have spontaneously created Taiwanese Mandarin, which does not serve as anyone's native language.

However, unlike the situation as reported in Rickford (1987), there is no social mobility along the continuum, in the sense that one does not move from the lower spectrum of the continuum to the higher spectrum as one is elevated to better social status. In fact, there is no exemplar model of Taiwanese Mandarin in general. Take the speech of Chen Shuibian, the new president of Taiwan as an example. His speech has remained more or less the same over the last two decades or so since he started his political career. Of course, considering the present make-up of the society in Taiwan, he may be consciously creating his own linguistic image. In today's Taiwan, following the Beijing linguistic model can cost him or any other politically prominent figures their

---

you-meiyou Q sentences, see Cheng (1985).

political careers. Moreover, with only the exception of schoolteachers, nobody seems to be concerned with one's own speech, however different it is from the Beijing model.

The following is an attempt to define the details of the Taiwanese Mandarin continuum with reference to only the syntactic structures.

7. Syntactic Features of Taiwanese Mandarin

Previous literature on the characteristics of Taiwanese Mandarin has heavily concentrated on the phonological structures and occasionally lexical items. Only Kubler (1985) offers a balanced study. Yet it mentions only a handful of straightforward items without going into the real workings of the structures concerned. This paper shall attempt to define the continuum syntactically.

Basically and syntactically, we can define Taiwanese Mandarin as exhibiting a varying degree of mixing Mandarin and Southern Min syntactic structures with basically modified Mandarin phonology and modified lexical items. Assuming that phonology and lexical items remain constant, more Min than Mandarin syntax defines Taiwanese Mandarin at the lower spectrum of the continuum and more Mandarin than Min syntax defines the other end of the continuum. This claim is elaborated below.

a) The 有/*You* marker

有 (meaning to 'have') is probably the trademark[4] for Taiwanese Mandarin. But its discussions have been rather lopsided and oversimplified. First let us look at some linguistic data.[5]

    i. a. 我真的有看到他進來。(I really did see him come in.)

        b. 他有沒有來？ (Did he come?)

    ii. 我有像她那麼厲害就好了！

       (I really wish I were as smart as she is!!)

---

[4]   Another equally well known, prominent trademark of Taiwanese Mandarin is the heavy use of sentential particles such as 啦/*la*: 多謝啦！(Thank you!) 好了啦！(Alright!).

[5]   Many of the data are from my own observations, but an Ntnu BBS posting called 漫談台灣通俗語法 ([作者] Gonzaley (UP TO YOU) [看板] ENG91A [標題] [閒聊] 慢談臺灣通俗文法[時間] Fri May 26 20:18:08 2000) is consulted and used with the author's email permission.

   iii. 沒考上啦！他沒有在認真讀書嘛！ (He did not pass the examination. He was not really working very hard at it.)

   iv. a. 年齡差個三、四歲也沒有所謂。(It would not matter even if the age discrepancy were 3 or 4 years.)

      b. 這個有夠貴！ (This is really expensive!)

(i) illustrates the occurrence of *You* in Taiwanese Mandarin in the context of action verbs where it is not called for in standard Mandarin, corresponding to the Mandarin word 了/*le*.[6] This is the only occurrence of *You* that is referred to in most literature dealing with Taiwanese Mandarin, but the scope of Taiwanese Mandarin *You* is much wider than this. In (ii) it occurs with a state verb; in (iii) it occurs with the progressive aspect; and in (iv) it occurs with a stative idiomatic expression.

You as in (i) is the most stable of the four features and is a built-in feature of the most standard Taiwanese Mandarin, which separates Taiwanese Mandarin from standard Mandarin. It occurs in the highest spectrum of the continuum, as observed in the speech of Dr. Ma Yingjiu, the mayor of Taipei, who has no Min roots. To facilitate the following discussion, *You* (i) will be referred to as perfective *You*, *You* (ii) as stative *You*, and *You* (iii) as existential *You*. *You* (iv) is a totally different element; it will be tentatively referred to here as 'blanket *You*', in the sense that it corresponds to the southern Min *You* (*u*), whose negative counterpart is 無 (*bo*). It is used regardless of the syntactic or the semantic contexts and occurs in the lowest spectrum of the Taiwanese Mandarin continuum.

Thus the examples above illustrate a syntactic demarcation of the various phases, not stages, of the continuum. At the lowest end, there is a blanket replacement of Min *u* with *You* when one switches code to Mandarin. At the highest end of the spectrum, *You* is consistently used only where standard Mandarin *le* is used. Taiwanese Mandarin continuum is therefore defined on the relaxation of the syntactic and semantic constraints of *You*. This is the central theme of this paper. The pertinent rules or constraints are presented below.

---

[6]   This is the so-called verbal 'le' as distinguished from the sentential 'le' (天氣好了).

You Rule 1: Replace Min *u* with *You* where *u* attributes action verbs

You Rule 2: Replace Min *u* with *You* where *u* attributes stative verbs

You Rule 3: Replace Min *u* with *You* where *u* attributes aspects

You Rule 4: Replace Min *u* with *You*

The interactions between these rules and the Taiwanese Mandarin continuum is illustrated below. We may informally state that on the far-left end, we observe verbatim translation from southern Min and on the far-right free translation.

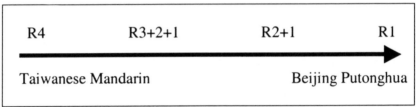

Figure 1 The Use of You in the Taiwanese Mandarin-Putonghua Continuum

b) 說/*Shuo* as a marker

i.   他覺得(*juede*)說應該花錢的時候就要花。[7] (He is of the opinion that money must be spent when it is necessary to do so.)

ii. 我們出去比比看說![8] (Well, why don't we go outside and size it up!!)

iii. 他突然發現到說銀行的存款不見了。(He suddenly discovered that the savings at the bank had disappeared.)

In standard Mandarin, *Shuo* as found in the examples above does not occur. This is Southern Min syntax. In (i), we have a complementation structure following the verb *juede*. In the sentence, *Shuo* acts as a complementiser or a complementation

---

[7]   Other *juede* -related verbs include 想*xiang*, to think; 感覺*ganjue*, to feel that; 認為*renwei*, to have the opion that; 以為*yiwei*, to make a wrong assumption that; and even *jiang* for some speakers.

[8]   The BBS postings also list similar items, e.g., (i) 你快過來說! (why don't you come quickly!)(ii) 你給我安靜說! (Why don't you shut up!) (iii) 過去看一下說! (Why don't you go over and take a look!) The posting does not mention such cases as given in footnote 5.

marker, corresponding rather closely to English 'that'. A similar structure appears in early vernacular Mandarin literature, e.g., 某某人說道…… (somebody said that...) but has disappeared in modern Mandarin. However, *Shuo* in the example (ii) is not a complementation marker, as it is in Taiwanese Mandarin sentences (i) and (iii).

Shuo in (ii) is different. It is an utterance-concluding marker, a discourse marker devoid of any lexical import. It does not occur after regular declarative sentences, only after threatening or suggestive imperatives[9]. Its Min parent is the marker 講 '*jiang*; to utter), which occurs also sentence-initially, but not (yet) in Taiwanese Mandarin. *Jiang* in Southern Min is a generic utterance verb, not *shuo*. This may explain the fact that Taiwanese Mandarin uses *jiang* as a primary utterance verb and the lower-ranking *shuo* as a discourse marker. Wang et al. (2000) also reports the occurrence of *shuo* as a sentence-initial discourse marker, though the present author does not share the analysis in that light.

Neither the case (i) nor (ii) is observed in the highest spectrum of the Taiwanese Mandarin continuum, e.g., not in Dr. Ma Yingjiu's speech. We can thus stipulate the following.

Shuo R1: Add *Shuo* to follow complementation verbs such as *juede*

Shuo R2: Add *Shuo* to suggestive imperative sentences

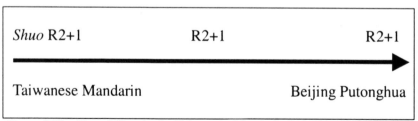

Figure 2 The Use of Shuo in the Taiwanese Mandarin-Putonghua Continuum

The following syntactic features of Taiwanese Mandarin can be analysed in a similar fashion. They are listed below with minimal glosses in standard Mandarin and in English to avoid repetition.

---

[9] I understand that this definition is a bit too severe. We should make allowance for more neutral imperatives.

c. 行/*Xing* as a modal verb

1) 這本書不行看. (這本書可不能/不許看) (You mustn't read this book!)

2) 這幾個字不行打哩! (這幾個字打不出來!) (I cannot input these characters!)

3) 你不行唱歌! (你不可以/不許唱歌!) (You mustn't sing!)

4) 不行你去! (你去不行！) (You mustn't be the one to go!)

5) 你不行那麼快! (You mustn't walk that fast!)

6) 你不行高興![10] (You mustn't feel so good about it!)

d. 輸/*Shu* with an overly extended 'range'

1) 陳水扁在那場選舉中輸了市長一職。(Chen Shuibian lost the mayor's seat at that election.)

2) 巴西隊輸了一場重要的比賽。 (Brazil lost an important match.)

3) 他們搶輸了地盤後,...... (他們在搶地盤的事情上失利後,......) (After they lost the territory…)

e. 不錯/*Bucuo* as a lexicalised state

1) 這本書不錯看喲！ (This is an interesting book to read.)

2) 那間店的牛肉不錯吃！ (That restaurant makes delicious beef.)

3) 馬友友的大提琴演奏真不錯聽. (Yoyo Ma's cello performance is super.)

f. 用/*Yong* with overly extended instrument

1) 不用搬椅子。我可以用站的吃。(No need to get me a chair! I can eat it standing.)

2) 不值錢的東西也是用買來的。 (Even worthless things were purchased.)

3) 來不及了！趕快用跑的去。 (Hurry up, you'll be late! Run!!)

g. **Verbal fillers and discourse markers**

1) 對呀: 我叫沈律偉. 對呀... (My name is Shen Luwei. '*Right*'!)

2) 然後: 我叫XXX, 今年X歲,...對呀!...然後...我是從XX來的啦! 然後..., 我希望...... (My name is XXX and X-years old. '*Right*', '*Then*'. I am from XX. '*Then*', I hope…)

---

[10]   These six examples are taken from BBS postings.

3) 那: 那…, 我叫 XXX, 今年 X 歲,...對呀!...那…我是從 XX 來的啦! …那…我希望…… (My name is XXX and X-years old. '*Right*', '*So*', I am from XX.' '*So*', I hope…)

h. Intrusive 來/*Lai*

1) 無線電視台主播: '回到<<整點新聞>>. 今天早上,西門町鬧區傳出來了一起火警...' (Cable TV: … This morning, a fire broke out in the busy section of Ximending…)

2) 無線電視台主播:'…突然,右邊的路口轉出來了一輛箱型車,娃娃車司機...' (Cable TV: … Suddenly, a van emerged from the right, and the driver of the school van…)

i. Sentence-initial tag questions

1) (高雄市長謝長廷): 會不會我選民進黨黨主席讓人以為……? ((Xie Changting, major of Kaohsiung): Is it possible that people will think that my running for the chairmanship of the DPP party will …?)

2) 會不會他不來我們就不能去? (Is it possible that we won't be able to go unless he comes first?)

3) 要不要我們明天一起去陽明山? (Shall we go to Yangming Mountain together tomorrow?)

4) 可以不可以你們兩個人先過去看一下? (Can you two go and take a look first?)

5) 好不好我們來聽一首歌? (Shall we listen to a song?)

8. Concluding remarks

The political arena in Taiwan is such that votes determine everything and language has become a key instrument in gaining voters' confidence and eventually their votes. Insisting on or maintaining the traditional standards or values no longer attracts votes. This has given a tremendous boost to the social and political status of Southern Min, which in turn has rapidly shaped the rising fortune of Taiwanese Mandarin in Taiwan. This paper attempts to quantify Taiwanese Mandarin in terms of its syntactic features, and has suggested ways of defining the continuum of Taiwanese Mandarin in purely syntactic terms.

It has to be noted that the syntactic continuum does not coincide with the phonological continuum. That is, one can be employing a higher spectrum of the syntactic continuum yet at the same time employing a lower spectrum of the phonological continuum. President Chen Shuibian is a good example of this mix. It is hoped that phonological and lexical studies of Taiwanese Mandarin can be carried out in ways suggested in this paper, so that a better definition of Taiwanese Mandarin will be established in a not too distant future.

12 Beyond the Textbooks: Kinds of Sociolinguistic Variation in International Cities

Björn H. Jernudd

Hong Kong Baptist University

Sociolinguistics textbooks and the Hong Kong student

Internationally distributed textbooks in sociolinguistics that are conveniently available to me rely on examples that are very remote from my Hong Kong students' experience. The undergraduate students do not have the background knowledge to understand the social realities that provide much stock in trade textbook content about language behaviour in remote places. To these students, the Lower East Side of New York, Norwich, Glasgow, Detroit, the American Black experience, the Quebec situation, and so on, are mere names that may trigger no more than a recall of a rather fuzzy impression of the Americas and Great Britain. But this impression is usually without any specific knowledge of locality or society that facilitates classroom interaction. What are teachers of sociolinguistics in Hong Kong going to do?

The topic of the linguistic variable is a good example of this conundrum. An undergraduate course in sociolinguistics anywhere cannot really omit this topic. Yet, this is what teachers usually experience when teaching this topic: Students in Hong Kong do not know what is 'class' or the living reality that a 'socio-economic index' describes. Teachers can take time in class to try to explain as best they can the class concept in relation to situations in foreign lands and peoples' living conditions, and/or they can attempt a discussion whether there is 'class' in Hong Kong. Both courses of action take disproportionate time relative to the pace of the textbook. They are also radically different options. The first option at least has some justification in an English Major because it teaches about class that *is* important in the UK.

Project work forces students to come face to face with variable language use. I teach an English Major programme at the Hong Kong Baptist University and local English usage would seem relevant. However, is the linguistic variable the critical concept that should be introduced to deal with the situation of English in Hong Kong? I would think not. Linguistic variability described in standard textbooks does not characterise differences between people's ways of using English in Hong Kong. Study of alternation of pronunciation of a particular phoneme has been shown to be useful to describe 'the developmental pattern of learners' of English in Hong Kong (Wong & Setter n.d.) but social meaning is not carried by some particular variables across the widely varying manifestations of English voices heard in Hong Kong. Instead, variety, accent, even foreign accent if understood as an interrelated bundle of linguistic features, would be relevant concepts – albeit not developed into the delicate matter of single-measured linguistic variability for a subject at introductory level at least.

As concerns Cantonese, which is spoken by the great majority of the people of Hong Kong, there is a well-known set of phonological variables. When students in my course do their team projects on these variables, the outcomes of each team, which work on a different variable of their choice, are always the same. The data show correlations of variability with age, education and gender. The students usually bring up 'lazy pronunciation' to signal the prescriptive purist norm that some educators and Chinese language authorities tout for Cantonese. However, class and indices of socioeconomically stratified living conditions do not come up in their analysis. The situation in Hong Kong is simply different from standard examples in dominant texts in regard to the social dimension.

With age as the major correlating factor and gender a modulating influence, what remains to be said about the reason for studying the variable is that there is change in speech. Since Cantonese is a spoken language paralleled by a differently anchored written language, change in speech announces itself as the cause of the patterns of variability and itself demands explanation. The prescriptive norm has been implicated as a retarding, conservative reaction; and education has been implicated as a channel for communicating that norm. A particular education or 'more' education would produce a higher awareness of the correctness norm which speakers would switch on in the more 'formal', as my students would say, speech situations.

There is another interesting and I think now recurring result from the student projects. Several projects have produced data that show what appears to be a reversal of language change, on the Cantonese variable /g^w/. Why is that? Students suggest that migration has brought people with such speech into Hong Kong that counters the change in progress. Students also suggest that the very rapidly expanding educational system in Hong Kong has successfully mediated the prescriptive norms to such an extent that they have not only retarded but also (temporarily, for some speakers) reversed the language change in progress. Bauer and Benedict (1997: 336) already suggested the possibility of reintroduction of the labialised velars because of 'the introduction and greater use of Putonghua in Hong Kong after 1997'.

Their project findings may not bring the students closer to the class concept although they now do begin to appreciate processes of language change – that reflect *something* in societal organisation, most forcefully developmental change. The international textbooks and local teaching opportunity meet at least on the utility of variability data to understand processes of social developmental change in relation to language change.

Several scenarios about the teaching of sociolinguistic topics in Hong Kong present themselves. If the goal is an in-depth area study of the major English-speaking communities overseas, in Britain, North America, and Australia, sociolinguistics in its internationally received form, including the international textbooks, fits in well with students' learning about social organisation. If the goal is undergraduate teaching about language and society in Hong Kong, and especially for the English Majors, sociolinguistics instructors need to develop their own localised teaching materials and textbooks. There is a *Course Guide* on *Language and Society in Hong Kong* for The Open University of Hong Kong's subject A331 written by Dr. Kingsley Bolton with the help of other sociolinguists in Hong Kong for Hong Kong students (Open University, 2000). This is the right way to go.

Sociolinguistics textbooks and trans-city realities

The prominent internationally distributed textbooks do not appear to reflect much of what is exciting about the city as a plurilingual hub in today's world. The sociolinguistics (sub-)discipline appears to have settled down to predictable content that textbooks reflect. There may be a value to presenting the same content in basic training. Still, if one were to introduce contemporary 'hub'-related topics into a textbook, what would they be?

Hong Kong is a spatially significant plurilingual hub. Hub is a spatial concept. What is it about hubs that we may wish to bring to students' attention – and to our own?

Hong Kong is spatially differentiated in a manner that implicates linguistic differentiation. Spatial differentiation is of course the subject matter of urban geography and sociology (see, e.g., Spates & Macionis, 1987) but language is not a highlight for these disciplines. In the sociolinguistics literature, space and spatial differentiation are concepts that are often used (taken for granted perhaps), or implied, certainly known by researchers and authors, but not normally overtly discussed. In Hong Kong, I suggest that no one would dispute the following socio-spatial facts:

a)   There is The Peak, a strongly expatriate, upper income, formerly access-proscribed area with a high incidence of use of English and an expectation of high English proficiency among people.

b)   There is the Mid-levels housing district on Hong Kong Island, not formerly proscribed but heavily upper income and expatriate, professional, with a clear English cityscape of services.

c)   The Central district on Hong Kong Island is a professional services and banking, work, and tourist space; English has a distinct presence because of the character of the work which links Hong Kong to the world. Most professional foreigners work in Central, I would think, and their shared language in and with others in Hong Kong is English. The headquarters of the most important departments of the bilingual civil service are concentrated in Central and nearby districts; there are hotels, shopping areas of particular character, and so on.

d)   Tsimshatsui is tourist space on the mainland facing the island's Central district (and famously connected by the Star Ferry) with hotels and shopping for visitors whose shared language when in Hong Kong (and when not from China) is English.

More items can be added to the list but I wish to proceed to address the question: What about the rapidly changing communicative patterns and repertoires in other Hong Kong neighbourhoods, such as the villages, in the New Town housing districts in the New Territories, and so on? And what about the concurrent changes in peoples' living arrangements for shopping, leisure, and children's care, etc., which condition communicative opportunities? Space is use of space and people live and communicate in these spaces in particular ways. Hong Kong has been and is changing in a spectacular manner in use of space, and consequently in communication patterns.

Furthermore, there are people who have to be mentioned in sociolinguistics teaching in Hong Kong who have their counterparts in other hubs around the world. These groups share in transnational, or should I rather say trans-city, communications and movements. Trans-city phenomena are critical to understanding the contemporary city and Hong Kong (Smith, 2001). I have in mind investigating phenomena such as:

Firstly, the communicative patterns of the domestic workers. Do they live lives communicatively confined to the locality of Hong Kong? I would assume not: their daily lives embrace communication with fellow domestic workers in the Middle East, Singapore and elsewhere, kin who have emigrated to North America, and with home networks in different parts of the Philippines. Their working, family-personal and leisure lives are interdependent with their globally dispersed communication partners. Their communicative networks extend in complex patterns far beyond Hong Kong. The domestic worker networks link with religious, labour rights, and other complex trans-city networks. Language use is delicately intertwined with the structure of these complex networks.[1] Other examples are Chinese ethnic diasporas, Koreatown in Los Angeles with its domestic and overseas networks, and migrant seasonal labour anywhere.

---

[1]   Constable (1997) describes the situation of Filipina domestic workers in Hong Kong, with references.

Secondly, professional expatriate groups (from America, Europe, Australia, South Asia, and Southeast Asia...). Expatriate networks exemplify transnational educational behaviour, local reproduction of country-of-origin language in ethnic-specific social and business activities, etc.

Thirdly, the many families now in Hong Kong who have members who migrated into Hong Kong – and left Hong Kong? Migrated from Hong Kong overseas – and returned?

The city is truly a plurilingual hub. As an interactive space, what is the city like? Cities show very different realities. In the then and now, just think of Hong Kong's rapid change, for example, with renewed immigration from China since the early 1980s; or think of the two demographic changes closely related to Hong Kong's change of sovereignty in 1997: the globalised Hong Kong families, and the (relatively speaking) massive outflow of British civil servants and the consequences of these changes on people and communications.

In making comparisons across the world, many cities may appear to be very similar in their international function, yet there are profound differences between them from region to region. For example, today's American city has its quite distinct areas of migrant activity with profound language correlatives, its Korea-town and Chinatown, which are local as much as they are 'hubs' far beyond the city; with profound linguistic consequences locally and beyond at points of origin, return and exchange, and interdependently so (cf. the Mixtec 'bifocal border crossers' (Smith, 2001: 160); or the Hmong refugees from Laos (Smith, 2001: 175)). In Sweden, migrants were settled according to national and city planning; one outcome was Rinkeby, an all-migrants suburb in Stockholm in which people created their own Swedish speech variety (Bijvoet, 2000).

As far as social change and language communication are concerned, Hong Kong has it all (for an inspiring overview of change in Hong Kong by a social geographer, cf. Li, 1997). There is intensive housing development, with movement of people to new towns, that condition daily-weekly movements, that sharpen socio-spatial residential patterns, that determine choice of schools and entertainment, that perhaps even push some people across the 'local' border. All these processes have consequences on language communication. There are neighbourhoods of course. Where I live, the children meet in the park. Growing up together has profound linguistic consequences. Different people share activities differently. I have some random questions:

a)   What are the villages like today? Are they as trans-city as they are local? What is the role of language variety in reconstituting and safeguarding village identity and village rights? Perhaps study of some village-based networks in the New Territories of Hong Kong will reveal intriguing transnational links, also with language consequences?

b)   Where are the migrant concentrations? There are sediments of older and younger migrant settlement areas in Hong Kong – who moves out, who stays? With what linguistic correlatives? What are migrants' movements and communication networks?

c)   What is happening on the other islands inhabited by a sizable population like Lama and Lantau? Are they ethnic foci for festivals, or more?

d)   How do the New Towns constitute themselves in terms of social communication?

e)   Profoundly important are of course professional networks, business networks, which precisely by their trans-city nature require international communication in the shared English language; and national communication in Putonghua. What do we know about these communications?

f)   What about the transnational and trans-city NGO networks, the greens or human rights organisations, the entertainment networks?

How do we capture the transnational networks in Hong Kong, especially in relation to their linguistic consequences? We sociolinguists need to rethink what we teach about the linguistically complex plurilingual and intra-linguistically differentiated city hub environments. These are the environments in which most university students find themselves. Therefore, these are the environments they need to understand in order to make a difference themselves in their lives after graduation.

13 Patterns and Variations in Language Attitudes and Language Choices among Bruneians

Mukul Saxena & Peter Sercombe
Universiti Brunei Darussalam

Brunei Darussalam is a plurilingual nation. Not only do a number of varieties of Malay occur, but also a number of other distinct Austronesian indigenous languages, codes of Chinese, Arabic and English, as well as other East and South Asian languages. There have been a number of sociolinguistic studies regarding individual ethnolinguistic groups in Brunei (see annotated bibliography, Martin, 1996a). There have also been studies of language choice among these groups (for example, Jones et al., 1993; Jones, 1995; Ozog, 1996; Martin, 1998; McLellan, 1997).

For the last ten to fifteen years, Brunei has been undergoing rapid changes as a result of a number of intra- and international developments, for example, the implementation of a bilingual education system and the availability of satellite television as well as the Internet. Such changes and their effects require continual reappraisal of patterns and variations in language attitudes and language choices among Bruneians. This paper, which is part of an ongoing study (see Saxena et al., 2000), makes use of primary data to consider patterns and variations in language attitudes and language choices among Bruneians, in particular among the younger generation.

In providing sociolinguistic profiles of Brunei, earlier research by Jones et al. (1993), Jones (1995), Ozog (1996) and Martin (1998) drew their data largely, though not exclusively, from questionnaire surveys. McLellan and Noor Azam (1998) have further built on this body of research relying mainly on participant observation and interviews.

Our study draws data from case studies and surveys conducted by 16 undergraduate students studying for a degree in

TESL (Teaching English as a Second Language) at the Universiti Brunei Darussalam. It devolves from a cumulative process which was part of a course on Bilingualism during which the students were inducted into theories, methodologies and practices within the field of Bilingualism. In order to develop a deeper understanding of the main issues involved, students were asked to develop their own bilingual profiles on the basis of how these are shaped by patterns of language use in their families, communities, and by the national *Dwibahasa* (Bilingual) Education Policy. The end result was a project report. For their individual research projects students employed an eclectic methodological approach involving 'Language Diaries' spanning two weeks, 'Questionnaires', 'Interviews' and 'Ethnographic Observations'. The present study reanalyses the questionnaires they administered, as well as drawing insights from general classroom discussions on their findings, and the discourses they produced in their report writing.[1]

We begin, in the next section, with a brief outline of relevant historical events in Brunei. Subsequently, we present the most pertinent features of the survey findings. Our main focus in this paper, however, is on qualitative dimensions as these have been found to reveal more about language attitudes, values and choices in our data. We continue by considering some of the underlying reasons behind these with respect to a number of current and historical processes. Finally, we summarise our overall findings in relation to the debate about the reproduction theorists' position that dominant and hegemonic ideologies are impenetrable (cf. Gal, 1998).

A Brief Historical Overview of Sociolinguistic Processes in Brunei

The following is a brief overview of significant historical processes which are relevant to the interpretation of language attitudes and language choices of Bruneians given later in this paper.

---

[1]   We are grateful to our students for allowing us to draw on these materials for the writing of this paper as well as for further use in the teaching of this course.

Table 1 **Significant Historical Processes in Brunei**

Period	Significant Historical Processes
1906	Establishment of British Residency
1906-1916	'vernacular' (i.e., Malay) schools for boys
1919	English school in Labuan with some places for Bruneians
1928	Elementary English available to govt. employees
1928	Discovery of oil; English-speaking foreigners
By 1938	Two mission schools
1951	Brunei town govt. English school; two trained English teachers from UK & Malaya
1954-1959	Brunei's education development plan using oil revenues; 133 Bruneians undergoing teacher training; expatriate teachers from Ceylon, India, Malaya, Philippines, UK & Australia
1959	Formulation of State Constitution & Language policy: Malay or Bahasa Melayu enshrined as state language (national survey reflected this choice) and re-emphasised as an essential constituent of *Melayu Islam Beraja* (MIB – Malay Islamic Monarchy)
1959-1984	Expansion in number of schools
1962	Establishment of the National Education Policy following recommendations by 1959 Baki-Chang Report of Education Commission of Brunei. Emphasis on national unity and loyalty of citizenry.
	Internal revolt: 'This is an important point in the history of education in Brunei and in the role of English in the state. Had the revolt not occurred, then Brunei would have followed the same education model as Malaysia. Today there would be no bilingual education system and Malay would be the main medium of instruction in all Bruneian schools.' (Jones 1997: 18)
1974	Implementation of Report of Brunei Education Commission: first recommendation not implemented to make Malay main medium of instruction in national primary and secondary schools. Decline in relations with Malaysia; also, absence of diplomatic relations with Malay-medium-education Indonesia; consequence was that Britain became solution for Malay-medium students at tertiary level; English-medium students had already studied there.
1984	Brunei gained full independence from British protectorate status
1985	• Implementation of National Bilingual Education System with subjects in Malay & English • Establishment of national university; programmes in Malay, English & Arabic
1988	Integration of Institute of Education with university
1991	Publication of first Brunei Malay dictionary by *Dewan Bahasa dan Pustaka* (Language & Literature Bureau)

As can be seen from the historical events listed above, since vernacular schools were first introduced in 1906 in Brunei, there has been a gradual but increasing development and dispersal of formal education, at primary, secondary and tertiary levels. These processes have been accompanied by a simultaneous dissemination of Standard Malay and English (leading to a consolidation of capital, in cultural and linguistic terms, Bourdieu 1977). Further details of individual events listed in the table above can be found in Hussainmiya (2000), Jones (1997) and Singh (1984).

Language Background & Language Use: Some Broader Trends

This section presents information regarding knowledge and use of languages reported by 125 people in surveys. These surveys were conducted by students in their broader networks in the community.

Responses to knowledge of languages in the survey were elicited on a three-point scale. A list of languages and dialects reported are provided in Table 2 below. Though not comprehensive, it is nonetheless indexical of the plurilingual nature of Brunei.

It can be seen from the table that the majority of people in the sample claim a high level of knowledge of Brunei Malay, Standard Malay and English. This is reflected in the raw scores, means and medians. In addition, the data show the descending order of numerical importance of languages claimed.

Information regarding language use was elicited on a three-point scale ('very often', 'sometimes' and 'never') with a range of interlocutors in family and non-domestic domains. Tables 3, 4 & 5 containing quantitative data on language use are provided at the end this paper.

As can be seen in Table 3, under the 'very often' category, an overwhelming number of informants choose Brunei Malay as the language that they use in the family domain, indicating the use of Standard Malay and English is insignificant. It is only under the category 'sometimes' (in Table 4) that a significant number of informants choose English; a much smaller number choose Standard Malay.

Table 2 **Languages known (N=125)**

Languages	Only a little (%)	Reasonably Well (%)	Quite well (%)	Mean	Median
Brunei Malay	12 (10)	18 (14)	95 (76)	2.7	3
Standard Malay	8(6)	27 (22)	82 (66)	2.6	3
English	14 (11)	34 (27)	72 (58)	2.5	3
Kedayan	34 (27)	22 (18)	7 (6)	1.6	1
Kampong Ayer	22 (18)	29 (23)	9 (7)	1.8	2
Tutong	16 (13)	11 (9)	11 (9)	1.9	2
Dusun	5 (4)	5 (4)	5 (4)	2	2
Belait	5 (4)	4 (3)	1 (0.8)	1.6	1.5
Bisaya	1 (0.8)	1 (0.8)	3 (2)	2.4	3
Murut	1 (0.8)	1 (0.8)	0	0	0
Iban	10 (8)	3 (2)	2 (2)	1.5	1
Hokkien	10 (8)	6 (5)	15	2.2	2
Hakka	4 (3)	1 (0.8)	5 (4)	2.1	2.5
Cantonese	15 (12)	9 (7)	4 (3)	1.6	1
Mandarin	5 (4)	10 (8)	12	2.3	2
Hainanese	3 (2)	1 (0.8)	0	1.5	1
Foochow	3 (2)	3 (2)	0	2	2
Teochew	1 (0.8)	1 (0.8)	0	1.5	1.5
Arabic	35 (28)	0	6 (5)	1.5	1

However, as we see in Table 5, in both the categories 'very often' and 'sometimes', the reported use of English with colleagues is much higher in the domains of work and education, albeit Brunei Malay is reportedly used 'very often' by a much greater percentage of informants. With respect to interaction with friends, the percentage of English used also increases but is still less than a third the amount of Brunei Malay reported. Therefore, it can be seen that Brunei Malay still remains the pre-eminent code in Brunei.

Case Studies: Language Choices, Language Attitudes & Values among Young Bruneians

In this section, we focus on three main themes relevant to this paper that emerge from students' case studies: some of the factors shaping language choices; code-switching/code-mixing; and attitudes and values associated with languages and language choices. We quote, verbatim (as in the indented texts below), representative samples of recurring discourses produced in students' writings.

Factors shaping language choices

The following statement supports the general survey finding that Brunei Malay is the predominant code in our sample.

It can be seen from the table (diary) that my first and foremost choice of language is Brunei Malay in almost all do- mains and contexts (places), with most interlocutors, and it is used to speak about most topics. This implies that for me, Brunei Malay is the predominantly used language.

However, other languages are used in conjunction with Brunei Malay. The most important of these that emerge from students' case studies include Brunei English and Standard English. It is important to note here that English in Brunei is emerging as a distinct variety (i.e., Brunei English) through a process of nativisation (see, e.g., Cane, 1993 & 1994; Mossop, 1996; Martin et al., 1996; Hjh Rosnah et al., 2000).

Regarding factors shaping language choices, Ozog (1996: 183) claims that topic is not significant in determining language choice among Bruneians. However, group discussions in the classroom and the following statements (among others) suggest that while interlocutors seem to play an important role, topic and domain are also significant.

...my language choice is determined by first and foremost who I am interlocuting with. Then other things need to be taken into account such as the domain I am in and how formal the situation is. The topic being discussed also influences which language is to be utilised.... With the people I have interviewed through the questionnaire, their language choice is similarly governed by basically the four factors above (interlocutor, domain, formality, and topic at hand).

... the language diary discloses ... that I tend to choose one language or another depending on the interlocutor and topic of conversation. Occasionally the domain, and at times, even the place (context) where the interaction takes place, also become important determiners of my language choice.

The following statements provide further evidence about the ways in which various factors shape the choices of different codes.

... the setting or place of interaction (context) may also play a small part in determining the choice of different languages. From the table, it can be seen that the formality of the university (UBD), and particularly when the topic of conversation is of academic nature, may trigger the use of Standard English. It should be noted that when academic matters are discussed at home, (with sisters), the language used is a code mix of Brunei Malay and Brunei English, but it switches to Standard English when discussed at the university. The same occurs with friends. Therefore, the setting or place of interaction does play a role, however small, in determining my patterns of language choice.

...most of the language used is Brunei-Malay but in some cases, such as when I am teaching my younger brothers and sisters concerning an educational topic, I tend to shift my language to English or in Standard Malay, depending on the subject.

...personal and family matters are usually discussed mostly in Brunei Malay, and sometimes in Brunei English ...

Besides interlocutor, domain and topic, network also plays an important role in the code choices individuals make:

I believe that the use of English in this area is due to the fact that my colleagues [TESL undergraduates] and I are a small group and I feel comfortable talking in English to them because I interact with them almost every weekday. Hence the nature of our friendship which is quite close provides me with the confidence to use English.

I speak more English with my friends at the university than my friends from outside the university.

As the findings so far suggest, the code choices individuals make are influenced by a number of macro factors, viz., interlocutor, topic, domain and network. As we shall see later, age is also an important factor in this regard. Students' writings as well as classroom discussions point out that saliency of any particular factor for a code choice is not always easily predictable. It appears though that Standard English is aligned more towards formality and Brunei English and Brunei Malay towards informality over and above other variables.

Purposes of Codeswitching/Codemixing

We move on now to look at what students have to say about code-switching/code-mixing. In the context of Brunei, code-switching/code-mixing as an unmarked choice has been shown to be evident in both informal (Ozog, 1996) as well as in formal interactions (McLellan, 1997). In our study, the following quotations also point towards such practices:

> ... code mixing and code switching of Brunei Malay and other languages/dialects, a common phenomenon for me, occurs when speaking with almost all interlocutors.

> Mixing of both languages (Brunei Malay and English) ... is a very usual way.

> I also use code mixing/switching to make my interlocutors feel at ease and 'welcome' in the conversation; probably the Malay words in the code-mixed utterance serve to identify with them as members of a Bruneian community, thus making them 'feel at home'.

> With my girl friends I've known for a long time I feel at ease talking to them in English because I know them well they would not dub me as a snob when I code-mix.

> I usually code-mix Brunei Malay and English.

> Brunei Malay is often code-mixed with English, especially if the topics of conversation are of general, up-to-date matters such as English music, movies, fashion, and books, etc. (general chat).

> In the case of the extended family from my mother's side, the dominant language is Brunei Malay. Code switching between Brunei Malay and English can only be seen when the technical jargon of the English language cannot be translated in Malay.

> ... code mixing is often used for jocular purposes with my siblings, as well as in informal and relaxed environments.

> Fixed phrases and common sentences in English tend to be used in the home domain quite frequently among me and my brothers and sisters. For example, phrases such as 'Oh my God' are usually code mixed with a Malay sentence. Jokes and Sarcastic remarks are sometimes produced in English and this occurs when the jokes and sarcasm are of Western culture.

As is evident from the above statements, the broader and narrower functions of code-switching/code-mixing in students' networks are generally topical, informal and affective in nature.

Attitudes & Values towards Brunei Malay, Standard Malay, Brunei English & Standard English

In the following subsection we discuss the reasons why students' language practices, as described by themselves so far, are shaped by certain attitudes and values they hold. The following statements reflect, in both general and specific terms, the attitudes and values that students ascribe to Brunei Malay, Standard Malay, Brunei English and Standard English.

Re: Brunei Malay

This shows that I have a great pride in using my own language [Brunei Malay] in formal and informal situations.

The dialect [Brunei Malay] gives me a sense of belonging in the Bruneian community, as well as social and group identity. In addition, I find that I tend to use Brunei Malay to show respect, particularly when speaking to older people, even though they understand English. To me, addressing an older person with the pronoun 'you', even without intending to, conveys a certain note of rudeness, as opposed to the word 'kita'.

… Brunei Malay 'describes' me as a Bruneian – it gives me social identity and serves as a statement of membership of the community I belong to.

These statements reinforce earlier findings by Martin (1996b) that Brunei Malay is a source of pride and an identity marker for many Bruneians.

Re: Standard Malay

… I am not comfortable with and find it [Standard Malay] quite hard to use …

If I do use Standard Malay I would feel uncomfortable and foreign to the language.

Standard Malay in my perspective will always be a foreign language to me and I would only use it in a very formal occasion as well as in education or when speaking to a Malaysian counterpart.

Both standard Malay and English are learnt at school where formal learning of the language are conducted. Most of the participants pointed out that Standard Malay is as foreign as the English language and some of the participants had difficulty in that Standard Malay.

… I considered it [Standard Malay] as a foreign language for me even though Brunei Malay is my mother tongue.

Standard Malay began to decline in From 6. … English has

replaced Standard Malay which isn't much of a loss since I do not identify with the language.

As we can see here the attitudes towards Standard Malay position it as a 'foreign language' which leads to a sense of 'awkwardness' [the term used by students in classroom discussion] as a means of using it as a spoken language. While Martin (1996b) does not explain the reason, he makes the observation that the use of Standard Malay out of context would 'make the speaker appear at best idiosyncratic and at worst pedantic and pretentious' (ibid.: 33).

Re: Brunei English

Bruneian English is reserved for very close family members (who speak and understand English) and friends. For me, the language serves as rapport between the interlocutors and me, and somehow indicates membership of a particular group. Particularly, in the friendship and family domains, where the environment is saturated with casualness, it feels natural to use Brunei English together with Brunei Malay...

... conversations are mostly conducted in Brunei Malay, except with my closest friends, with whom Brunei English is the 'norm' or agreed code of speech, to be used in most occasions. With them, Brunei English seems more natural; I feel 'at home' and find it easier to convey ideas and messages in this language. One reason for this is because I am trying to accommodate a friend who is not fluent in Malay. However, I never thought to use Standard English even with her; this may probably be due to the fact that the language sounds stuffy and too formal to have a place in our friendship...

Re: Standard English

With Aisah [pseudonym], there is more Brunei Malay than English, but sometime I catch her using English with me in a way she rarely behaves, for instance when we are out shopping and she realises someone is staring at us for no reason. She would switch to English and speak it with an attitude. I think the reason for her switch and atypical behaviour is that she thinks that person is in awe of her, and she might as well give that person another reason to be in awe of. In Brunei, if one speaks good English, he/she is deemed to be very educated. They would say that person's English is 'belaing' (meaning sounds very native-like).

In some cases I use a high standard of English all the time.

This is usually when I wish to diverge from the interlocutor (shop assistant), when I want something to be done very quickly (especially to waiters) and when I wish to show that I am capable of purchasing an expensive item. This shows that I perceive English as a very high status language and it denotes economic status and as well as intellect. However I also use very simplified form of English to Chinese hawkers. This shows that I am converging to the language used by the interlocutor.

Standard English... is used to talk about academic and other important matters, as well as in formal environments, particularly with my lecturers at UBD and the students whom I taught at the tuition at the school. However, when used with local speakers, its employment often serves several subtle functions, among which are to distance myself in a conversation, to intimidate (with my 'sophistication'), to show disrespect (as opposed to using Brunei Malay), or simply just to show off that I am an educated person. In other words, I only use this language when I particularly dislike the interlocutor.

Students' attitudes and values reflected in the types of statements above suggest that knowledge of Standard English is related to power, social and economic status, and levels of educational attainment. At the same time, use of Standard English in certain contexts is considered inappropriate and its use can lead to being 'ridiculed' as well as being perceived as highly 'disrespectful':

When I reached government school, my perfect English made me an outsider. I was often ridiculed for being 'too good' in English...

At home I don't use English except when I know I am not going to be ridiculed.

... my father on a few occasions tends to speak in English to me although I would answer back in Brunei-Malay. These occasions are sometimes in the presence of guests who are not Malay. The reason I don't answer back in English is because I feel that it is very rude to speak to your elderly in English. Therefore, to show respect, I stick to speaking in Brunei-Malay to my parents.

I never use English to anyone who is older than me it would seem rude, impolite and raising myself above him or her.

I don't go down to Miri often, but when I do, I meet up with my Uncles, Aunties and cousins and only speak in Hakka with them. It would be really out of line for myself and my siblings to speak in English to them, even though I know that they can understand English. I guess this is what my Mother warned us as 'remembering the language your mother taught you', speaking in a foreign language such as English, would cause disrespect (and loss of 'face') to our Mother.

As pointed out earlier, the above statements clearly suggest that age is an important factor in language choice patterns among people in students' networks. At the same time, sanctions are in place against the use of Standard English in informal and intimate domains.

Statements by students themselves can perhaps best summarise patterns of language choice with regard to Standard Malay, Standard English, Brunei Malay and Brunei English as well as the values and attitudes associated with these.

The reason that they would like their children to know the Malay language is to preserve the Asian culture as well as to promote national identity of the country. And the main reason that they would like their children to know the English language is due to that the English language has prestige and knowledge of the language could assist their children for further education overseas and have better employment opportunities either in the country or internationally.

The non-standard languages [Brunei Malay and Brunei English] are extensions of local dialect, i.e., they are expressions of a 'regional' identity' which I feel is of utmost importance. However, for matters of business/formal inter-actions, it may be best to retain the use of 'standard' languages [Bahasa Melayu and Standard English], since it would be unwise to assume that one's regional variety be understood by all!

For both Brunei Malay and Brunei English, it gives me a sense of belonging when I use it with other fellow Bruneians I am proud to be able to know these two non standard varieties.

Processes Shaping Language Choices And Language Attitudes & Values

Language choices, as well as language attitudes and values evident in students' discourses can be seen as categorising the standard codes (Standard Malay & Standard English) and the non-standard codes (Brunei Malay & Brunei English) along the sociolinguistic dimensions of power and solidarity. An obvious question springs to mind: how and why has such a categorisation entered students' consciousness?[2] A range of past and present processes (as given in Table 1) need to be taken into account in order to deal with this question.

The cultural and linguistic capital of Standard English draws its legitimate market value from: (a) the establishment of the British residency and Brunei's ongoing close relations with Britain reinforced through a continuing military presence, Brunei Shell, and the British legal system; (b) English's upwards reversal of fortune: since the 1962 political rebellion and the period of decline in political and diplomatic relations with Malaysia during the mid-1970s; (c) the national *Dwibahasa* Education Policy and a traditional British style of education; (d) its role in tertiary education both locally and overseas; (e) the increasing importance of English as an integral part of the globalisation process.

The cultural and linguistic market of Standard Malay has been established through: (a) long standing links and geographical proximity with Malaysia and Indonesia; (b) reinforced by the rise to power of the ethnic Malays in the Southeast Asian archipelago and especially the role accorded to Malay/Bahasa Melayu in the 1959 Brunei Constitution; (c) the implementation of the Bilingual Education policy; (d) the requirement for the acquisition of an O-level credit pass in Malay to obtain officer level positions in government service.

Despite these ongoing supporting historical processes, the cultural and linguistic capitals of the legitimate codes, Standard

---

2   Relevant analytical and descriptive terms are learnt during the university bilingualism course, but what counts is the ways in which students have chosen these terms to organise their sociolinguistic experiences, through observation and introspection.

Malay and Standard English, do not seem to be completely saturated in the collective consciousness of the population, largely because of the development of cultural and linguistic capital of the non-standard varieties, Brunei Malay & Brunei English (whether as 'alternatives' or in 'opposition'; see Woolard (1985) for a discussion on this distinction). The following historical and current processes have an important bearing on the development of variation in the linguistic market as the values associated with the standard varieties are perceived to be exonormative, rather than endonormative.

Brunei Malay derives its cultural and linguistic capital from: (a) being the language of the most powerful indigenous ethnic group; (b) use in both formal and informal domains for most topics, as well as its role as a *lingua franca* among various ethnic groups in Brunei; (c) Brunei's progression to full independence from British protectorate status in 1984; (d) since 1984, its development as a symbol of national identity, as an alternative to Standard Malay, reflected in its increased legitimisation through corpus elaboration by the National Language and Literature Bureau and its increasing use in formal contexts (cf. Martin, 1996b: 34-35).

The nativisation of English as Brunei English can be seen as part of an ideological process. In the recent history of Brunei, since the implementation of the Bilingual Education policy and the proliferation of English mass media, Standard English as a code has been made available to more and more people in the country. A consequence of this is that (for instance as evident from students' accounts) it is becoming a part of habitual language use (along with other codes) of more and more Bruneians. However, the increasing status of Malayness, particularly through the ideology of *Melayu Islam Beraja* (Malay Islamic Monarchy), has been developing the national consciousness which, for some at least, appears to position Standard English as 'foreign' (i.e., external) and 'inappropriate' in a number of contexts. So, for 'English' to become Bruneian, it seems to be undergoing a process of recontextualisation. This means, for example, whereas the use of Standard English at home or with elders might be construed as 'inappropriate', it may be tolerated in the form of Brunei English.

This situation seems to suggest that each context has its own discrete norms of appropriate behaviour. This leads us to question the structural-functional approach (Fishman, 1967, 1971 & 1972) and reproduction theory (e.g., Bourdieu, 1977), both of which seem to suggest that norms of appropriacy apply only to formal situations and get relaxed in informal situations (Woolard, 1985). According to these perspectives, use of vernaculars in the formal domain is seen as an encroachment, whereas the transgression of the standard code in informal domains is seen as permissible (Martin-Jones, 1989: 109). However, if one gets ridiculed for using a standard language in the 'informal' domain, then obviously the norms of behaviour for 'informal' domains do not permit its use, because the 'informal' domain has its own set of rules, which do not form a part of 'society-wide' norms. The issue here is that this informal versus formal distinction may not be accurate in the sense that informal implies a relaxation of rules, whereas our data clearly suggests that informal situations have their own distinct sets of rules.

Conclusions

Our findings corroborate earlier research findings that Brunei Malay is still the predominant choice in Brunei, despite recent internal as well as international developments. The use of Standard Malay is highly restricted. It is mostly used in the written form in classrooms and in government offices, as pointed out by those mature students who have been in employment; or it is used in formal speeches, and even there it is interspersed with Brunei Malay vocabulary. Standard English is mostly used in educational contexts, whether it is to do with topic or domain. Sometimes, it is also used in non-educational contexts, as a symbol of power and authority.

Brunei English seems to be used more than Standard English and Standard Malay, particularly by people in younger age groups. Its use is particularly facilitated by close networks of friends, more so the ones associated with the educational domain. However, it is also used in cross-ethnic encounters, where Brunei Malay may be less appropriate, and even in the family domain, particularly among siblings. More often than not, in many of these situations code-switching/code-mixing between Brunei Malay and Brunei English is the unmarked choice.

A close look at the attitudes and values and a number of historical and current sociolinguistic processes suggests that the statuses of the standard codes are not fully established in the collective consciousness. This is mainly due to the increasing importance of Brunei Malay and the ongoing recontextualisation of English as Brunei English, albeit as an alternative, rather than as an oppositional form.[3]

Woolard (1985) and Gal (1998) have argued against the reproduction theorists' position that dominant and hegemonic ideologies are impenetrable. Drawing on the practices of working classes and minorities, they have shown that saturation of dominant ideologies is seldom complete in the collective consciousness of the populace. Our findings from the Bruneian context not only support their argument, but they further reveal that even a dominant group, like the Brunei Malays, could be involved in or even initiate such a sociolinguistic change. In the context of Brunei, multiple layers of interests, viz. individual, familial, community, national, regional (i.e., within the Malay archipelago) and international, put competing demands on people's linguistic resources in their daily encounters. Such a situation makes it difficult for any ideology to reach saturation point in the collective consciousness of the local populace.[4]

---

[3] In forthcoming work we are further exploring the issue of recontextualisation, as an extension of nativisation, of English as Brunei English.

[4] The point made about recontextualisation will also be discussed in relation to the reproductionists theorists' position.

Appendix

Table 3 **Patterns of Language Choice (very often) with Family Members**

Interlocutor (row total)	Brunei Malay	Standard Malay	English	SM + Eng*	BM + Eng*	BM+ SM*	BM + SM + Eng*
Mother's mother (49)	37 (76%)	8 (16%)	3 (6%)	---	---	1 (2%)	---
Mother's father (36)	30 (83%)	3 (8%)	2 (6%)	---	---	1 (3%)	---
Father's mother (42)	39 (93%)	1 (2%)	1 (2%)	---	---	1 (2%)	---
Father's father (31)	29 (94%)	---	1 (3%)	1 (3%)	---	---	---
Mother (77)	63 (82%)	4 (5%)	6 (8%)	---	2 (3%)	1 (1%)	1 (1%)
Father (78)	67 (86%)	1 (1%)	6 (8%)	---	1 (1%)	1 (1%)	2 (3%)
Brother (78)	67 (86%)	1 (1%)	6 (8%)	---	1 (1%)	1 (1%)	2 (3%)
Sister (78)	58 (74%)	1 (1%)	6 (8%)	2 (3%)	7 (9%)	3 (4%)	1 (1%)
Spouse (50)	38 (76%)	1 (2%)	3 (6%)	---	3 (6%)	4 (8%)	1 (2%)
Children (39)	30 (77%)	1 (3%)	2 (5%)	---	1 (5%)	2 (5%)	3 (8%)

(N=125)

* SM = Standard Malay, BM = Brunei Malay

Table 4 **Patterns of Language Choice (sometimes) with Family Members**

Interlocutor (row total)	Brunei Malay	Standard Malay	English	Brunei Malay	Standard Malay	English
Mother's mother (8)	6 (75%)	---	2 (25%)	6 (75%)	---	2 (25%)
Mother's father (4)	2 (50%)	---	2 (50%)	2 (50%)	---	2 (50%)
Father's mother (7)	4 (57%)	2 (29%)	1 (14%)	4 (57%)	2 (29%)	1 (14%)
Father's father (4)	1 (25%)	2 (50%)	1 (25%)	1 (25%)	2 (50%)	1 (25%)
Mother (35)	10 (29%)	1 (3%)	23 (65%)	10 (29%)	1 (3%)	23 (65%)
Father (28)	3 (11%)	1 (4%)	22 (78%)	3 (11%)	1 (4%)	22 (78%)
Brother (35)	6 (17%)	1 (3%)	24 (69%)	6 (17%)	1 (3%)	24 (69%)
Sister (46)	8 (17%)	1 (2%)	33 (72%)	8 (17%)	1 (2%)	33 (72%)
Spouse (11)	---	---	11 (100%)	---	---	11 (100%)
Children (15)	2 (7%)	1 (13%)	12 (80%)	2 (7%)	1 (13%)	12 (80%)

(N=125)

Table 5 **Patterns of Language Choice (very often [vo] & sometime [st]) with Colleagues & Friends**

Interlocutor	Brunei Malay	Standard Malay	English	SM+ Eng	BM+ Eng	BM+ SM	BM+SM +Eng
Colleagues (vo) (107)	48 (45%)	1 (1%)	28 (26%)	2 (2%)	19 (18%)	2 (2%)	7 (7%)
Friends (vo) (106)	62 (58%)	1 (1%)	20 (19%)	2 (2%)	13 (12%)	2 (2%)	6 (6%)
Colleagues (st) (47)	13 (28%)	3 (6%)	24 (51%)	5 (11%)	---	2 (4%)	---
Friends (st) (53)	15 (27%)	2 (4%)	36 (67%)	1 (2%)	---	---	---

(N=125)
* SM = Standard Malay, BM = Brunei Malay

14 Sociolinguistic Survey Research in Brussels: Some Methodological Issues

Rudi Janssens
Centre for the Interdisciplinary Study of Brussels,
Vrije Universiteit Brussel

1. Introduction

Daily conversations are a spontaneous social activity that rarely becomes an object of study. In a multilingual environment, however, the dynamics behind the choice of a particular language in which communication takes place are less evident. On the one hand, language is a carrier and producer of the culture of a given group. In this respect, the use of a language refers to membership of a specific group or community. On the other hand, language use often expresses complex social meanings and codes of conduct. One person might use several languages, depending on the situation. If one wishes to analyse a sociolinguistic situation these different meanings and codes have to be unravelled. In the past the theoretical framework has often been narrowed down to majority/minority theories, where the minority group slowly adapts to the language of the majority with bilingualism as an in-between stage. But an urban linguistic environment is often subject to high population fluctuations and a general linguistic overview is frequently lacking or unreliable. The linguistic situation in many urban centres is generally too complex to fit into a majority/minority framework. At the same time the importance of language makes governments require a precise overview of the linguistic situation on which to base language policy.

One of the most common approaches for obtaining such a representative view of the language situation in a city is the application of survey research. The present contribution deals with some methodological problems inherent to this type of research, mainly focusing on the operationalisation of linguistic variables. The chief problem introduced here is the operationalisation of identification of language groups within a multilingual area. Three grounds for operationalisation will be discussed. First is the official/political status of a language. Although language policy seldom recognises all the languages spoken in a given region, it undeniably has a strong impact on the probability of survival of these languages. The mother tongue of the speakers is a second basis, although several definitions can be used here. The level of competence is the last operationalisation to be treated here.

This contribution attempts to show how one can deal with these kinds of problems and restrictions to the survey approach. The presentation is based on the experience with survey research in Brussels. The organisation of the research project at the Centre for the Interdisciplinary Study of Brussels will be briefly introduced.

2. Survey of the role of language in Brussels

Because of the lack of understanding of actual language relationships in urban centres in general and in Brussels in particular, the Centre for the Interdisciplinary Study of Brussels first set itself the task of gathering reliable basic data so as to provide a solid base for on-going discussions about linguistic communities, and for exploring the perceptions, possibilities and expectations of the inhabitants of Brussels towards a community that is based on people with a different linguistic and/or cultural background. Another goal is to mark the contours of a future 'Brussels Model' that may serve as an example for dealing with similar linguistic diversity in Europe. In the following the objectives and methods of the research itself will first be briefly introduced so as to provide a general framework for a detailed discussion of operationalisation and for providing an example of the way sociolinguistic research can be tackled (without claiming this is the best or only way to deal with it).

2.1 Objectives

The key objectives of this sociolinguistic approach adopted by the Centre were to build up a representative picture of linguistic relationships in Brussels, to come to a clearer understanding of the dynamics generating these linguistic relationships, and to gain insights into (linguistic) identification processes.

Where previous research concentrated on the relations between the French and Dutch-speaking inhabitants of Brussels, this project explores language use within the broader multi-linguistic reality of the city. A picture, for example, about language shift emerges from linking the actual language use (who speaks what language, when, and with whom) with social, economic and demographic background variables.

However, given the fact that we cannot rely on data from previous research, it is not easy to make any clear statement about language shift. A possible alternative is to connect language use with important moments of transition. To this end the following groups were selected: people born in Brussels (and growing up in a multilingual environment), Belgians born in Wallonia or Flanders (who moved from a monolingual to a multilingual environment in which their native language is officially recognised), Brussels inhabitants with Turkish or Moroccan roots (who migrated to another linguistic, ethnic and cultural environment where their religion is often considered as a threat for the native culture) and wealthy European Union civil servants and executives (who grew up in a different linguistic environment but share similar cultural values). For these groups, language use is linked to three transitions where the importance for language shift has already been proven in past studies by Louckx (1982) and De Metsenaere & Witte (1990). The three transition factors are migration, marriage and the choice of language of education for children. To explore the effect of the choice of the language of education, a group of non Dutch-speaking parents whose children are enrolled in Dutch-language schools is also included.

The most difficult challenge is to link language use with the identity of persons from a different cultural background. According to 'Core Value' theory (Smolicz, 1981 & 1992) the importance of language for personal and group identification is highly significant. Language is more than a means of communication and plays a crucial role in entering into interpersonal networks and for the perception of others. In Brussels, the situation is even more complex since language is not only a cultural marker but also a political one. Hence, linguistic identity plays a decisive role in the search for an acceptable type of society for all the inhabitants of Brussels.

The social relevance of this study goes well beyond the limits of Brussels. It is self-evident that in the first instance this study must be of some real advantage to Brussels and its inhabitants. Day-to-day language behaviour and the perception of the multilingual environment influence the individual interactions of various groups living and/or working in Brussels, as well as the frame of reference within which speakers of other languages are judged.

Being able to evaluate and analyse this identification process is of vital importance, therefore, not only in grasping the diverse connotations associated with the concepts 'Brussels' and 'Brussels inhabitant', but also in preparing the future of the city itself, in assessing how successful the 'Brussels model' is. As a multicultural, multilingual metropolis with its own problems, the Belgian capital finds itself in the company of other multilingual cities (Jerusalem and Sarajevo, to mention only two), where the course of living of various groups side by side with one another does not always run as smoothly as one would hope. Without assuming the Brussels model as a shining example, we would claim that any insights gained into the situation in Belgium might well contribute to a clearer understanding of the mechanisms at work in other multilingual cities.

2.2 Method

The above goals can only be attained by means of a sociological and microlinguistic study, in which the macro-context also plays an essential role. Only in this latter context do we find the situational elements that explain specific, individual language behaviour. A recent example of just such a multi-disciplinary approach is given in Lüdi & Py (1995).

The basic empirical data were collected by interviewing a sample group of individuals. This sample had to represent all Brussels inhabitants as well as combine representativeness with feasibility and practicability. The following procedure was followed:

First, a representative random sampling of 2000 respondents resident in the conurbation and aged between 18 and 70 was selected. The interview topics (see below) presupposed a minimum age (the over-eighteens, while, generally speaking, the over-seventies were not only less readily available but also more difficult to interview.). In this study, the geographical spread of the sample was restricted to the area contained by the official Brussels boundary, even though this does not correspond to the real sphere of influence of the capital. Any attempt to constitute a representative sample of the entire Brussels region would have posed enormous demarcation problems.

Second, within the representative sample, however, a number of groups are under-represented or altogether absent. This is true of those subgroups that live in Brussels yet are numerically small and too few in number in any random sample to allow representative generalisations to be drawn. The same applies to that section of the population that works in the Brussels conurbation and therefore, though not resident, helps to determine the picture there (commuters from Wallonia and Flanders, and affluent Euro-officials from the periphery). Four particular subgroups were also questioned: 250 foreign speakers from the Mediterranean area, 250 commuters, 250 affluent Euro-officials and 250 non Dutch-speaking parents of children attending Dutch-language schools in Brussels. (This group represents those Brussels inhabitants who are gradually being educated in the city's Dutch-language schools as a result of the great attraction these schools have for non Dutch-speaking children. The repercussions of this influx of children speaking other languages on language use, language teaching and education in general in these schools are the subject of other research projects. What no one has been able to assess so far is the possible influence of this process on identification and individual identification with the cultural communities in Brussels.)

The above research is based on a thoroughly tested questionnaire built up along three major lines of inquiry:
• background variables of a social, intellectual and demographic nature to provide information on socio-professional status, material living conditions, family composition, educational level, place of birth (also of parents and grandparents), history of geographical mobility, and relations with the region of origin, etc.
• actual language use in various domains, on various topics, in various situations, with various speakers: acquired languages; language use with parents/grandparents; language of education;

viewing, listening and reading language; language use within the family (with partner, children, and others); language use in informal situations (with friends, neighbours) and formal situations (shopping, contacts with institutions, etc.); language use in the workplace, and so on.

The concepts of language domains, topics of conversation, conversational context, 'who speaks what language to whom and when', were presented in the work of Fishman (1972). Lüdi & Py (1995) have demonstrated the ways in which network analysis makes it possible to refine these concepts: identity, identification, attitudes, views regarding Brussels, the languages spoken in Brussels, Flanders, and the Flemish Community, etc.

Third, although the analysis of the questionnaire may result in a general view of the relation between language and identity, some questions remain unanswered. Especially the function of language as a formative element, in-group dynamics and the possible alternatives of cohabitation within a multicultural environment need further exploration. These problems were analysed, based on a qualitative approach.

Fourth, besides a macrological approach consisting of a survey and a detailed study of specific groups, a micrological study was also carried out. The latter operationalised the concept of network, a relatively recent approach designed to examine day-to-day interactions of particular individuals in a meaningful communicative context. Results provide insights into decisive moments relating to the (social) life and organisation of the (social) individual.

Although the concept of social network dates back to the fifties, it was not until the 1970s that it attracted the attention of sociolinguists (cf. Milroy, 1980). The basic postulate of this approach is 'that people interact meaningfully as individuals, in addition to forming parts of structured, functional institutions' (Milroy, 1980: 45-6). In trying to explain social behaviour the links that exist between individuals are considered to be more important than social or personal attributes. In other words, the 'other' plays an important role in making the individual into what s/he is and/or what s/he wants to be. More than elsewhere this seems to be the case in Brussels, where the interaction between two unevenly balanced official languages plays a dominant role in the organisation of the individual self.

Characterising this approach are the three major concepts of density, multiplexity and clustering. Density denotes the number of links, multiplexity the nature of these links (e.g., employee, tennis partner, etc.), while clusters are the segments or compartments of networks with relatively high density, such as are found within kinship relations or occupational groups.

Network analysis is based on fieldwork carried out by a researcher contacting various individuals who will serve as entries to a particular number of networks. Since the possibilities are enormous, it was decided to take as a starting point a number of bilingual young urban professionals. The networks are built up by way of the pyramidal system. Because of the labour-intensive nature of such work, no more than 15 networks were singled out.

3. Conceptualisation and operationalisation of language in Brussels

The following section concentrates on one aspect of the approach taken, namely the conceptualisation and operationalisation of language. First the political definition of linguistic communities in Brussels is discussed. Then, a search for the operationalisation of 'mother tongue' is presented. Finally the notion of 'linguistic competence' and its importance for the operationalisation of language in a multilingual setting is discussed.

3.1 Political status of a language and linguistic communities

The status of a particular language depends on its official recognition by parliament. The grounds on which such a decision is made might be quite different. Sometimes it is linked to the country's heritage (like the Irish language that has historical and cultural importance but is only spoken by a small minority over the country). Other times, economic arguments are decisive (like English in Puerto Rico, where the local population is pre-dominantly Spanish-speaking, but where the benefits of common-wealth status with the US made English an official language as well). In Belgium however, there is no single language that has official status all over the country.

Language conflicts between the French- and the Dutch-speaking communities have repeatedly dominated Belgian political life. The subsequent negotiations between the two groups gave rise to a complex and continuing transformation process of state reform. To fully understand the importance of language use in Brussels, it is necessary to: first, briefly introduce the constitutional system of the country from a language-related perspective. Second, introduce the principles on which Belgian language policy is based. Third, give an overview of the situation in Brussels. And finally describe the nature of the data on which current language policy is based.

3.1.1 The principle of territoriality

The Belgian constitution recognises three official languages: French, Dutch and German. These three languages do not have equal legal status all over the country but are spoken in restricted areas. As Figure 1 shows, Belgium consists of two main language communities divided by a linguistic frontier: the Dutch-speaking Flemish community in the northern part of the country, and the French-speaking Walloon community in the south. Near the eastern border, there is a small German-speaking minority, making up the third language community of the country. Every municipality belongs to one of these language communities and is unilingual, with two exceptions: municipalities with 'language facilities' on the one hand, and Brussels on the other. Twelve municipalities in Flanders (six on the linguistic frontier and six on the periphery of Brussels) have facilities for their French-speaking inhabitants, four in Wallonia for their Dutch-speaking ones. Brussels is a bilingual French/Dutch region.

The basic idea behind Belgian language policy is the principle of territoriality: i.e., the official language of a particular municipality depends on the territory in which it is situated. Municipalities with language 'facilities' only give restricted rights to residents who prefer to speak French or Dutch in some situations. The exception is Brussels where two languages, French and Dutch, have equal status. Of course, this only refers to the official use of the language (in administration, education, etc.) but does not say anything about private use.

To complete the picture, it is necessary to say a few words about regions and communities. The three language communities do not correspond to the three regions: Flanders, Wallonia and Brussels. Flanders is a unilingual region (Dutch-speaking community), Wallonia is unilingual apart from a small area where German is spoken (French-speaking and German-speaking communities) and Brussels is bilingual (Dutch-speaking and French-speaking community). Each region and each community has its own jurisdiction and its own parliament and government or council. Flanders however has only one government for regional and community affairs. For Brussels, this implies that the regional matters (for instance economy, employment, environment and the protection of nature) are the responsibility of the Brussels Regional Government, while community matters (like culture and education) are decided by the Flemish or the French-speaking Community (see Figure 2).

3.1.2 The bilingual Brussels Capital Region

Historically, the language conflicts between the Dutch-speaking and Francophone Brussels language communities resulted in the so-called bilingual 'Brussels Model'. However 'bilingual' does not imply that an inhabitant of Brussels is regarded as bilingual. What it means is that French and Dutch have an equal status. The application of complex language legislation guarantees that members of either community can use their own language in administrative, municipal and regional services. Every citizen is considered to be a member of either the Dutch-speaking or the French-speaking community, although no sub-nationality exists and individuals are not considered as such.

Somebody with an identity card in Dutch can easily have a driving licence in French. Nevertheless, the difference between Dutch- and French-speaking citizens has its importance. For the local elections, bilingual lists are accepted, but for the regional elections, only unilingual lists are allowed so that every representative can be labelled as being Dutch- or French-speaking. The linguistic affiliation determines whether the representative will also be a member of the French or Flemish Community Commission. Both commissions bear responsibilities for the institutions of their own language community. Both can act as an organising and subsidising power on community issues such as cultural and

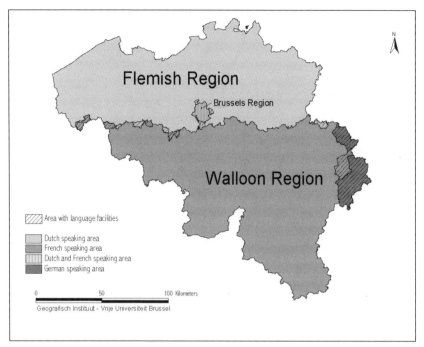

Figure 1 Ethnic groups and protected minorities in Belgium

educational matters and those which 'concern the individual'. This is a perfect illustration of the nature of bilingualism in Brussels: the representatives of the language communities manage the unilingual institutions, and all citizens can use their facilities.

Brussels is politically bilingual. The democratic system is based on the relation between the two linguistic communities. The established equilibrium between these communities depends on the fact that the majority in Belgium speaks Dutch, but that the Dutch-speaking community is a minority in Brussels. At both the regional and the national level, a guaranteed participation of the minority groups secures this balance of power. Moreover, both language communities are assured of being represented in the national or (for Brussels) regional council. Where on the federal level the number of representatives is fixed for every electoral district, the elections in Brussels are a kind of French-Dutch win-lose situation. The number of Flemish and French-speaking representatives changes according to the number of votes Flemish and French-speaking parties get. This relation between both language communities and the problems inherent to its governmental

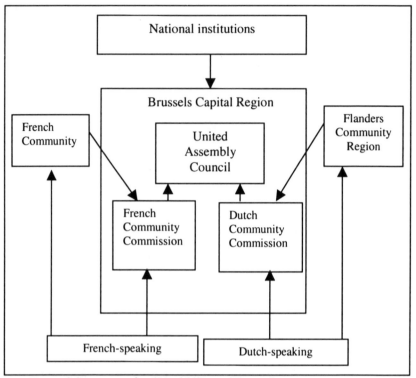

Figure 2 Structure of political bilingual Brussels

implementation predominantly determines political life in Brussels. Brussels is not just a city or a region, but the bilingual capital of a federal state.

Because the Dutch-speaking communities in Flanders and Brussels are considered as one, as are the French-speaking communities in Brussels and Wallonia, governmental decisions on community matters cannot be implemented for the inhabitants of Brussels. On the institutional level, this kind of political bilingualism might work, but on the individual level, if a decision affecting the Flemish or French-speaking community is taken, it cannot be applied within the Brussels Capital Region, unless corrective or additional measures are taken.

Sociolinguistically speaking however, Brussels is a multilingual city where, as in all comparable European cities, a variety of languages are used. Apart from both communities, Brussels has within its limited confines dozens of different cultural and linguistic groups. Primarily boosted by an economic reality, cities have always been a major pole of attraction for foreigners and people from the countryside. The demand for unskilled labour after the Second World War resulted in an increasing number of immigrants from Southern Europe, followed by a substantial group respectively from North African and Turkey International institutions such as the EU and NATO, together with the implant of major international companies, attracted a vast number of highly qualified Western Europeans. Therefore, bilingualism does not refer to the actual linguistic situation, but to the (political and cultural) relations between the indigenous language communities of Belgium.

3.1.3 Brussels language data

The study of the current language situation in Brussels, given its status, is interesting. Although data about the Brussels language situation are few, yet figures about the strength of both language communities are often cited and appear in political discussions.

Till 1947 language censuses were held on a regular basis. Their results were the only official source presenting a supposedly representative overview of the Belgian linguistic situation. But these figures were highly unreliable, especially for the Brussels area. First of all, the census results played a conclusive role in the decision on the language statute of the municipalities. Due to the Frenchification of the Brussels region, more and more Flemish municipalities got a bilingual status. The censuses were considered as a kind of political referendum, rather than the collection of scientific data on which government policy could be founded. A second problem lay in the design of the questionnaire itself and the way questions were phrased. Different inter-pretations and translations of the notion of 'mother tongue' were used, sometimes even depending on the interviewer: the language first learnt, the language best spoken, and the language most used. As a consequence, the results of two censuses as well as those of two municipalities within the same census were difficult to compare. The first question one has to ask when confronted with linguistic data or statements based on similar figures of mother tongue speakers is: who has commissioned the study? Language censuses are seldom neutral or pure scientific data, but rather political instruments guiding the language policy of political agents.

Given the theoretical political model with two community commissions, the results of the elections are often considered as an alternative source of data about the language situation, complementing the findings of the censuses. Since on a regional level bilingual lists are prohibited, all members of the regional parliament are elected on either Flemish or French-speaking lists and considered as representing their own language community. So the number of votes obtained by adding the results of the Flemish parties on the one hand and the French-speaking ones on the other, serves as an indicator of the size of both language communities. This estimate relies on the axiom that the members of the Dutch-speaking community vote for Flemish parties, as those of the French-speaking community prefer French-speaking parties. This way of thinking can be illustrated by the fact that the electronic voting procedure is designed such that first the voter has to decide whether he or she will vote for a Flemish or French-speaking party, before a personal choice between the different political parties can be made.

The importance of language in Belgian political life is also illustrated by the fact that there are no political parties that bid for the public's favour in all regions of the federal state. During the federalisation process every political family split up into an independent Flemish and French-speaking (and even German-speaking) party. But in Brussels the link between the language community and the language of the political party does not seem to be an absolute one. Research confirms (see Janssens, 2001) that some members of the Dutch-speaking minority tend to vote for French-speaking parties.

However, it does not come as a surprise that the figures of the linguistic majority are overrated in the final estimation. This is also the case for other derived measures from administrative acts, such as the language in which a tax declaration is returned, the language of a driving licence, etc. Another measure used to assess linguistic affiliation is the language of somebody's identity card. Although several languages do appear on that card, the language in which the address of the person is written counts as the language of the card. Consequently, a bilingual ID card does not exist. Nevertheless, seven per cent of the respondents claim to have a bilingual Belgian ID card. Remarkably, the younger the interviewees are, the more they think they have such a bilingual card (respectively +65y: 4.5%; 41y-65y: 5.3%; 26y-40y: 6.6% and -25y: 13.5%). This might be an indication of the fact that the younger generation of Brussels inhabitants has a different attitude towards the traditional language situation.

At the same time, this finding illustrates one of the main weaknesses of this political approach, namely the lack of an intermediate bilingual position and the casualness with which it is assumed that every inhabitant of Brussels can be considered as a member of the Flemish or the French-speaking community. Where in a multilingual society bi- or multilingual speakers are essential to make the community work, the political concept of bilingualism in Brussels ignores this. It recognises bilingual services but does not label citizens as bilinguals.

The fact that the gap between the official recognition of two languages and the day-to-day experience of reality is obvious does not reduce the impact of the political way of thinking. The political debate and the language policy of the government still take this view as the starting point. Partial inaccurate data and a narrow view on bilingualism gave rise to all sorts of myths and political-ideological polemics. But often, they play a crucial role in the decision-making process.

3.2 Language groups and mother tongue in Brussels

The political definition of language communities is an illustration of the monolinguistic ideal of assigning one language to one person, preferably with all persons using the same language living in the same monolinguistic geographical area. But even in the Europe of nation states, this does not exist (apart from Iceland). The way a multilingual society is forced into a two-community-model (for the Brussels example) is not a linguistic but rather a political and psychological battle. A multilingual environment however can only function when people do speak more than one language. According to Fishman (1978), a basic definitional property of speech communities is that they cannot be defined as communities of those who speak the same language. The problem with language is that it is a fluid characteristic to mark a community, since somebody can easily change language, especially when one is in a minority position in a bi- or multilingual environment. To classify people into language groups the notion of mother tongue is often introduced. Nevertheless, if one refers to language as the central marker for a speech community, to which language does one refer: the language a person spoke within the family where he or she grew up, in the family where he or she lives now, and the one that person uses most frequently, etc.? So there is no unique criterion either, and as is the case with the political approach, the content of mother tongue is often an ideological choice. According to Skutnabb-Kangas and Phillipson (1989), in general four grounds can be discerned on which this choice can be based: origin, function, competence and identification. These four options will be briefly discussed and illustrated by the experience of the research on the Brussels situation.

Origin can be interpreted in two ways one of which refers to the historical background of the region and/or the language communities or groups. The other interpretation refers to the family situation of the respondents. In the Brussels situation, both interpretations have their importance. The first interpretation is closely related to the political implementation of language policy. As already mentioned previously, the Dutch-speaking communities in Flanders and Brussels are considered as one community, so are the French-speaking communities in Brussels and Wallonia. Both communities have a different view on the status of Brussels. In general, the Flemish political and cultural elite considers Brussels as a Flemish city. Legally Brussels is the capital of the Flemish Community and holds the seat of its government, although it is situated within a different language region. To understand this point of view, one has to go back to the 19th century when the majority of the citizens of Brussels spoke Dutch. French was the language of the political, cultural and economic elite; Dutch was considered as the language of the working class even in Flanders. The hierarchical relation between these two languages meant that for Dutch-speakers, the use of French was identified as an element of upward social mobility, especially in the capital. Therefore, a process of Frenchification took place. Based on this historical evolution, a part of the current French-speaking population in Brussels is considered as having Flemish roots. The fact that Brussels is surrounded by Flemish territories lends credence to the aforementioned point of view. According to the view of the French-speaking community, however, Brussels is a French-speaking city because the majority of the population speaks French in its daily life, and that French is the dominant language in administration and education (two measurable features). These opposite views highlight the problem of defining both language communities. This operationalisation problem can be illustrated by the notion of French-speaking Flemings, which refers to those citizens with a Flemish background using the French language as their mother tongue. According to the Flemish vision, 'Dutch' as a language and 'Flemish' as an ethnic category are often used as synonyms, whereas the Francophone vision takes language as the central marker and considers everybody speaking that language as a member of their community notwithstanding his or her ethnic background. In general, the problem can be stated as follows: how can we define and discern a language community in a bilingual/multilingual society?

In this contribution, a second interpretation of origin will be used as the ground for categorisation. We will use the language(s) one spoke with his/her parents and the language(s) these parents spoke with each other as the standard on which language communities will be defined[1]. The advantage of this operationalisation is that a language community can indeed be used as an exclusive and exhaustive category, that mixed-language families can be included and that both elements of language and origin can be combined. This option is not purely arbitrary. Based on his analysis of the Frenchification process of Dutch-speaking immigrants in Brussels, Louckx (1982) concludes that the language spoken with the parents was the least susceptible to change. Our choice is to some extent a choice for stability. Nevertheless, we are well aware of the fact that a language community is but a theoretical construct which is deployed to gain

---

[1]   The operationalisation of language groups is based on the answers to the following questions: *Which language(s) did your parents speak with each other? Which language(s) did you use in conversations with your father? Which language(s) did you use in conversations with your mother?*

a clearer insight into language use and language relations in Brussels. Because the word community might be misleading, we will use the expression 'language group'[2]. In general, five categories can be discerned: Dutch-speakers, French-speakers, traditional bilingual speakers (Dutch/French), new bilingual speakers (French combined with another language other than Dutch) and respondents raised in a family where neither Dutch nor French are/were used. According to our findings (see Table 1), about 50% of the adults are French-speaking, 10% Dutch-speaking and 10% bilingual Dutch/French. The majority within these groups is Belgian. The small percentage of non-Belgian Dutch-speakers is from the Netherlands, the French-speaking non-Belgians are mainly from France and other countries. Apart from these language groups, two other linguistically more hetero-geneous groups can be discerned: new bilinguals combining French and another language other than Dutch (about 10%), and a group raised in a linguistic environment where neither Dutch nor French was used (about 20%).

The information in Table 1 is based on a survey gathering data on more than 2500 adult (≤18) inhabitants of Brussels. The survey is based on a representative sample of all adult inhabitants. The fact that the questionnaires were only available in Dutch, French, English, Arabic and Turkish means that the number of Dutch- and

Table 1 **Language groups in Brussels**

Language groups	Brussels inhabitants	Belgian nationality	Non-Belgian nationality
Dutch-speakers	9.3 %	10.9 %	2.9 %
French-speakers	51.7 %	62.8 %	9.2 %
Traditional bilinguals	10.1 %	12.2 %	0.4 %
New bilinguals	9.1 %	7.4 %	15.9 %
Other language speakers	19.8 %	6.2 %	71.7 %
	2,521	1,995	526

---

[2]   The word 'community' is not only dismissed because of its political definition in the Belgian context. In sociological literature, 'community' is used in three meanings: as a locality, as a network of interrelationships and as a particular type of social relationship referring to a common 'feeling' (Worsley, 1987). Because none of these meanings can be applied here (it's used in a migration context where the interrelations are the subject of the study and not presupposed) 'group' is more appropriate.

French speakers and the respondents from other EU-member states might be slightly over-represented, while some Asians, Africans and elderly people of non-Belgian origin might be slightly under-represented. However, this does not distort the representative character of Table 1 and the rest of this contribution.

A second possibility to categorise people into language groups is to concentrate on the function of the language: in which domain does the speaker use a particular language? An example of this classification method was illustrated when discussing the use of administrative formalities to decide about the size of the two traditional linguistic communities in Brussels[3]. Even though the variable 'mother tongue' is not conducive to precise measurement, it is interesting to see how the language one uses at home might differ from the language used on the street. As an illustration, we present the figures of language use of the respondents with the local authorities (language use with local civil servants in the town hall), with medical personnel and with the local shopkeeper.

Table 2 **Oral communication with local civil servants**

Language communication	Dutch	French	Traditional bilingual	New bilingual	Other
Dutch	48.7 %	0.5 %	5.1 %	1.7 %	1.2 %
French	40.9 %	97.5 %	85.8 %	94.3 %	96.2 %
Both Dutch / French	10.3 %	1.9 %	9.1 %	3.5 %	1.0 %
Other languages	---	---	---	0.4 %	1.4 %

Table 3 **Language used with GP and in hospital**

GP / Hospital	Dutch	French	Traditional bilingual	New bilingual	Other
All Dutch	27.6 %	0.5 %	3.1 %	---	0.2 %
All French	42.7 %	91.9 %	81.6 %	90.0 %	74.0 %
Both Dutch / French	24.6 %	5.5 %	13.4 %	6.3 %	1.6 %
Also other languages	5.2 %	2.2 %	1.9 %	3.6 %	24.1 %

---

[3] The question asked sounds as follows: Which language do you speak when you address a civil servant of your local municipality? Possible answers: *1*. Dutch; *2*. French; *3*. Both Dutch and French; and *4*. Other language (same for GP, hospital and local shop).

Table 4 **Language used in local shop**

Local shop	Dutch	French	Traditional bilingual	New bilingual	Other
All Dutch	19.8 %	0.9 %	4.1 %	---	---
All French	49.2 %	94.9 %	83.1 %	83.3 %	63.1 %
Both Dutch / French	30.4 %	3.2 %	12.3 %	2.0 %	2.0 %
Also other languages	0.5 %	0.1 %	0.5 %	14.8 %	34.5 %

As one may notice, the language use in daily life is predominantly French, notwithstanding the linguistic variety of the speakers. The tables, show that although Dutch is an official language just as French is only for administrative matters do Dutch-speakers use more Dutch then French in their formal contacts. In general, the language the people of Brussels use at home is often different from the one they use on the street. To an outsider, Brussels seems to be a French-speaking city.

A third aspect defining mother tongue is identification. This process of identification works in two ways; one can identify oneself as a (native) speaker of a given language, or one can assign somebody to a specific language group or community. This aspect can be illustrated by the notion of French-speaking Flemings, referring to those citizens with a Flemish background using the French language as their mother tongue. From the Flemish point of view, they are assigned to the Flemish community according to the linguistic background of their ancestors. But how far can we go back, one, two, three... or more generations? Or does the use of the French language prove that they identify themselves with the French-speaking community? The identification process is a very complex one and requires an extensive battery of survey questions to measure. Moreover, identification with a language group or community has a political connotation as well. That makes it even more difficult to use identification as a base for categorisation.

A last option for categorisation is competence which will be treated more substantially in the next section.

3.3 Linguistic competence

A second possibility to describe the language situation is to determine the range of a language. The respondents were asked how well they could understand, speak, read or write languages.

The following figures are based on self-reported knowledge of the French, Dutch and English language. The interviewees could rate their competence level as: excellent, good, reasonable, knowing a few expressions, or, not knowing the language at all[4]. Given the fact that most respondents master the French language which can be considered as the *lingua franca* in Brussels, it may suffice to present the respondents' self-rating of their Dutch skills as summarised in Table 5.

Table 5 **Self reported knowledge of Dutch by adult citizens of Brussels**

Level of competence	Understanding	Speaking	Reading	Writing
Don't know language	16.1 %	17.4 %	20.2 %	21.6 %
Know few expressions	14.9 %	19.6 %	15.0 %	20.0 %
Reasonable knowledge	29.9 %	29.7 %	27.2 %	26.5 %
Good knowledge	17.9 %	14.7 %	17.5 %	14.3 %
Excellent knowledge	21.2 %	18.7 %	20.1 %	17.6 %

Figure 3 is based on the speaking skills of the respondents and is conceived as an indication of how fluently they are able to communicate in the Dutch, French and English languages. As the figure shows, 95.6 % of all adult inhabitants of Brussels claim to speak good French, 33.3% can have conversations in Dutch and the same percentage in English. Only 3% do not reach a 'good' competence level for one of these three languages. One has to take into account that these figures result from self-reported knowledge and reflect the ratings the respondents gave themselves. On the one hand, there might be some interference between the actual knowledge of a language and its attractiveness; on the other hand, it is the only possibility to obtain an indication of language competence based on survey research. However, the above figures illustrate the function of French as the *lingua franca* in Brussels. Almost every Brussels adult is able to engage in conversations in French. With Dutch or English, a third of the

---

[4]   Question sounds: The following questions deal with your linguistic competence. Specify for the languages given if you are able to understand, speak, read or write them. Choose one of the following categories: 1. an excellent, fluent knowledge; 2. a good, practical knowledge; 3. reasonable, I can get by in this language; 4. I know a few words and expressions; and 5. I don't know the language.

population can be reached. Although both Dutch and English seem to have a similar range, about 23.1% of the adult population do not know the English language at all, while for the Dutch language this figure drops to 17.4%. It is clear that English is no alternative to French, given its restricted range compared to the *lingua franca*, but for some it might be an alternative for the Dutch language.

To obtain a better insight into who speaks which language, Table 6 combines both speaking skills and linguistic background based on the language situation in the family where the respondents grew up. Of course, if some respondents are for instance considered as monolingual French-speakers, it does not imply they do not speak any other language but French, but only that they do not master Dutch or English on a 'good' speaking level. Just as one has to be aware of the fact that not all possible categories are included in the table and that the listed categories are not exclusive ones: all trilingual speakers are also bilingual, but are only listed as trilinguals.

That English is not a threat to French is confirmed by the high percentages of monolingual French speakers among the non-traditional language groups. Among the 'new' bilinguals, of which most were born in Brussels, Dutch is spoken by almost one fourth, mainly due to the educational system, but English seems to be more popular. This is also the case for the respondents raised in French-speaking families. Respondents from Dutch-speaking families have the highest degree of traditional bilingualism; about 90% have a good knowledge of both official languages. However, the fact that the youngest generation is raised in Dutch-speaking schools causes their knowledge of the French language to decrease. The same phenomenon is observed among the French-speakers in relation to the Dutch language. Only for the traditional bilinguals is the phenomenon of language loss among youngsters not observed.

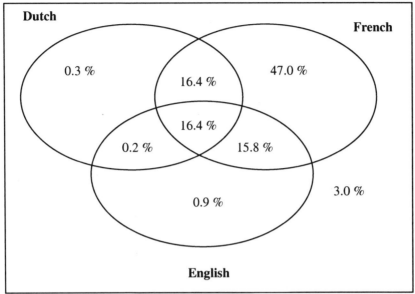

Figure 3 Good/excellent speaking skills

Table 6 **Speaking skills Dutch/French/English of language groups in Brussels**

Proficient speaking skills in	Dutch	French	Traditional bilingual	New bilingual	Other
All three languages	38.4 %	15.1 %	26.4 %	14.0 %	5.4 %
Dutch/French	52.2 %	11.0 %	44.1 %	8.6 %	2.8 %
Dutch/English	1.3 %	---	---	---	0.2 %
French/English	1.3 %	18.5 %	1.9 %	21.7 %	20.3 %
Only French	0.8 %	55.4 %	27.2 %	54.8 %	51.7 %

4. Conclusion

There are good reasons to take language use figures with a grain of salt. There is no single international standard to compare sociolinguistic research findings from studies on different cities or different moments in time, since everybody uses their own operational definition of the concepts concerned. If one wants to develop a standard, it has to be a robust measure. The best choice here is the language used in the family of origin. This measure has two main advantages: it does not change over time, and it is possible to assign more than one language to a person. But this operationalisation can only provide a partial view of the linguistic situation of a city or a region. It only focuses on the linguistic background of the citizens as the starting point of a possible evolution.

The second important variable is linguistic competence. Apart from the language spoken at home, many people living in a multilingual area speak another language as well. Urban society can often only function with bi- or multilinguals. Linguistic competence, however, is hard to measure in large-scale surveys where one can only rely on the self-perception of the respondent. This does not give an objective measure of linguistic knowledge, but is a personal evaluation of the degree of satisfaction with communication in the different languages used.

One may master a particular language, but the question is if one uses it as well, in what circumstances and with whom. This type of question forms a third crucial part of the survey questionnaire. From this kind of data, the function of a language within a group or a broader community can be derived. The function can be influenced by the local (ethnic) community, the political constellation, the economic situation, geographical aspects, and family composition, etc.

These three aspects form the basis of every sociolinguistic research project. They are crucial data before one can go deeper into the analysis of the process of language shift or linguistic identification. Often however, the operationalisation of the linguistic variables is based on the political context and in this respect starts from the particularity of the local situation. However, the growing impact of multilingualism and the problems it poses will increase the demand for comparability and co-operation.

15 Research on a Multilingual City: The Case of Brussels

Els Witte
Director, Centre for the Interdisciplinary Study of Brussels

1. The development of an unexplored field of study

From a linguistic point of view the Belgian capital is one of the more interesting cities in Europe. Massive immigration from European Union, Mediterranean and other countries has transformed it recently into a kaleidoscope of languages. This has considerably increased the complexity of the language situation that existed before such developments, which was characterised by a certain degree of French-Dutch bilingualism.

If the current language situation is compared to that of two centuries ago a radical language shift can be seen to have occurred. During the last quarter of the 18th century Brussels was an almost homogeneously Dutch-speaking city situated in the Flemish part of the country. By the time of the last linguistic census in 1947, however, things had changed drastically. Only one out of four members of the Brussels community considered themselves a speaker of the Dutch language. Although 50% of the self-declared Francophones testified that they knew the Dutch language or other Dutch dialect, the number of French monolinguals had increased tremendously. In the course of 150 years, language behaviour had changed to the advantage of French-speakers. These processes of change have made Brussels a fascinating topic of historico-sociolinguistic study.

The political ramifications of the linguistic changes in the capital are manifest. Brussels has become the focus of a conflict between the Dutch- and French-speaking communities of Belgium. Their respective positions are as follows: Francophones make appeal to their individual freedom of language rights – apparently in an attempt to slow down the Dutch-speaking community's efforts to contain Frenchification of Brussels and its outskirts. On the other hand, the Dutch-speaking community insists that the capital of bilingual Belgium, with a Flemish majority in the country as a whole, be strictly bilingual and governed accordingly. The Belgian capital became even more of a conflict area for these communities as the country gradually transformed into a federal regime.

It may be hard to find a better example of a social matter with high topical value such as sociolinguistic conflict in Brussels to illustrate the hypothesis that scientific understanding of social phenomena always lags behind their evolution. Twenty years ago Brussels was entirely unexplored from a social scientific perspective. Sociolinguistic and historical questions remained unanswered, and the role that Brussels played for the two language communities had not been analysed. Not only was research non-existent, but various myths were kept alive for political reasons. The need was felt for a research centre that would draw an adequate, unbiased picture of the city's historico-sociolinguistic situation.

In 1977, as a member of the Department of Contemporary History at the Vrije Universiteit Brussel (VUB), I took the initiative to look into this need in depth. The aims were to dismantle a number of myths and misunderstandings, take stock of recurrent language shifts, and explore factors of language choice in the light of policy options. The complexity of the matter required multidisciplinary teamwork. Staff answered calls for co-operation from several human science disciplines at the VUB (including sociologists of language, political sociologists, linguists, geographers, communication scientists, psychologists and legal experts). This led to the establishment of the *Centrum voor de Interdisciplinaire Studie van de Brusselse Taaltoestanden* (Centre for Interdisciplinary Study of the Brussels Language Situation) in 1978.

The aim of the Centre was to scrutinise social, economic, demographic, political and psychological factors, and to build a forum where these factors could be synthesised. A genuine interdisciplinary strategy, however, proved difficult to realise for a number of reasons (such as an absence of resources, research traditions, preliminary study material, and deficient primary source material). The Centre resorted to a strategy where its hypotheses would spring from a variety of complementary strategies. Actual research would then adopt the methodologies and topics proper to each discipline. At the same time, common frameworks were developed. These also tied in with models on social integration processes and social mobility patterns. The observation that language use is status-related required social issues to be taken into account. By the same token, the roles of diversified structural and external factors, such as family ties, education, the working environment, etc. were considered. Research into political decision-making processes, on the other hand, focused on the roles of dominant political classes, strategies commonly applied by social elites, and the so-called 'consociational' democracy model. After years of co-operation on a number of central research themes (migration, education, etc.) a multidisciplinary and holistic approach emerged that is fairly exceptional in the human sciences.

2. Description of the process of language shift

One of the Centre's priorities was a scientific reconstruction of the process of language shift that occurred in and around Brussels. This task proved very difficult. Available census data were of dubious value, since they abstract from primary linguistic elements. Data from different census efforts proved difficult to compare. Moreover, the socio-psychological and political climate in which these census data were collected did not guarantee sound interpretation. Members of the Flemish community, who had reasons to believe that Francophones were using the data to foster the Francophone status of Brussels, demanded that language censuses be abolished in 1961. No statistical data are available for any period since then.

Each study that was undertaken by the Centre consequently had to begin with a time-consuming structuring of source material. Not only did the available census data require a critical reading; they also had to be complemented. Various demographic sources were investigated in order to draw language-geographical conclusions. The observation that immigration was a vital link between urbanisation and Frenchification inspired research on this topic. A lack of uniform data on the linguistic proportion in the recruitment areas of the immigrants also called for comparative linguistic maps of Belgium. In order to investigate distribution patterns over the last thirty years, address files were set up per neighbourhood by using individualised data of socio-cultural associations. At the end of the 1990's we finally undertook an extensive survey, thanks to the financial support of several scientific institutions.

Interesting results were obtained with respect to diachronic aspects of language contact. These allowed the dismantling of a long persistent myth, by which it was believed that the Frenchification of Brussels had already been well on its way in the Middle Ages. There is good counter evidence that the language situation of Brussels hardly differed from that of any other Flemish city in the 18th century. Critical assessment of source material and complementary studies revealed that the influx of a Francophone population only began during and after the French occupation (1794-1815). At the time of Belgian independence in 1830, immigration from Wallonia, the Francophone part of the country, rose sharply when Brussels became the capital of the new state. Frenchification then stagnated, to resume again at a faster pace at the turn of the century. Language shift to French in the 19th century occurred in concentric circles with the Brussels municipality as its centre. Similar patterns of Frenchification were observed in neighbouring boroughs.

Much work remains to be done on a detailed inventory of the processes of language shift to French that occurred since the First World War. A study of the interwar period is in progress. Investigation of the Brussels language situation after 1950 has proved more difficult. Notwithstanding the abolition of language censuses in 1961, various estimates have been made at different times, most of which were inspired by political motives and cannot stand up to scientific scrutiny. The impact on the language situation of immigration from European Union and from Mediterranean countries, such as Morocco and Turkey, is an equally crucial question, which is gradually getting more of the Centre's attention.

Taking the multicultural and multilinguistic realities as a starting point, the Centre is now categorising the current, linguistic behaviour of the different groups living in the Region of Brussels-Capital. This research goes beyond the bi-polarised image of Dutch-French language use, replacing it with one that allows for representation of how multilingualism and complex combinations of language codes are currently manifested. The study also analyses the dynamics of language shift in greater detail. The language experience of different generations within different groups have been compared, and the changing political, social and economic realities are taken into account, with the aim to depict both intra- and inter-group dynamics. The extent to which language use affects individual and group identity in Brussels has also been addressed. The 'traditional inhabitant of Brussels' has been portrayed, along with specific groups that are seen to influence the current language image of Brussels, i.e., Mediterranean immigrants, commuters from Flanders and Wallonia, civil servants working for the European institutions, families of non-native speakers of Dutch who nevertheless send their children to Flemish schools and youngsters studying in Brussels. Complementary to this sociological investigation is a parallel (socio)linguistic research project which analyses the use of languages in Brussels by means of social network analysis. This approach enables us to account for the way a language is used in Brussels from the viewpoint of the underlying dynamics that incite speakers to apply language in a certain way, regardless of the cultural differences between them. By correlating social network variables a clear view will be obtained of the sociolinguistic system that supports the use of languages in Brussels.

A first partial study concerning the use of Dutch has recently been published. (Janssens, 2001) One of the most striking results of the investigation shows that one third of the Brussels population alleges that it has a good mastery of the language. We need no longer look at Dutch as the language of the Flemish inhabitants of Brussels, and as an important language simply because of the size of the group that uses it as its mother tongue, but rather as a language that plays an important role in the social, economic, cultural and political life of the city.

3. Language use, social integration and social mobility

As mentioned above, the Centre intended to operate on the understanding that language behaviour varies according to social situation, and that it is largely determined by social relations.

These relations are considered to be extensions of the power relations that define social groups using a particular language. Social groups may be expected to aspire to identification with higher social strata and with dominant social classes through the acquisition of the latter's language. Upward social mobility can consequently be taken to be a factor of language change. Socio-historical research contributions have consistently looked for correlations between social stratification and language use. Taking as a starting point the most complete and reliable language census from the middle of the 19th century, additional research was carried out on a number of specific groups. Factor and cluster analyses were applied to this extensive research material, and a survey of 11,000 individuals was analysed with the aid of computer programmes.

The study of the Brussels language situation in the 19th century shows that indigenous residents of Brussels were still largely Dutch-speaking in that period. People born in Brussels, no matter which social class they belonged to, considered themselves Flemish. As for the large group of poor immigrants from Flemish Brabant and Flanders, there is no evidence of Frenchification either. They tended to settle in homogeneous Dutch neighbourhoods and maintained their language. Immigration from Wallonia and France, on the other hand, was an important factor of Frenchification. This group showed a very diversified social background, including higher and intellectual classes that imposed a strong Francophone influence. In these classes, linguistically mixed marriages proved an important cause for Frenchification as well. Data on these groups provided convincing evidence that the language barrier in the 19th century was simply a social barrier. The process of language shift to French grew most strongly among intellectuals and civil servants. This fact explains why, as time went on, Brussels became deprived of a monolingual Dutch-speaking upper middle class.

The Frenchification of broad layers of the middle and working classes around the turn of the century and in the interwar period cannot be explained as the result of immigration from French-speaking regions only. Links between the specific social composition of the lower middle classes and of the working classes in Brussels had to be explored in some detail. It is relevant to note the absence of a genuine industrial proletariat. Brussels had a sizeable group of highly skilled labourers in the luxury and precision industries, and many worked in small-handicraft businesses and services. Social polarisation did not occur in the capital and many inhabitants were eager to rise on the social ladder. Concurrently, the middle class promoted a strategy of class integration that furthered the process of Frenchification. The habit of speaking French was already a well-established pattern among the middle class, which was integrated into urban society. The involvement of the lower social strata in the upward mobility movement and in the social integration process implied these strata shift to speaking French as well. They first became bilingual and after two generations a large number of them became unilingual French speakers.

Does this instrument of language integration suffice to explain why Brussels evolved towards bilingualism and multilingualism? This question has been addressed by the Centre, along with questions as to socioeconomic factors that determined the post-war waves of Frenchification in the neighbouring boroughs, the socio-psychological mechanisms that operated during the German occupation period (1940-1944), and the extent to which language integration occurred among groups of migrants. As to the last question, immigrants from Latin countries, the Arabic countries and Turkey are an important focus of research interest. Investigations are under way on how their language use is linked with the improvement of their social position. The recent increase in bilingualism in certain social strata is being analysed within the same framework. The results of these studies will be published in the near future.

4. External structures as factors of language shift

The publication of the sociological study, *The Flemings between Flanders and Wallonia* (Language and Social Integration, vol. 5) has contributed considerably to the understanding of external structures on language shift. This book discusses the results of elaborate surveys of Flemings who migrated into Brussels. Their language behaviour seems to have been influenced substantially by linguistically mixed marriages and by the language situation in the borough where they settled. Their working environment proved to be a less decisive factor.

The role of other contemporary structures and organisations has been analysed in a set of complementary studies. Such analyses have been accomplished on the media and the advertising sector. A content analysis of the newspaper *Le Soir* indicated that it strongly encouraged Frenchification, and that the paper's representation of Flemings underwent an interesting evolution that ran parallel with the socioeconomic and political development of Flanders. More recent analytical content investigation into the attitudes of two trend-setting newspapers shows that newspapers regard themselves as the defenders of their respective communities. Research into television viewing habits, by contrast, showed that the TV-medium tends to encourage bilingualism. The advertising industry has also undergone a thorough change in the past few decades and fitted its activities accurately to the distribution pattern and size of the Dutch- and French-speaking communities in Brussels. English is nowadays more frequently used than some years ago.

Investigation of language usage in the medical sector has also been conducted. An analysis of recruitment and the localisation patterns of Brussels doctors showed the proportion of Dutch-speaking doctors to be significantly lower than that of the actual Flemish presence. Research is also being done on the quality of communication between patients and physicians in the health care centres in Brussels. The fact that more often than not the 30% of Dutch-speaking patients cannot be helped in their own language – which is their fundamental right – formed the starting point of this project. The formulation of this problem is not limited to the use of Dutch, but is expanded to language use in general. Hence, communication policies concerning Francophones and speakers of other languages have also received due attention. What are the field-specific problems? How has this situation evolved and what measures can be taken to ensure improved communication? Central to this investigation is the direction taken by the patient. It appears that patients and doctors develop strategies in order to avoid linguistic problems, for example, by making their most frequent contacts with hospitals where there are no language difficulties.

In addition to these studies, extensive diachronic research was carried out for two sectors. The first is education. Research findings reveal that since the beginning and throughout the 19th century, education was an entirely Francophone affair, which nevertheless lacked a massive Frenchifying impact because of prevailing illiteracy. This situation changed towards the end of the 19th century. By means of so-called 'transitional courses' for Flemish children, French was taught in a very efficient manner. These transitional courses were abolished after World War 1, when French-speaking domination was restored and the number of Flemish schools was reduced to a minimum. It was not until the 1960s that a change took place. The expansion of the Dutch-speaking school structure since the middle of the 1960s has been given much attention. Studies have led to the remarkable observation that increasingly large proportions (currently 30%) of children from French-speaking families choose to attend Flemish schools. These figures may reflect bilingual aspirations of some Francophones, and their reaction against the concentration of migrants' children in French-speaking schools. The influx of Francophones in Flemish kindergarten and primary schools has stopped the decline of these schools, and reversed the trend to one of growth that continues today.

Several scholars have collaborated in the Centre's research project on non-native speakers of Dutch attending Flemish schools. Earlier studies had already addressed processes of language acquisition and language use in the bilingual context of Brussels. In addition to historical research into the position of the Dutch language in Brussels, sociolinguists also paid attention to language acquisition and language use in a 'language-mixed' context. New developments in Brussels now call for an update of these research questions, and inspire the Centre to examine processes of language acquisition by non-natives. The project aims at analysing the main factors that cause problems with non-natives in the Brussels education system. It seeks to determine the effects of a large non-native group on both the teacher and the native pupils, and puts forward proposals as to future strategies, particularly practical tools that can help educators to respond to the specific needs and problems of non-natives. Certain scholars also plead for Content and Language Integrated

Learning, where subjects like physical education and the plastic arts are taught through the medium of both languages.

Social life as expressed by the activities of cultural associations has also been a focus of research. On the Flemish side, a strong impact of literary associations and of the theatre was observed until 1930. The extent to which the Flemish population was involved in, and the functions of, contemporary socio-cultural life have been studied in detail. On the Francophone side, the flourishing cultural life in Brussels has been reconstructed from its origins until the mid-1960s. The main functions of these cultural associations can be identified quite unequivocally: on both sides, where influence is largely situated on a political level. It is a well-known phenomenon that intellectuals are at the centre of nationalist movements. This was also the case in the Flemish and the Walloon movements. Traditionally, the Flemish associations have played a mobilising role in linguistic and political issues. On the other hand, the Walloon organisations have always efficiently opposed the spread of bilingualism in the capital, while at the same time being at the core of anti-Flamingant conflict in Brussels. The cultural communities became autonomous from the beginning of the 1970s. A comparison of these communities on the level of their organisation and financial policy revealed their aims and goals to differ considerably.

The above shows that many blind spots remain, despite considerable research efforts. The economic sector, for instance, is a field that needs to be examined more closely. Today, only sparse information exists on the potential pressure for language shift exerted by various professional associations, such as trade unions, associations from financial, economic and liberal professions, etc. Research material collected on the Brussels health care system, as well as on the impact of the administration and the judicial system on language behaviour is insufficient.

5. The political approach

Research on the political evolution of Brussels has made more considerable progress. This allows for a clear picture of the period up to the crisis years of the 1930s. In 1988, the Centre organised a colloquium on the so-called 'language compromise' of 1963, where the 1945-1960 period was given much attention. Many aspects of the political evolution over the past decades have been analysed, which help to identify the main lines of its developments.

One of these developments is the initial powerlessness of Flamingantism. The Flemish Movement did not get off the ground under the bourgeois regime when it adopted a poll-tax voting system (1830-1893), and when it extended voting rights to men aged over 25 years (1894-1914). Many Flemish associations were politically active but lacked results in Brussels. The movement operated in a city governed by Francophone liberalism, at a time when French-speaking progressive liberals appealed to the middle classes, which also assimilated the mainly French-speaking social democratic leaders of the working class. As a result, the Flamingants could not form their own electoral base.

The introduction of universal male suffrage in 1919 hardly changed this position of powerlessness. Flemish electoral lists recruited their supporters almost exclusively in Flemish Brabant. Moreover, low correlations were found between the number of Dutch-speaking people in Brussels and the number of actual voters for Flemish lists. Since the turn of the century, the Walloon movement managed to gain a power position within the liberal party. This fact considerably slowed down Flamingantism within the party.

Research into decision-making on the national level concerning Brussels shows an obvious connection between, on the one hand, the emancipation of Flanders and, on the other, the Flemish presence in the capital. Legislation during the period between 1873 and 1940 tended to compensate for Flanders' monolingual status by providing a special status for Brussels. This strategy did not give a fair chance to the development of any true bilingual policy. Moreover, the authorities encouraged Frenchification of public and private life. This severely hampered the chances for an increase in the political status of bilingualism. Another explanation for the lack of success of the Flemish Movement in Brussels is the fact that the capital was by no means the movement's main priority. As a compensation for their loss of influence in Flanders, the Francophones can be said to have devoted themselves successfully to the preservation and expansion of their position in Brussels. The collaboration of a number of Flemish nationalists with the German occupier during the Second World War did not improve Flanders' post-war position. The Movement was discredited after the war, and as a consequence, Flemish demands concerning Brussels were almost entirely disregarded by French-speaking Belgium.

This situation changed towards the end of the 1950s, when Flanders and the Flemish Movement underwent new and strong revival as a result of economic, demographic and socio-cultural developments. More ardently than ever, the recognition of the Flemings' socio-political rights in Brussels was sought. The Movement's main demands were to halt Frenchification in Flemish Brabant, to enhance bilingualism in the Brussels local institutions and the establishment of an efficient system of control. This Flemish offensive was supported by various political organisations and pressure groups and resulted in two spectacular mass mobilisations. The subsequent 1963 language compromise granted a number of Flemish demands. The Francophones naturally considered these as an infringement on their position and as a frontal attack on the most prestigious language. They responded by creating a very successful Brussels political party defending the Francophone position, the *Front démocratique des Francophones* (FDF). The powerful position of this party was one of the reasons why the 1963 language pact and its implementation were eroded, reversed and devalued.

Towards the end of the 1960s Brussels became part of the conflict between the different communities and regions in the country. Both in Flanders and Wallonia federalism gained ever more advocates. By 1970 the country was split up into communities and regions: the communities dealing with socio-cultural matters and the regions with economic matters. In this conflict Brussels played a central role. Anxious about the fact that the influence of Brussels would be reduced and that in a bipartite federal Belgium, the capital would fall under Flemish rule, the Francophones preferred the capital to become a third region. The Flemings, who maintained that the capital should play a linking role in the federalist state, rejected this option. On the other hand, the

Flemings, like the Francophones, made full use of the opportunities provided by the policy of cultural autonomy. They established their own institutions in order to reinforce the Dutch-speaking community in the capital.

The representative institutions, which the government created in 1980 for the Flemish and Walloon Communities, signified an important transfer of competencies from the national level to that of Communities and Regions. However, not until 1988 could consensus be reached on the status of Brussels. Brussels-Capital became the country's third Region, with a directly elected Parliament (the Council of the Brussels-Capital Region) and a Brussels Government which has extensive competence on regional matters. As a compensation for this fundamental concession, the Flemings were given formal guarantees for their participation in regional powers. Members of the Council of the Region of Brussels-Capital are categorised according to language group (some 65 belonging to the French-speaking group and 12 to the Dutch-speaking group), which have an equal representation in the Brussels Government. This Government is made up of five members elected by the Council. In addition to the Minister-President, it comprises two Ministers for the French-speaking group and two Ministers for the Dutch-speaking group. Decisions must be made by consensus, an 'alarm procedure' is provided for, and other mechanisms have been established that guarantee Flemings effectively participate in governing the Region. The French-speaking and Dutch-speaking groups meet separately to exercise community powers. These community institutions can operate fairly autonomously, acting as an organising authority in matters relating to culture, education and individual persons, and presenting a forum where each community can establish its own cultural identity. Bi-community-issues are negotiated and coordinated by the Joint Community Commission.

The language positions in the Capital appear to have been pacified by the institutional arrangements designed for the area, and by the priority of attention that politicians nowadays pay to its social, economic and financial problems. But some conflicts still remain. In the first place there is the problem of the implementation of the language laws. These have been established as a protection mechanism for the Flemings in public institutions. From the beginning of their implementation in 1963 they were a cause of friction. The French-speaking majority in the different institutions tended to result in a minimalist implementation of the laws. Studies by the Brussels Centre concentrate on the analysis of implementation and of the attitude of the different parties *vis-à-vis* the tasks and the functioning of control organs. It appears that language laws still remain a very delicate part of the Brussels model.

Much of the pacification process depends on the electoral position of the Flemings in Brussels. For the Flemings in Flanders, Brussels is not an attractive city. As a result they remain a minority in the capital. Their political parties therefore ask for a guaranteed number of representatives in both the parliament and the local councils. The Centre is also monitoring this strategy, while ongoing questioning of the Brussels model is triggering further political-institutional research. Demands to reshape it in some ways make new research on this topic particularly relevant. In 1998 the Centre organised a multidisciplinary conference on the subject, together with many other specialists from Belgian universities, and with contributions from Switzerland and Canada for comparative research.

During the last decade the political world has shifted part of its attention to the municipalities on the outskirts of Brussels, which are part of the Flemish territory. The impact of the expanding capital appears grafted on to pre-existing situations of language friction. In organising a conference on this issue (1993) the Centre investigated the impact of economic and social changes, of migrations from Brussels and the role played by the system of the so-called 'language facilities' conceded to the French-speaking majority of these municipalities.

Other projects emphasise the Centre's socio-political research, one of which participates in the federal government's Inter-university Research Programme on the integration of ethnic minorities. This consists of an exhaustive historic-comparative study to determine the impact of social politics on the integration of ethnic minorities living in a capital city. Key research questions consider the historical articulation of national policies on immigration and integration, the components of specific local migrant policies, the implementation of these at different levels (Region - Community - National), as well as the social reality of immigration, integration and the formation of minorities within the city. These questions are addressed in different contributions to the fourth issue of *Brussels Themes,* on the basis of an evaluation of the Brussels migrant policy and its feasibility within the political-institutional construction of the Region of Brussels-Capital.

A second research project that links up to the previous one considered the attitudes of Turkish and Moroccan migrants living in Brussels-Capital. A broad survey of 600 migrants aimed at depicting the attitudes of both groups on multilingualism, schooling and education facilities, language and employment. The survey also sounded out opinions on cultural preservation and adaptation to the perceived values and norms of Belgian society. The Moroccan and Turkish migrants were also examined as to their knowledge and perceptions of the Brussels political institutions and so-called language situations.

Another project focuses on processes of minority statuses and on the distribution and acquisition of identity within the migrant communities. It studies the field of friction between minority status and identity constructing with first generation Muslim migrants. The complexity of this problem calls for an in-depth analysis of different domains. This includes an analysis of the Flemish Catholic Trade Union (ACV) discourse on migrants since 1964, as well as a detailed study of the operations, goals and motives of the Brussels migrants from the Arabic section within the union. This case study is based on archive and other source material, participant observation and interviews. It is expected to clarify the discourse that this community applies and reproduces. The discourse analysis is intended to help understand processes of categorisation and problem fixing, and the way in which these processes affect identity building.

At the beginning of 1999 three new politically oriented projects were launched. The first is a three-part project concerned with the Flemish communities surrounding Brussels that give facilities to Francophones. The first part takes a close look at the history of the legislation and its political development to date. The second comprises an assessment of the implementation of the facilities-system. This requires analysis of the internal administrative working of recruitment profiles of municipal employees and policy makers and of the activities of governing bodies. In a third part everyday language use in these communities is analysed. An in-depth analysis is planned of the social background of the populations; of their attitude towards the language groups; of the role language plays in their political and cultural identity, and of how the facilities influence their choice of residence.

Another project deals with the Flemish Movement in Brussels between 1945 and 1993. This links up with the quantitative electoral research into the Flemish presence in Brussels mentioned earlier. It focuses on questions concerning the interaction between political parties and independent groupings, the underlying ideology and frame of reference. Also the influence and attitudes of the organisations towards policy making and their reactions towards Francophone strategies are looked into.

The third project deals with nation-building processes. Despite the flow of international literature on these processes, the historical analysis of the Belgian case remains limited, despite the fact that Belgium has known several nation-formation tendencies since 1945. Brussels forms the epicentre in which a complex political-ideological mix of identities has arisen as a continuation of the federalisation process. Consequently, various political-cultural movements have attempted to solidify these identities. National festive holidays and accompanying symbols, rituals and myths give meaning to this pursuit. The issue has been approached by means of a systematic investigation of the political and cultural role of Belgian, Flemish, Francophone, Walloon and Brussels festive holidays in the capital. This approach also allows for a comparative analysis of identity-building forces.

All these research issues show that from a political point of view the recent period is particularly interesting. The consequences of legislation on bilingualism on the one hand, and the establishment of monolingual structures on the other, provoked a number of interaction processes. The way in which immigrants do or do not integrate adds to the complexity of this problem. At the same time a seemingly paradoxical evolution can be pointed out: the stronger the tendency for a separate Brussels region, the stronger the demand for bilingualism and multilingualism seems to become. Brussels is more than ever a highly relevant political field of tension, and research can contribute in a meaningful way to controlling this tension.

6. Comparative projects undertaken by the Centre

One of the Centre's options was to broaden its research capacity beyond one university, by co-ordinating dispersed initiatives. Colloquia were organised to improve contacts with other scientific institutions, and a Study Series was launched. From 1978 to 1990 thirteen volumes were published in the series *Language and Social Integration*, and subsequently seven volumes have appeared in the new series, *Brussels Themes*.

Contacts with the Canadian Research Centre of Laval University led to a first synthesis report in 1983. Also, a French volume was published by the *Editions de l'Université Libre de Bruxelles*. In 1986 international interest in multilingual cities gave rise to an English summary published by *Multilingual Matters Ltd.* A new, updated synthesis report is currently in progress.

Funding by the European Commission allowed the Centre to launch a comparative study between Brussels and Jerusalem as of 1995. The Centre co-operated with the Université Libre de Bruxelles (ULB), the Facultés Universitaires Saint Louis (FUSL), and the Israel Palestine Centre for Research and Information (IPCRI), in a comparative study on different ethnic groups and communities within one city. Possibilities of conflict management and resolution must effectively be addressed today against a background of nationalist uprisings and continuing conflicts in several polarised cities (Sarajevo, Nicosia, Jerusalem and the like). Even if Brussels presents a very 'mild' case of polarisation compared to Jerusalem, the two conflict situations have a number of common grounds and points of comparison Brussels is sometimes presented as a 'model' for pacification of community relations. The research project seeks to determine to what extent the new political structure in Brussels has solved the divide between the communities, the role it has played for each of these communities, and whether Brussels turns out to be a factor of polarisation or unification for Belgium. The political-institutional model has been evaluated and the extent to which legal provisions guarantee that minorities participate in policy. By highlighting certain elements in the Brussels model questions arise whether these can help solve the conflict situation in Jerusalem, as well as how guarantees for minority groups can contribute to solving social conflicts. The publication *Brussels-Jerusalem: Conflict Management and Conflict Resolution in Divided Cities* reports on this research co-operation.

In 1999 the Centre became the hub of a Scientific Research Network, financed by the Flemish Institute for Scientific Policy. The goal of this network on 'Research on Brussels and other multilingual cities/capitals' is to provide further analysis of the Brussels situation by internationalising the topic. This enables the exchange of interdisciplinary research findings between different national and international institutions. The focus of attention ranges from political-cultural and sociolinguistic to demographic-geographic and politico-judicial aspects. Such interaction between the members of the research network allows for a confrontation between studies on various aspects of similar issues, for example, a comparison between the Brussels language situation and those of Montreal and Swiss cities.

The future will see a systematic follow-up of the path trodden to date. Keeping the original perspective in sight, new trends can be investigated and the delicate Brussels model, with its complex balances, can be tested against ever more similar models throughout the world, thereby extending the internationalisation of research at the VUB-Centre.

References

Acton, W. R. & De Felix, J. W. (1986). Acculturation and mind. In J. M. Valdes (Ed.). *Culture Bound.* (pp. 20-32) New York: Cambridge University Press.

Adiv, E. (1980). *An Analysis of Second Language Performance in Two Types of Immersion Programs.* PhD. Thesis, Department of Second Language Education. Montreal, Canada: McGill University.

Afrendras, E. & E. Kuo. (Eds.). (1981). *Language and Society in Singapore.* Singapore: RELC Press.

Akashi, Y. (1970). *The Nanjing Chinese National Salvation Movement, 1937-1941.* New York: Paragon.

Allwright, R. L. (1984). The importance of interaction in classroom learning. *Applied Linguistics 5:* (156-171).

Andersen, R. (1983). Introduction: A language acquisition interpretation of pidginization and creolization. In R. Andersen (Ed.). *Pidginization and Creolization as Language Acquisition.* (pp.1-56) Rowley, Mass.: Newbury House.

Asker, B. (Ed.). (1998). *Building Hong Kong on Education: Teaching Language Culture.* Hong Kong: Longman

Assuied, R. & Ragot. A. M. (2000). *Evaluation des compétences cognitives des élèves en situation d'apprentissage bilingue.* Rapport terminal. Région autonome Vallée d'Aoste.

Baetens Beardsmore, H. (2ⁿᵈ ed.). (1986). *Bilingualism: Basic Principles.* Clevedon: Multilingual Matters.

Baetens Beardsmore, H. (1993). European models of bilingual education: Practice, theory and development. *Journal of Multilingual and Multicultural Development.* 14, 1 & 2: (103-120).

Baetens Beardsmore, H. (1993). *Report to the Ministry of Education of Brunei Darussalam on the Visits to Schools and Discussions with Ministry Officials, August 1993.*

Baetens Beardsmore, H. (1995). The European school experience in multilingual education. In T. Skutnabb-Kangas (Ed.). *Multilingualism for All,* (pp. 21-68). Lisse: Swets and Zeitlinger.

Baetens Beardsmore, H. (1998). Language shift and cultural implications in Singapore. In S. Gopinnathan, W. K. Ho, A. Pakir & V. Saravanan (Eds.). *Language Education & Society in Singapore – Issues and Trends* (2ⁿᵈ ed.). (pp. 85-98). Singapore: Times Acad. Press.

Baetens Beardsmore, H. (1999). Consolidating experience in plurilingual education. In D. Marsh & B. Marsland (Eds.). *CLIL Initiatives for the Millennium,* (pp. 24-30). University of Jyväskylä: Continuing Education Centre.

Baetens Beardsmore, H. (1999). *Language Policy & Bilingual Education in Brunei Darussalam,* in *Bulletin des Séances/ Medelingen der Zittingen, Académie Royale des Sciences d'Outre-Mer/Koninklijke Academie voor Overzeese Wetenschappen.* *45*, 4: (507-523).

Baetens Beardsmore, H. (Ed.) (1981). *Elements of Bilingual Theory.* Vrije Universiteit Brussel.

Baetens Beardsmore, H. (Ed.). (1993). *European Models of Bilingual Education.* Clevedon: Multilingual Matters.

Baetens Beardsmore, H. & Kohls, J. (1988). Immediate pertinence in the acquisition of multilingual proficiency: the European schools. *Journal of The Canadian Modern Language Review,* 44, 2: (240-260).

Baetens Beardsmore, H. & Swain, M. (1985). Designing bilingual education: Aspects of immersion and European School Models. *Journal of Multilingual and Multicultural Development,6:* (1-15).

Baker, C. (1993). *Foundations of Bilingual Education and Bilingualism.* Clevedon: Multilingual Matters.

Baker, C. (1996). *Foundations of Bilingual Education and Bilingualism.* (2nd ed.). Clevedon: Multilingual Matters.

Baker, C. & Eversley, J. (Eds.). (2000). *Multilingual Capital.* Battlebridge Publications.

Baldauf, R. B. & Kaplan, R. B. (Eds.). (1998). Language planning in Malawi, Mozambique and the Philippines. *Journal of Multilingual and Multicultural Development. Vol.19:* (5&6).

Baldauf, R. B. & Kaplan, R. B. (Eds.). (1999). Language planning in Nepal, Taiwan and Sweden. *Journal of Multilingual and Multicultural Development. Vol.20:* (4&5).

Bamgbose, A. (1991). *Language and the Nation: The Language Question in Sub-Saharan Africa.* Edinburgh: Edinburgh University Press.

Bauer, R. S. & Paul, K. B. (1997). *Modern Cantonese Phonology.* Berlin and NY: Mouton de Gruyter.

Berman, R. & Slobin, D. (Eds.). (1994). *Relating Events in Narrative: A Crosslinguistic Developmental Study.* Hillsdale, NJ: Erlbaum.

Bickley, V. (Ed.). (1988). *Languages in Education in a Bi-lingual or Multi-lingual Setting.* HK: Institute of Language in Education, Education Department.

Bijvoet, E. (2000). *Nya svenska ungdomsvarieteter - uppfattningar och attityder.* http://www.uib.no/uno/forskning/sammendrag/ [last updated 13.12.00]

Bloom, A. (1981). *The Linguistic Shaping of Thought: A Study in the Impact of Language and Thinking in China and the West.* Hillsdale, NJ: Lawrence Erlbaum.

Bloomfield, L. (1927). *Literate and Illiterate American Speech.* 1927, 2: (432-439). (Reprinted in Hymes 1964)

Bloomfield, L. (1933). *Language.* New York: Holt, Rinehart and Winston.

Board of Education. (1973). *Report of the Board of Education on the Proposed Expansion of Secondary School Education over the Next Decade.* Hong Kong: Government Printer.

Bostwick, M. (2001). English immersion in a Japanese school. In D. Christian & F. Genesee (Eds.). *Case Studies in Bilingual Education.* Alexandria, VA: TESOL.

Bourdieu, P. (1977). *Outline of a Theory of Practice.* New York: Cambridge University Press.

Bourdieu, P. (1982). *Ce que parler veut dire. L'économie des échanges linguistiques.* Paris: Fayard.

Broeder, P., Extra, G. & Van Hout, R. (1993). Richness and variety in the developing lexicon. In C. Perdue (Ed.). *Adult Language Acquisition: Cross-Linguistic Perspectives Vol.I:* (pp. 145-163). Cambridge: Cambridge University Press.

Bronckart, J. P. (1988). Fonctionnement langagier et entreprises normatives, In G. Schöni, et al. (dir.). *La langue française est-elle gouvernable?* (109-132.). Neuchâtel/Paris, Delachaux-Niestlé,

Brown, H. D. (1986). Learning a second culture. In J. M. Valdes (Ed.). *Culture Bound.* (pp. 33-48) New York: Cambridge University Press.

Bruner, J. (1982). The formats of language acquisition. *American Journal of Semiotics* 1: (1-16).

Bruner, J. (1983). Child's talk. *Learning to Use Language.* Oxford: Oxford University Press.

Bruner, J. (1985). The role of interaction formats in language acquisition. In J. Forgas (Ed.). *Language and Social Situations,* (pp. 31-46). New York: Springer.

Bruner, J. (1999). Folk pedagogies. In J. Leach & B. Moon (Eds.). *Learners and Pedagogy.* (pp. 4-20). London: Paul Chapman Publishing/Open University Press.

Brusselse Thema's. (1992-2000). (7 volumes). *Brussels Themes - Thèmes Bruxellois.* Brussels: VUB Press.

Bullock, R. (1975). *The Bullock Report.* HMSO

Burstall, C., Jamieson, M., Cohen, S. & Hargreaves, M. (1974). *Primary French in the Balance.* Slough, Eng: NFER Publishing.

Byram, M. & Ó Riagain, P. (1999). Towards a framework for language education policies in Europe. Linguistic Diversity for Democratic Citizenship in Europe. Innsbruck, Austria. 10-12 May 1999 (ref.: DECS/EDU/LANG (99) 6 rev.).

Cane, G. (1993). A Description of the Spoken English of Educated Bruneian Speakers of English in the 1990's. PhD. Thesis, University of Strathclyde.

Cane, G. (1994). The English language in Brunei Darussalam. *World Englishes*, 13, 3: (351-360).

Cenoz, J. & Genesee, F. (1998a). (Eds.). *Beyond Bilingualism: Multilingualism and Multilingual Education.* Clevedon: Multilingual Matters.

Cenoz, J. & Genesee, F. (1998b). Psycholinguistic perspectives on multilingualism and multilingual education. In J. Cenoz & J. Genesee (Eds.). *Beyond Bilingualism: Multilingualism and Multilingual Education,* (pp.16-32). Clevedon: Multilingual Matters.

Cenoz, J. & Valencia, J. F. (1994). Additive trilingualism: Evidence from the Basque Country. *Applied Psycholinguistics, 15:* (195-207).

Cheng, R. (1985). A comparison of Taiwanese, Taiwan Mandarin, and Peking Mandarin. *Language,* 61:2 (352-377).

Cheng, T. C. (1949). *The Education of Overseas Chinese – A Comparative Study of Hong Kong, Singapore and the East Indies.* Unpublished MA dissertation. University of London.

Cheung, D. C. K. (1990). The language of success. *The South China Morning Post.* 15 January 1990.

Cheung, D. C. K. (1997). 'New education policy socially divisive'. *The South China Morning Post.* 1 November 1997.

Clark, E. (1995). *The Lexicon in Acquisition.* Cambridge: Cambridge University Press.

Cloud, N., Genesee, F. & Hamayan, E. (2000). *Dual Language Instruction: A handbook for Enriched Education.* Boston, MA: Heinle and Heinle.

Clyne, M., Jenkins, C., Chen, I., Tsokalidou, R. & Wallner, T., (1995). *Developing Second Language from Primary School: Models and Outcomes.* Deakin: NLLIA.

Colonial Office, Great Britain. (1950). *Colonial Annual Review: Hong Kong.* London: H.M. Stationery Office.

Colonial Office, Great Britain. (1962). *Colonial Annual Review: Hong Kong.* London: H.M. Stationery Office.

Commission of the European Communities. (1995). *White Paper: Teaching and Learning-Towards the Learning Society.* Objective IV. Council of Europe, Brussels, DGV.

Constable, N. (1997). Maid to order in Hong Kong. *Stories of Filipina Workers.* Ithaca and London: Cornell University Press.

Council of Europe. (1998). *Recommendation No. R (98) 6 of the Committee of Ministers to Member States concerning Modern Languages.* http://cm.coe.int/ta/rec/1998/98r6.htm.

Council of Europe. (2001). *Common European Framework of Reference for Languages: Learning, Teaching, Assessment.* Cambridge: Cambridge University Press.

Coyle, D. (1994). Science in French in the national curriculum: a pilot study. In R. Budd, Chaux, C. O'Neil, D. Arsndorf & U. Gaber (Eds.). *Subject Learning and Teaching in a Foreign Language.* (pp. 151-179). Triangle 13. Paris: Didier Erudition.

Coyle, D. (1999a). The next stage. Is there a future for the present? The legacy of the communicative approach. In *Francophonie.* (pp. 13-16). March 1999. UK: Association for Language Learning.

Coyle, D. (1999b). *Breaking the Rules of the Game: Adolescent Voices Speak Out.* Unpublished PhD thesis, University of Nottingham.

Coyle, D. (1999c). Theory and planning for effective classrooms: Supporting students in Content and Language Integrated Learning contexts. In J. Masih (Ed.). *Learning Through a Foreign Language* (46-62). London: CILT (Centre for Information on Language Teaching and Research).

Coyle, D. (2000a). Meeting the challenge-the 3Cs curriculum. In S. Green (Ed.). *New Perspectives on Teaching and Learning Modern Languages.* (pp. 158-182). Clevedon: Multilingual Matters.

Coyle, D. (2000b). Raising the profile and prestige of modern foreign languages in the whole school curriculum. In K. Field (Ed.). *Issues in Modern Foreign Languages Teaching.* (pp. 12-17). London: Routledge Falmer.

Coyle, D. & Leith, J. (1996). Content-oriented language learning. *Comenius News issue, 7, 1996.* (pp. 6-7). London: CILT (Centre for Information on Language Teaching and Research).

Cummins, J. (1976). The influence of bilingualism on cognitive growth: A synthesis of research findings and explanatory hypothesis. *Working Papers on Bilingualism 9:* (1-43).

Cummins, J. (1979). Linguistic interdependence and the educational development of bilingual children. *Review of Educational Research, 49:* (222-251).

Cummins, J. (1981). The role of primary language development in promoting educational success for language minority students. *Schooling and Language Minority Students: A Theoretical Framework,* (1-50). Los Angeles, CA: Evaluation, Dissemination, and Assessment Center.

Cummins, J. (1984). *Bilingualism and Social Education: Issues in Assessment and Pedagogy.* Clevedon: Multilingual Matters.

Cummins, J. & Swain, M. (1986). *Bilingualism in Education*. London and NY: Longman.

Day, E. & Shapson S. (1991). Integrating formal and functional approaches in language teaching in French immersion: An experimental study. *Language Learning, 41*, 1: 25-58.

De Metsenaere, M. & Witte, E. (1990). Taalverlies en taalbehoud bij de Vlamingen in Brussel in de negentiende eeuw. *Bijdragen en mededelingen betreffende de geschiedenis der Nederlanden*, jrg *105*, 1: (1-37).

De Pietro, J. F., Matthey, M. & Py, B. (1989). Acquisition et contrat didactique: les séquences potentiellement acquisitionnelles dans la conversation exolingue. *Actes du troisième Colloque Régional de Linguistique* (Strasbourg, 28-29 avril 1988). (99-124). Strasbourg, Université des Sciences Humaines/Université Louis Pasteur.

Department of Chinese, Translation and Interpretation. (1994). [renamed Chinese and Bilingual Studies in 1995]. *Report of the Language Proficiency Perception Survey*. Commissioned by the Education Commission.

Devolder, I. (1989). *Language Proficiency Compared: The Relevance of Immediate Pertinence in Second and Third Language Learning*. Unpublished B.A. Dissertation, Vrije Universiteit Brussel.

DfEE (1999). The national curriculum for England and Wales. *Modern Foreign Languages*. (Curriculum 2000).

Dietrich, R. (1990). Nouns and verbs in the learner's lexicon. In W. Dechert (Ed.). *Current Trends in European Second Language Acquisition Research*, (pp. 13-22). Clevedon: Multilingual Matters.

Donato, R. (1996). *The Contributions of Vygotsky to Understanding Learning in Foreign Language Classrooms*. Unpublished paper delivered at AILA Conference, Jyvaskyla, Finland

Dorian, N. (1982). Language loss and maintenance in language contact situation. In R. Lambert & B. Freed (Eds.). *The Loss of Language Skills*. (pp. 44-59). Rowley, Mass Newberry House.

Ducrot, O. & Todorov, T. (1972). *Dictionnaire encyclopédique des sciences du language*. Paris: Seuil.

Dulay, H. & Burt, M. (1977). Remarks on creativity in language acquisition. In H. Dulay, et al. (Eds.). *Viewpoints on English as A Second Language*, (pp. 95-126). New York: Regents.

Eagle, S. (1999). The language situation in Nepal. In R. B. Baldauf & R. B. Kaplan (Eds.). *Language Planning in Nepal, Taiwan and Sweden*. Special Issue of the *Journal of Multilingual and Multicultural Development*. Vol. 20: (4&5).

Education & Manpower Branch. (1993). *School Education in Hong Kong: A Statement of Aims.* Hong Kong: Government Printer.

Education Commission. (1999). *Education Blueprint for the 21ˢᵗ Century: Review of Academic System: Aims of Education. Consultation Document.* Hong Kong: Government Printer.

Edwards, J. (1991). *Implementing Bilingualism: Brunei in Perspective.* Volume 1 of the collected papers from the Bilingualism and National Development conference held in Brunei, 9-12 December 1991.

Edwards, J. (1994). *Multilingualism.* London: Penguin.

EEC. (1990). Joint Conference of the Commission of the European Communities and the Council for Cultural Co-operation of the Council of Europe: *Secondary Schools and European/International Education in Europe: Mobility, Curricula and Examinations.* Namur, 21-23 May (mimeo, unpublished).

Egger, K. & Lardschneider-McLean, M. (2001). Trilingual schools in the LadinValleys of South Tyrol, Italy. In D. Christian & F. Genesee (Eds.). *Case Studies in Bilingual Education.* Alexandria, VA: TESOL.

Ellis, R. (1986). *Understanding Second Language Acquisition.* Oxford: Oxford University Press.

Ellis, R. (Ed.). (1999). *Learning a Second Language Through Interaction.* Amsterdam/Philadelphia: John Benjamins: Studies in Bilingualism 17.

European Commission. (1995). White Paper on education and training. *Teaching and Learning – Towards the Learning Society.* Luxemburg: Office for Official Publications of the European Communities.

Firth, A. & Wagner, J. (1997). On discourse, communication and (some) fundamental concepts in SLA research. *The Modern Languages Journal* Vol 8, No. iii.

Fishman, J. A. (1967). Bilingualism with and without diglossia: diglossia with and without bilingualism. *Journal of Social Issues.* 23: (29-38).

Fishman, J. A. (1971). *Advances in the Sociology of Language.* vol. 1. The Hague: Mouton.

Fishman, J. A. (1972). Domains and the relationship between micro- and macro-sociolinguistics. In J. J. Gumperz & D. Hymes (Eds.). *Directions in Sociolinguistics: The Ethnography of Communication.* (pp. 435-453). New York: Holt, Rinehart & Winston.

Fishman, J. A. (1972). Essays by Joshua A. Fishman. *Language in Socio-cultural Change.* Stanford University Press.

Fishman, J. A. (1978). *The Sociology of Language. An interdisciplinary social science approach to language in society.* Rowley Massachusetts.

Fromm, E. (1948). *Man for Himself.* London: Routledge and Kegan Paul, Ltd.

Fromm, E. (1982-1989). *Haven oder Sein (zhanyou haishi shengcun).* Tr. by Guan Shan, Beijing: Sanlian Press.

Gajo, L. (2001). *Immersion, bilinguisme et interaction en classe.* Paris: Didier, coll. LAL.

Gajo, L. & Mondada, L. (2000). *Interactions et acquisitions en contexte.* Fribourg: Editions Universitaires.

Gajo, L. & Serra, C. (2000). Acquisition des langues et des disciplines dans l'enseignement bilingue: l'exemple des mathématiques. *Etudes de Linguistique Appliquée,* (120).

Gal, S. (1998). Cultural bases of language-use among German-speakers in Hungary. In P. Trudgill & J. Cheshire (Eds.). *The Sociolinguistics Reader: Multilingualism and Variation. Vol.1.* (pp. 113-126) London: Arnold.

Gao, Y. (1994). Productive bilingualism: an empirical study (shengchan xing shuangyu xianxiang kaocha). *Foreign Language Teaching and Research (waiyu jiaoxue yu yanjiu)* 97, 1: (59-64).

Gao, Y. (2001). *Foreign Language Learning: "1+1>2".* Beijing: Peking University Press.

Gao, Y., Li, Y. & Li, W. (2001). *English Language Learning and Self-identity Construction: Three Cases of College English Majors.* Paper presented at the International Symposium on ELT in China, May 2001, Beijing.

Gardner, R. C. (1982). Social factors in language retention. In R. D. Lambert & B. Freed (Eds.). *Loss of Language Skills.* (pp. 24-43). Rowley, Mass: Newbury House.

Gardner, R. C. (1985). *Social Psychology and Second Language Learning.* London: Edward Arnold.

Gardner, R. C. & Lambert, W. E. (1972). *Attitudes and Motivation in Second Language Learning.* Rowley, Mass: Newbury House.

Garner, J. (1997). 'Proposals repeating mistakes of the past'. *The South China Morning Post.* 8 May 1997.

Genesee, F. (1976). The role of intelligence in second language learning. *Language Learning, 26:* (267-280).

Genesee, F. (1981). A comparison of early and late second language learning. *Canadian Journal of Behavioral Science, 13:* (115-127).

Genesee, F. (1983). Bilingual education of majority-language children: The Immersion experiments in review. *Applied Psycholinguistics, 4:* (1-49).

Genesee, F. (1987). *Learning Through Two Languages: Studies of Immersion and Bilingual Education.* Rowley, MA: Newbury House.

Genesee, F. (1991). Second language learning in schools settings: Lessons from immersion. In A. Reynolds (Ed.). *Bilingualism, Multiculturalism, and Second Language Learning,* (pp. 183-201). Hillsdale, NJ: Lawrence Erlbaum.

Genesee, F. (1994). Integrating language and content: Lessons from immersion. *Educational Practice Report: 11.* Santa Cruz, CA: The National Center for Research on Cultural Diversity and Second Language Learning.

Genesee, F. (2001). Bilingual first language acquisition: Exploring the limits of the language faculty. In M. McGroarty (Ed.). *Annual Review of Applied linguistics: Language and Psychology, Vol.21:* (pp. 153-168). New York: Cambridge University Press.

Genesee, F. & Lambert, W. E. (1983). Trilingual education for majority language children. *Child Development, 54:* (105-114).

Genesee, F., Holobow, N., Lambert, W. E. & Chartrand, L. (1989). Three elementary school alternatives for learning through a second language. *Modern Language Journal, 73:* (250-263).

Global, R. (30 Sept 2000). www.glreach.com/globstats/refs.php3

Goebl, H. (1989). Spracheinheit – unité de la langue – unità della lingua – unidad de la lengua. Bemerkungen zur Problematik des Sprachunitarismus. In F. H. Riedl & T. Veiter *Fédéralisme, régionalisme et droit des groupes ethniques en Europe.* Hommage à Guy Héraud. Wien, Wilhelm Braumüller, (162-171).

Graddol, D. (1997). *Language: the Next Generation, the final report and recommendations of the Nuffield Language Inquiry 2000.* The Nuffield Inquiry, UK.

Graddol, D. (1997). *The Future of English.* London: British Council.

Grin, F. (1997). *Langue et différentiels de statut socio-économique en Suisse.* Berne, Office fédéral de la statistique.

Grin, F. (1999). *Compétences et récompenses: la valeur des langues en Suisse.* Fribourg: Editions universitaires.

Grosjean, F. (1985). The bilingual as a competent but specific speaker-hearer. *Journal of Multilingual and Multicultural Development 6:* (467-477).

Guiora, A. (1972). Construct validity and transpositional research: toward an empirical study of psychoanalytic concepts. *Comprehensive Psychology 1, 2:* (139-150).

Gülich, E. (1986). L'organisation conversationnelle des énoncés inachevés et de leur achèvement interactif en situation de contact. *DRLAV* (34-35).

Hammerly, H. (1991). *Fluency and Accuracy: Toward Balance in Language Teaching and Learning.* Clevedon: Multilingual Matters.

Hanvey, R. G. (1990). Cross-cultural awareness. In W. Hu (Ed.). *Selected Readings in Intercultural Communication*. Changsha: Hunan Education Press.

Harley, B. (1993). Instructional strategies and SLA in early French immersion. *Studies in Second Language Acquisition, 15*: (245-259).

Hassan, R. (Ed.) (1976). *Singapore: Society in Transition*. Kuala Lumpur: Oxford University Press.

Hawkins, E. (Ed.). (1999). *30 Years of Language Teaching*. London: CILT (Centre for Information on Language Teaching & Research).

Home Affairs Department. (1974). *A Public Opinion Study on the Education Green Paper*. Hong Kong: Government Printer.

Housen, A. (1995). *It's About Time – The Acquisition of Temporality in English as a Second Language in a Multilingual Educational Context*. PhD thesis, Vrije Universiteit Brussel.

Housen, A. (1997). Teaching and Learning Second Languages in the European Schools. In K. Karavas-Doukas & Rea-Dickins (Eds.). *Proceedings of the Euroconference on The Teaching of Foreign Languages in Primary Schools in Europe*, (pp. 40-53).

Housen, A. (2000). Verb semantics and the acquisition of Tense-Aspect Morphology in English. *Studia Linguistica, 54*, 2: (249-259).

Housen, A. (forthcoming). A corpus-based study of the L2-acquisition of the English verb system. In S. Granger, J. Hung & S. Petch-Tyson (Eds.). *Computer Learner Corpora, Second Language Acquisition and Foreign Language Learning*. London: John Benjamins.

Housen, A. & Baetens Beardsmore, H. (1987). Curricular and extra-curricular factors in multilingual education. *Studies in Second Language Acquisition, 9*, (83-102).

Housen, A. & Pallotti, G. (forthcoming). Interlanguage development at primary school – The acquisition of English by young Italian-speaking learners in different socio-educational contexts. In P. Rea-Dickins (Ed.). *The Teaching and Learning of Foreign Languages in European Primary Schools*.

Hughes, R. (1968). *Hong Kong: Borrowed Place – Borrowed Time*. London: Andre Deutsch.

Humboldt, W. von, (1836). Über die Verschiedenheit des menschlichen Sprachbaues und ihren Einfluss auf die geistige Entwicklung des Menschengeschlechts. Berlin.

Hussainmiya, B. A. (2000). *The Brunei Constitution of 1959: An Inside History*. Bandar Seri Begawan: Brunei Press.

Hymes, D. (1964). *Language in Culture and Society*. New York: Harper & Row.

Hymes, D. (1974). *Pidginization and Creolization of Languages*. Cambridge: Cambridge University Press.

Irving, E. A. (1914). *The Educational System of Hong Kong*. HK: Government Printer.

Jacobs, K. & Cross, A. (2001). The seventh generation of Kahnawà:ke: Phoenix or Dinosaur. In D. Christian & F. Genesee (Eds.). *Case Studies in Bilingual Education*. Alexandria, VA: TESOL.

Janssens, R. (1999). Aspecten van het taalgebruik in Brussel. E. Witte, A. Alen, H. Dumont & R. Ergec (Eds.). *Het statuut van Brussel - Bruxelles et son statut*. (pp. 283-306). Brussel: Larcier.

Janssens, R. (2001). Over Brusselse Vlamingen en het Nederlands in Brussel (Flemish Residents and the Dutch Language in Brussels). In E. Witte & A. Mares (Eds.). *Brusselse Thema's – Brussels Themes – Thèmes Bruxellois 7* (pp. 43-83). 19 Keer Brussel, Brussels: VUB Press.

Jernudd, B. H. (1991). Culture planning in language planning: What do we know about culture loss, survival and gain in relation to language loss, survival and gain? In Volume 2 of the collected papers from the *Bilingualism and National Development* conference held in Brunei, 9-12 December 1991.

Johnson, R. K. (1983). Bilingual switching strategies: A study of the modes of teacher-talk in bilingual secondary school classrooms in Hong Kong. *Language Learning and Communication* 2(3): (267-285).

Johnson, R. K. & Swain, M. (Eds.). (1997). *Immersion Education: International Perspectives*. Cambridge: Cambridge University Press.

Jones, G. M. (1991). From here to eternity? Bilingual education in Brunei Darussalam. In Volume 1 of the collected papers from the *Bilingualism and National Development* conference held in Brunei, 9-12 December 1991.

Jones, G. M. (1995). *A Study of Bilingualism and Implications for Language Policy Planning in Negara Brunei Darussalam*. PhD Thesis, University College of Wales, Aberystwyth, HK.

Jones, G. M. (1996a). The bilingual education policy in Brunei Darussalam. In P. W. Martin, C. Ozog & Poedjosoedarmo (Eds.). *Language Use & Language Change in Brunei Darussalam*. (pp. 123-132) Ohio: Ohio University Press.

Jones, G. M. (1996b). Bilingual Education and Syllabus Design: Towards a Workable Blueprint. *Journal of Multilingual and Multicultural Development*. Vol.17: (2-4).

Jones, G. M. (1997). The changing role of English in Brunei Darussalam. In A. Brown (Ed.). *English in Southeast Asia*. (pp. 13-34). Proceedings of the first 'English in Southeast Asia' Conference (21-23 Nov. 1996). National Institute of Singapore.

Jones, G. M. (1998). Some observations on gender and educational achievement in Brunei Darussalam. *Awareness. Vol.5#1*. Singapore: Association of Women for Action and Research.

Jones, G. M., Martin, P. W. & Ozog, A. C. K. (1993). Multilingualism and bilingual education in Brunei Darussalam. *Journal of Multilingual and Multicultural Development*, Vol. 14: 1 & 2, (39-58). Clevedon: Multilingual Matters.

Joseph, J. E. (1996). English in Hong Kong: Emergence & decline. *Current Issues in Language & Society, 3*, 2: (166-179)

Kesckes, I. & Papp, T. (2000). *Foreign Language and Mother Tongue.* Hillsday, NJ: Lawrence Erlbaum.

King, Rex. (1982). Standards of English in Hong Kong. In Editorial Committee, Symposium on Language and Education in Hong Kong. (Ed.). *Language and Education*, (pp. 237-42). Hong Kong: 新雅印務有限公司.

Krafft, U./Dausendschön-Gay, U. (1994). Analyse conversationnelle et recherche sur l'acquisition. *Bulletin suisse de linguistique appliqu*ée, *59*: (127-158).

Krechel, H. L. (1996). Französisch als Vehikularsprache im bilingualen Sachfach Erdkunde. Buchloh, H., et al. (Eds.). *Konvergenzen: Fremdsprachenunterricht: Planung – Praxis – Theorie*, (7-33). Tübingen: Narr.

Kubler, Cornelius. (1985). *The Development of Mandarin in Taiwan: A Case Study of Language Contact.* Taipei: Students Books.

Kuo, E. (1976). *A Sociolinguistic Profile.* In R. Hassan (Ed.) *Singapore: Society in Transition.* (pp. 134-148). Kuala Lumpur: Oxford University Press.

Kuo, E. (1981). The sociolinguistic situation in Singapore: Unity and diversity. In E. Afrendras & E. Kuo (Eds.) *Language & Society in Singapore.* (pp. 39-62) Singapore: Singapore University Press.

Kuo, E. (1985a). *Measuring Communicatively in Multilingual Societies: The Cases of Singapore and West Malaysia.* QA/SEAMEO.

Kuo, E. (1985b). *The Use of Mandarin in Restaurants and Coffee Shops in 1981-83: An Attempt at An Assessment of the "Speak Mandarin Campaign".* QA/SEAMEO.

Lambert, W.E. 1974. Culture and language as factors in learning and education. Paper presented at the 8th annual TESOL conference.

Larking, L. (1994). Reading comprehension ability of primary 5 & 6 children in Malay and English in Brunei Darussalam. In M. L. Tickoo (Ed.). *Reading and Research in Writing.* (pp. 55-62) Singapore: Regional Language Centre.

Laurie, S. S. (1890). *Lectures on Language and Linguistic Method in School.* Cambridge: Cambridge University Press.

Leat, D. (1998). *Thinking Through Geography.* Cambridge: Chris Kington Publishing.

Lebrun, N. & Baetens Beardsmore, H. (1991). Trilingual education in the Grand Duchy of Luxembourg. In O. García (Ed.). *Bilingual Education: Focusschrift in Honor of Joshua A. Fishman,* (pp. 107-122). Amsterdam/Philadelphia, Benjamins.

Legutke, M. & Thomas, H. F. (1991). *Process and Experience in the Languages Classroom.* Addison Wesley: Longman.

Leith, J. (2000). The chattering classes (11-12). *TES* Curriculum Special Autumn 2000: Modern Languages.

Li, S. M. (1997). Hong Kong: From a colony to a model for China. In B. K. Won, et al. (Eds.). *Culture and the City in East Asia.* Oxford: Oxford University Press.

Long, M. (1996). The role of the linguistic environment in second language acquisition. In W. Ritchie & T. Bhatia (Eds.). *Handbook of Second Language Acquisition.* (pp. 413-468). San Diego: Academic Press.

Long, M. & Robinson, P. (1998). Focus on form. Theory, research, and practice. In C. Doughty & J. Williams (Eds.). *Focus on form in classroom second language acquisition.* (pp. 15-41). New York: Cambridge University Press.

Lord, R. (1974). English – how serious a problem for students in Hong Kong. *English Bulletin,* 6.3: (1-10).

Lord, R. & Cheng, H. (Ed.). (1987). *Language Education in Hong Kong.* Hong Kong: Chinese University Press.

Lord, R. & Tsou, B. K. (1979). *Studies in Bilingual Education.* Hong Kong: Hong Kong University & Heinemann.

Lord, R. & Tsou, B. K. (1986). *The Language Bomb.* Hong Kong: Heinemann Press.

Louckx, F. (1982). Vlamingen tussen Vlaanderen en Wallonië. *Taal en Sociale Integratie 5,* (348).

Lüdi, G. (1991). Construire ensemble les mots pour le dire. A propos de l'origine discursive des connaissances lexicales. U. Dausendschön-Gay, E. Gülich, & U. Krafft (Eds.). *Linguistischen Interaktionsanalysen. Beiträge zum Romanistentag 1987.* (pp. 193-224). Tübingen: Niemeyer.

Lüdi, G. (1994). Dénomination médiate et bricolage lexical en situation exolingue. *AILE 3,* (115-146).

Lüdi, G. (1999). Alternance des langues et acquisition d'une langue seconde. In V. Castellotti & D. Moore (Eds.). *Alternance des langues et contruction de savoirs.* (pp. 25-51). Cahiers du français contemporain 5.

Lüdi, G. & Py, B. (1986). *Etre Bilingue.* Berne, Lang.

Lüdi, G. & Py, B. (1995). *Changement de langage et langage du changement. Aspects linguistiques de la migration interne en Suisse.* Lausanne.

Lüdi, G., et al. (1998). Welche Sprachen sollen die Schülerinnen und Schüler der Schweiz während der obligatorischen Schulzeit lernen? Bericht einer von der Kommission für Allgemeine Bildung eingesetzten Expertengruppe. Gesamtsprachenkonzept an die Schweizerische Konferenz der Kantonalen Erziehungsdirektoren. Bern. http://www.romsem.unibas.ch/sprachenkonzept.

Lüdi, G., Pekarek Doehler, S. & Saudan, V. (2001). *Französischlernen in der Deutschschweiz. Zur Entwichlung der diskursiven Fähigkeiten innerhalb und ausserhalb der Schule.* Chur & Zürich: Rüegger.

Lüdi, G., Werlen, I. & Franceschini, R., et al. (1997). *Le paysage linguistique de la Suisse. Recensement fédéral de la population 1990.* Berne: Office fédéral de la statistique.

Luke, K. K. (Ed.). (1994). *Into the Twenty First Century: Issues of Language in Education in Hong Kong.* Hong Kong: Linguistic Society of Hong Kong.

Lyster, R. (1994). Négotiation de la forme: stratégie analytique en classe d'immersion. *Canadian Modern language Review, 50,* 3: (447-465).

Lyster, R. & Ranta, L. (1997). Corrective feedback and learner uptake: negotiation of form in communicative classrooms. *Studies in Second Language Acquisition, 19,* 1: (37-66).

MacDonald, T. (2000). Chapter 1: A new century: a new context in *Language: the Next Generation, the final report and recommendations of the Nuffield Language Inquiry.* (pp. 12-17). London: The Nuffield Inquiry.

MacWhinney, B. (1995). *The CHILDES Project: Computational Tools for Analyzing Talk.* Hillsdale, NJ: Lawrence Erlbaum.

Man, E. Y. (2001). Additive bilingualism – the teachers' perspective of what's missing and what's needed in the case of Hong Kong. Paper presented at Plurilingual Hubs in the New Millennium, January 2001, Hong Kong.

Martin, P. (1996). Code-switching in the primary classroom: One response to the planned and the unplanned language environment in Brunei. *Journal of Multilingual and Multicultural Development. Vol.17*: (2-4).

Martin, P. (1996a). An annotated bibliography of selected linguistic and ethnographic sources on Brunei Darussalam. In Martin, et al. (Eds.). (pp. 315-347).

Martin, P. (1996b). Brunei Malay and Bahasa Melayu: A sociolinguistic perspective. In Martin, et al. (Eds.). (pp. 27-36).

Martin, P. (1997). *Accomplishing Lessons Bilingually in Three Primary Classrooms in Negara Brunei Darussalam: Insights into the Dwibahasa Programme*. PhD. Thesis, University of Lancaster.

Martin, P. (1998). A sociolinguistic perspective on Brunei. *International Journal of the Sociology of Language, 130*: (5-22).

Martin, P., Ozog, C. & Poedjosoedarmo, G. (Eds.). (1996). *Language Use and Language Change in Brunei Darussalam*. Ohio: Ohio University Press.

Martin-Jones, M. (1989). Language power and linguistic minorities: The need for an alternative approach to bilingualism: Language maintenance and shift. In R. Grillo (Ed.). *Social Anthropology and the Politics of Language*. (pp. 106-125). London: Routledge.

Martin-Jones, M. (1990). Code-switching in the classroom: A discussion document. In ESF Network on Code-Switching and Languages. In Contact (Ed.). *Papers for the workshop on impact and consequences of code-switching: Broader Considerations. Brussels, Nov. 1990*, (pp. 79-110). Strasbourg: European Science Foundation.

Martin-Jones, M. & Romaine, S. (1985). Semilingualism a half-baked theory of communicative competence. *Applied Linguistics, 6*, (105-19).

McGuiness, C. (1999). *From Thinking Skills to Thinking Classrooms: A Review and Evaluation of Approaches for Developing Pupils' Thinking*. Research Report 115, DfEE: HMSO.

McLellan, J. (1997). English-Malay code-switching in Brunei: a domain-based analysis. In H. M. Said & S. Butler (Eds.). *English is an Asian Language: the Malaysian Context*. (pp. 164-174). Kuala Lumpur: Persatuan Bahasa Moden Malaysia/The Macquarie Library.

McLellan, J. & Noor Azam Hj Othman (1998). *The Myth of Widespread English: A Sociolinguistic Investigation*. 3rd Regional Conference on English in Southeast Asia: ASEAN Perspectives, Universiti Brunei Darussalam, 24-26 Nov.

Met, M. (1998). Curriculum decision-making in content-based instruction. In J. Cenoz & F. Genesee (Eds.) *Beyond Bilingualism: Multilingualism and Multilingual Education*. (pp. 35-63). Clevedon: Multilingual Matters.

Milroy, L. (1980). *Language and Social Networks*. Oxford: Blackwell.

Mohan, B. (1986). *Language and Content*. Reading, MA: Addison-Wesley.

Mossop, J. (1996). Some phonological features of Brunei English. Martin, et al. (Eds.). (pp. 189-208).

Nisbet, J. (1993). The thinking curriculum. In *Educational Psychology, 13*, (281-290).

Nuffield Language Inquiry. (1998). In A. Moys (Ed.). *Where Are We Going With Languages?* Nuffield Foundation, UK.

Nuffield Language Inquiry. (2000). The Final Report. Nuffield Foundation, UK.

O'Connor, J. & Seymour, J. (1990). *Introducing Neuro-linguistic programming.* Mandala Press.

Office for Standards in Education (OFSTED). (1996). *Handbook for the Inspection of Schools.* London: HMSO.

Open University. (2000). *Course Guide. A331. Language and Society in Hong Kong.* School of Arts and Social Sciences.

Ozog, A. C. K. (1991). Bilingualism in Brunei: English and Malay in the community. Volume 1 of the collected papers from the *Bilingualism and National Development* conference held in Brunei, 9-12 December 1991.

Ozog, A. C. K. (1996). Codeswitching in Peninsular Malaysia and Brunei Darussalam: A study in contrasting linguistic strategies. In P. Martin, et al. (Eds.). (pp. 173-188).

Pekarek, S. (1999). *Leçons de conversation: dynamiques de l'interaction et acquisition de compétences discursives.* Neuchâtel/Paris: Delachaux and Niestlé.

Peltzer-Karpf, A. (1997). Early Foreign Language Learning - The Biological Perspective. In B. Kettemann & I. Landsiedler (Eds.). *The Effectiveness of Language Learning and Teaching,* (pp. 90-104). Vienna: Zentrum für Schulentwicklung – Bundesministerium für Unterricht und kulturelle Angelegenheiten.

Perdue, C. (Ed.). (1993). *Adult Language Acquisition: Cross-Linguistic Perspectives* (2 vols.). Cambridge: Cambridge University Press.

Phillipson, R. (1994). *Linguistic Imperialism.* Oxford University Press.

Pica, T. (1984). Methods of morpheme quantification: Their effect on the interpretation of second language data. *Studies in Second Language Acquisition, 6*, (69-78).

Poon, A. Y. K. (2001). The Hong Kong case: additive bilingualism through education? Paper presented at Plurilingual Hubs in the New Millennium, January 2001, Hong Kong.

Py, Bernard (1996). Apprendre une langue dans l'interaction verbale. *Bulletin suisse de linguistique appliquée 63*, (11-23).

Reilly, J., Bates, E. & Marchman, V. (1998). Narrative discourse in children with early Focal Brain Injury. *Brain and Language, 61*, (335-375).

Rickford, J. (1987). *Dimensions of a Creole continuum: history, texts and linguistic analysis of Guyanese Creole.* Stanford: Stanford University Press.

Richards, J., Platt, J. & Weber, H. (Eds.). (1985). *Longman Dictionary of Applied Linguistics.* Essex: Longman.

Ripple, R., Jaquish, G., Lee, H. W. & Salili, F. (1984). Cognitive and affective costs of bilingual education: A look at the Hong Kong experience. *New Horizons No 25:* (74-81). (November, 1984).

Romaine, S. (1989). *Bilingualism.* London: Blackwell

Romaine, S. (1995). *Bilingualism* (2nd ed.). London: Blackwell.

Rosnah (Hjh) Haji Ramly, Noor Azam Haji Othman & McLellan, J. (2000). *Englishization and Nativization Processes in the Context of Brunei Darussalam: Evidence For and Against.* 5th English in Southeast Asia Conference, Curtin University of Technology, 6-8 December 2000.

Sato, C. (1990). *The Syntax of Conversation in Interlanguage Development.* Tübingen: Gunter Narr.

Saxena, M., Sercombe, P., Hj Mohd Yusop & Hairuni Hj Mohd Ali Maricar (2000). Atlas of the languages and ethnic communities of Brunei & Borneo: A project in progress. In M. Leigh (Ed.). *Borneo 2000: Language, Management and Tourism.* (pp. 206-211). Proceedings of the Sixth Biennial Borneo Research Conference, July 10-14. Sarawak: Universiti Malaysia Sarawak.

Schlegoff, E., Jefferson, G. & Sacks, H. (1977). The preference for Selfcorrection in the Organisation of Repair in Conversation. *Language* 53, (361-92).

Schulze, H. (1994). *Staat und Nation in der europäischen Geschichte.* München, C.H. Beck.

Schumann, J. (1978). The acculturation model for second-language acquisition. In R. C. Gingras (Ed.). *Second Language Acquisition and Foreign Language Teaching.* (pp. 27-50). VA: Center for Applied Linguistics.

Schumann, J. (1998). *The Neurobiology of Affect in Language* (A Supplement to *Language Learning*). U. of Michigan: Blackwell Publishers.

Serra, C. (1999a). Le développement de la compétence discursive et conversationnelle en français L2. Apprendre en deux langues à l'école secondaire. *Travaux Neuchâtelois de Linguistique Appliquée (TRANEL)* 30: (29-91).

Serra, C. (1999b). Entwicklung der Gesprächsfähigkeit. In O. Stern, B. Eriksson, Ch. Le Pape Racine, H. Reutener H. & C. Serra (Eds.). *Französisch - Deutsch. Zweisprachiges Lernen auf Sekundarstufe I.* (pp. 81-158). Chur/Zürich: Rüegger Verlag.

Siguán, M. (1987). Code switching and code mixing in the bilingual speaker: a cognitive approach. In G. Lüdi (Ed.). *Devenir Bilingue, Parler Bilingue,* (pp. 211-224). Tübingen: Niemeyer.

Singh, R. D. S. (1984). *Brunei 1839-1983: Problems of Political Survival.* Singapore: OUP.

Siu, K., et al. (1979). *The Final Report on the Effects of the Medium of Instruction on Student Cognitive Development and Academic Achievement.* Hong Kong: School of Education, Chinese University of Hong Kong.

Skutnabb-Kangas, T. (1981). *Bilingualism or Not: Education of the Minorities.* Clevedon: Multilingual Matters.

Skutnabb-Kangas, T. (2000). *Linguistic Genocide in Education – or Worldwide Diversity and Human Rights?* Mahwah, NJ: Erlbaum.

Skutnabb-Kangas, T. (Ed.). (1995). *Multilingualism for All.* Lisse:Swets and Zeitlinger.

Skutnabb-Kangas, T. & Cummins, J. (Eds.). (1988). *Minority Education: From Shame to Struggle.* Clevedon: Multilingual Matters.

Skutnabb-Kangas, T. & Phillipson, R (1989). Mother tongue the theoretical and sociopolitical construct of a concept. In U. Ammon *Status and Function of Languages and Language Varieties.* Berlin: Walter de Gruyter.

Skutnabb-Kangas, T. & Toukomaa, P. (1976). *Teaching Migrant Children's Mother Tongue and Learning the Language of the Lost Country in the Context of the Socio-Cultural Situations of the Migrant Family.* Tampere: University of Tampere.

Smith, M. P. (2001). *Transnational Urbanism. Locating Globalization.* Malden, Mass. & Oxford, UK: Blackwell Publishers.

Smolicz, J. (1981). Language as a core value of culture. In H. Baetens Beardsmore (Ed.). *Elements of Bilingual Theory.* (pp. 104-124) Brussel: Vrije Universiteit Brussel.

Smolicz, J. (1992). Minority languages as core values of ethnic cultures. A study of maintenance and erosion of Polish, Welsh and Chinese languages in Australia. In W. Fase, K. Jaspaert & S. Kroon (Eds.). *Maintenance and Loss of Minority Languages.* (pp.277-306) Amsterdam: John Benjamins Publishing Company.

Snow, M. A., Met, M. & Genesee, F. (1989). A conceptual framework for the integration of language and content in second/foreign language instruction. *TESOL Quarterly, 23,* (201-217).

So, D. W. C. (1984). *The Social Selection of an English-dominant Bilingual Education System in Hong Kong: An Ecolinguistic Analysis.* Ed. D. Dissertation. Honolulu: University of Hawaii.

So, D. W. C. (1986). *A Study on the Educational Language Preferences of Parents, Students & Teachers in Tsuen Wan, Kwai Chung & Tsing Yi.* The Association of Heads of Secondary Schools of Tsuen Wan, Kwai Chung & Tsing Yi District.

So, D. W. C. (1992). Language-based bifurcation of secondary education in Hong Kong: Past present and future. In Luke (Ed.). *Into the Twenty First Century: Issues of Language in Education in Hong Kong,* (pp. 69-95). Hong Kong: Linguistic Society of Hong Kong.

So, D. W. C. (1998). One country, two cultures and three languages: sociolinguistic conditions and language education in Hong Kong. In B. Asker (Ed.). *Teaching Language and Culture: Building Hong Kong on Education,* (pp. 152-175). Hong Kong: Addison Wesley Longman.

So, D. W. C. (2000). Achieving biliteracy and trilingualism without moi-based bifurcation of the schools: A plea for third-alternatives. In D. C. S. Li, A. Lin & W. K. Tsang (Eds.). *Language and Education in Postcolonial Hong Kong,* (pp. 9-34). Hong Kong: Linguistic Society of Hong Kong.

Spada, N. & Fröhlich, M. (1995). *COLT – Coding Conventions and Applications.* Sydney: National Centre for English Language Teaching and Research.

Spates, J. L. & Macionis, J. J. (1987). *The Sociology of Cities.* (2nd ed.). Belmont, CA: Wadsworth Publ. Co.

Stern, H. (1983). *Fundamental Concepts of Language Teaching.* Oxford: Oxford University Press.

Stevens, F. (1983). Activities to promote learning and communication in the second language classroom. *TESOL Quarterly, 17,* (259-272).

Sun, C. (2000). Hong Kong Needs a Bilingual Educational System. paper for the Workshop on 'Hong Kong After 1997'. HKUST.

Swain, M. (1985). Communicative competence: some roles of comprehensible input and comprehensible output in its development. Gass, S. & Madden, C. (Eds.). *Input in Second Language Acquisition.* (pp. 235-253). Rowley, Mass.: Newbury House.

Swain, M. (1996). Integrating language and content in immersion classrooms: Research perspectives. *The Canadian Modern Language Review, 52,* 4: (529-548).

Swain, M. (1998). Focus on form through conscious reflection. In C. Doughty & J. Williams. (Eds.) *Focus on form in classroom second language acquisition.* (pp. 64-81). New York: Cambridge University Press.

Sweeting, A. E. (1990). *Education in Hong Kong, Pre-1841-1941: Fact and Opinion*. Hong Kong: Hong Kong University Press.

Taal en Sociale Integratie-Language and Social Integration- Langue et Intégration Sociale. VUB Press, Brussels, 1978-1990 (13 volumes).

Thürmann, E. (1999). Eine eigenständige Methodik für den bilingualen Fachunterricht? In G. Bach & S. Niemeier (Eds.). *Bilingualer Unterricht: Grundlagen, Methoden, Praxis, Perspektiven*, (pp. 75-96). Frankfurt am Main: Peter Lang.

Thürmann, E. (2000). Zwischenbilanz zur Entwicklung der bilingualen Bildungsangebote in Deutschland (unpublished manuscript).

Titone, Renzo (1987). The psychological roots of code-switching. In Lüdi & Georges (Eds.). *Devenir Bilingue – Parler Bilingue*, (pp. 259-270). Tübingen: Niemeyer.

Tsou, B. K. (1976). Linguistic co-variants of cultural assimilation. *Anthropology Linguistics*.

Tsou, B. K. (1980). Critical sociolinguistic realignment in multilingual societies. In E. A. Afendras (Ed.). *Patterns of Bilingualism*. (pp. 261-286). Singapore University Press.

Tsou, B. K. (1981). The language of SWONAL (Speaker Without a Native Language): A study on semi-lingualism and accelerated creolization. In H. Baetens Beardsmore (Ed.). *Elements of Bilingual Theory*, (pp. 125-167). Brussels: VUB.

Tsou, B. K. (1983). Triglossie et Realignment Sociolinguistique. *Contrastes*. (10-15).

Tsou, B. K. (1986). Chinese and the cultural eunuch syndrome. *The Language Bomb*. (pp. 15-19). Hong Kong: Longman.

Tsou, B. K. (1991). Distribution of Chinese outside China. In S. A. Wurm, B. K. Tsou & D. Bradley (English Eds.). *Language Atlas of China* (English and Chinese editions). Longman (Asia): Hong Kong.

Tsou, B. K. (1993). Some Issues on Law and Language in the Hong Kong Special Administrative Region (HKSAR) of China. In K. Prinsloo, Y. Peeters, J. Turi & C. Rensburg (Eds.). *Language, Law and Equity*. (pp. 314-331). Pretoria: University of South Africa.

Tsou, B. K. (1997). *Aspects of the Two Language System and Three Language Problem in the Changing Society of Hong Kong*, In S. Wright & H.K. Holmes (Eds.). 1997, (pp. 22-33).

Tucker, G. R. (1998). A global perspective on multilingualism and multilingual education. In J. Cenoz & F. Genesee (Eds.). *Beyond Bilingualism: Multilingualism and Multilingual Education*, (pp. 3-15). Clevedon: Multilingual Matters.

Ullmann, M. (1999). History and geography through French: CLIL in a UK secondary school. In J. Masih (Ed.). *Learning Through a Foreign Language.* (pp. 96-105). London: CILT (Centre for Information on Language Teaching and Research).

Van Lier, L. (1996). *Interaction in the Language Curriculum: Awareness, Autonomy and Authenticity.* NY: Longman Group Ltd

Verstrepen, G. (1986). French as a third language in the Brussels European School. Unpublished B.A. Dissertation, Vrije Universiteit Brussel.

Wallraff, B. (2000). What global language? *The Atlantic Monthly, Vol. 286 (Nov.).* (52-66). Boston, MA: The Atlantic Monthly Grou

Wang, Y. F., Aya, K. & Chen, C. H. (2000). From 'prepositional' to 'expressive' meanings – *Shuo* ('say') in Chinese BBS talk and conversation produced by young people in Taiwan. *Proceedings of the 7th IsCLL,* (193-212). December 22-24, 2000. Chiayi, Taiwan.

Wells, G. (1986). The language experience of five-year-old children at home and at school. In J. Cook-Gumperz (Ed.). *The Social Construction of Literacy,* (pp. 69-93). Cambridge, MA: Cambridge University Press.

Wiesemes, R. (2000). *Towards a Theory of Practice in Bilingual Education* (working title). Unpublished thesis. University of Nottingham.

Witte, E. & Baetens Beardsmore, H. (Eds.). (1987). *The Interdisciplinary Study of Urban Bilingualism in Brussels.* Clevedon-Philadelphia: Multilingual Matters.

Witte, E., Alen, A., Dumont, H. & Ergec R. (Eds.). (1999). *Het statuut van Brussel. Bruxelles et son statut.* Brussels: Larcier.

Wode, H. (1981). *Learning A Second Language: An Integrated View of Language Acquisition.* Tübingen: Gunter Narr.

Wode, H. (1995). *Lernen in der Fremdsprache: Grundzüge von Immersion und bilingualem Unterricht.* Ismaning: Hueber.

Wolff, D. (1994). Der Konstruktivismus: Ein neues Paradigma für den Fremdsprachenunterricht? *Die Neueren Sprachen,* 93: (407-429).

Wolff, D. (1997). Bilingualer Sachfachunterricht: Versuch einer lernpsychologischen und fachdidaktischen Begründung. In H. J. Vollmer & E. Thürmann (Eds.). *Englisch als Arbeitssprache im Fachunterricht: Begegnungen zwischen Theorie und Praxis,* (pp. 50-62). Soest: Landesinstitut für Schule und Weiterbildung.

Wong, C. L. (1982). *A History of the Development of Chinese Education in Hong Kong.* Hong Kong: Po Wen Book Co. [In Chinese].

Wong, C. S. P. & Setter, J. S. (Eds.). Is it 'night' or 'light'? – How and why Cantonese-speaking ELS learners confuse syllable-initial [n] and [l]. Manuscript. The Hong Kong Polytechnic University.

Woolard, K. A. (1985). Language variation and cultural hegemony: toward an integration of sociolinguistic and social theory. *American Ethnologist.* 12, 4: (738-748).

Worsley, (1987). *New Introductory Sociology,* (3rd ed.). London: Penguin.

Wright, S. & Kelly-Holmes, H. (Eds.). (1997). *One Country, Two Systems, Three Languages: A Survey of Changing Language Use in Hong Kong.* Clevedon: Multilingual Matters.

Wurzel, J. (1988). *Toward Multiculturalism.* Yarmouth, Maine: Intercultural Press. Inc.

Zou, J. Y. [Tsou, B. K.] & You, R. J. (2001). *Hanyu yu Huaren Shehui.* Fu Dan Da Xue Chu Ben Shi yu Xiangguang Cheng Shi Da Xue Chu Ben Shi.

Index: Subjects

Index: Languages and Places

Index: Author

Acknowledgements

The editors express sincere thanks to Vrije Universiteit Brussel, Universiti Brunei Darussalam and The Hong Kong Polytechnic University (Grant code G-T340) for providing financial resources to have made the conference Plurilingual Hubs in the New Millennium and the publication of this volume possible. They wish to acknowledge the assistance of the seven colleagues who kindly acted as referees to help select the fifteen papers included in this volume and whose suggestions to the authors have enhanced the quality of this volume. The referees are from a variety of different countries but for obvious reasons have to remain anonymous.

We also wish to register Hugo Baetens Beardsmore's invaluable contributions to us throughout the editing process. He provided material input to the editing of this volume and it is only at his strong insistence that he is not included as one of the editors. Any weakness pertaining to the editing work, however, is solely our responsibility.

Finally we would like to thank all the members of the production team at the Department of Chinese & Bilingual Studies of The Hong Kong Polytechnic University for the care and the effort they have put into the compilation of this volume.

Daniel W.C. So
Gary M. Jones